Say but the Word: Poetry as Vision and Voice

Micheal O'Siadhail

SAY BUT THE WORD

Poetry
as
Vision
and
Voice

**Editors:
David F. Ford and
Margie M. Tolstoy**

Published by Hinds Publishing Ltd
13 Carlisle Avenue
Dublin 4
Ireland

First published 2015

ISBN-13 978-1-909442-02-3

Typeset in Agmena
Design by Bill Murphy Design
Printed in Ireland by Naas Printing

For Christina

Table of Contents

Acknowledgements

Each of the quotations used in this work has a footnote reference to a specific page in the book from which it is taken. Acknowledgement for the use of these quotations is made to the publishers of those works as listed below and as required by the Copyright and Related Rights Act, 2000, of Ireland: Allen Figgis for Brendan Kennelly, *Selected Poems*, Allen Figgis, Dublin, 1969. Arc for Mary O'Donnell, *The Ark Builders*, Arc, Todmorden, 2009. Baker Academic for Peter Ochs, *Another Reformation: Postliberal Christianity and the Jews*, Baker Academic, Grand Rapids, Michigan, 2011. Beacon for *The Philosophy of Paul Ricoeur: An Anthology of His Work*, Beacon Press, Boston, 1978. Bloodaxe for: Micheal O'Siadhail, *Our Double Time*, Bloodaxe, Tarset, 1998; Micheal O'Siadhail, *Collected Poems*, Bloodaxe, Tarset, 2013; Brendan Kennelly, *A Time for Voices: Selected Poems 1960–1990*, Bloodaxe, 1990; Tess Gallagher, *My Black Horse: New and Selected Poems*, Bloodaxe, 1995; Micheal O'Siadhail, *Globe*, Bloodaxe Books, Tarset, 2007. Brandon for Anthony Cronin, *Heritage Now: Irish Literature in the English Language*, Brandon, Dingle, 1982. Butterworth for Bertha S. Phillpotts, *Edda and Saga*, London, 1931. Cambridge University Press for: David F. Ford, *Christian Wisdom: Desiring God and Learning in Love*, Cambridge University Press, 2007; Charles Taylor, *Sources of the Self: The Making of the Modern Identity*, Cambridge University Press, 1989. Carcanet for Rainer Maria Rilke, *Sonnets to Orpheus with Letters to a Young Poet*, translated by Stephen Cohn, Carcanet, Manchester, 2000. Carl Winters Universitätsbuchhandlung, Heidelberg for *EDDA: Die Lieder des Codex Regius Nebst Verwandten Denkmälern*, herausgegeben von Gustav Neckel, Heidelberg, 1927. Carysfort Press for Marc Caball and David F. Ford, *Musics of Belonging: The Poetry of Micheal O'Siadhail*, Carysfort Press, Dublin, 2007. T&T Clark for *Essentials of Christian Community*, eds. David F. Ford and Dennis L. Stamps, T&T Clark, Edinburgh, 1996. Cló iar-Chonnachta for Cathal Ó Searcaigh, *Gúrú i gClúidíní*, Indreabhán, Conamara, 2006. Collins for William Shakespeare, *Collins Complete Works*, Glasgow, 1994. Columba for: Una Agnew, *The Mystical Imagination of Patrick Kavanagh: A Buttonhole in Heaven*, Columba Press, Dublin, 1998; Tom Stack, *No Earthly Estate: God and Patrick Kavanagh*, Columba Press, Dublin, 2002. Darton, Longman & Todd for Daniel W. Hardy and David F. Ford, *Jubilate: Theology in Praise*, Darton, Longman

& Todd, London, 1984. J. M. Dent for *The English Poems of George Herbert*, ed. C. A. Patrides, J. M. Dent, London, 1974; Dylan Thomas, *Collected Poems 1934–1952*, J. M. Dent & Sons Ltd, London, November 1952. Dolmen Press for Patrick Kavanagh, *Self-Portrait*, Dolmen Press, Dublin, 1964. Duquesne University Press for Emmanuel Levinas, *Ethics and Infinity: Conversations with Philippe Nemo*, Pittsburgh, 1985. Ecco Press for Czesław Miłosz, *Provinces*, The Ecco Press, New York, 1991. en.wikiquote for en.wikiquote.org/wiki/Samuel_Beckett#The_Unnamable_.281954.29. Faber & Faber for Seamus Heaney, *Field Work*, Faber & Faber, London, 1979; T. S. Eliot, *Collected Poems 1909–1962,* Faber & Faber, London, 1963; Louis MacNeice, p84, *Collected Poems*, Faber & Faber, London, 1966; Richard Wilbur, *New and Collected Poems*, Faber and Faber, London, 1989; W. H Auden, *Collected Poems*, ed. Edward Mendelson, Faber and Faber, London, 1976; Theodore Roethke, *Collected Poems*, Faber & Faber, London, 1968. Forlagt for Einar Skjæraasen, *Bumerke*, Forlagt, Oslo 1968. Fount for David Ford, *The Shape of Living*, Fount Paperbacks, London, 1997. The Free Press for: Ernest Becker, *The Denial of Death*, The Free Press, New York, 1973; Stephen Toulmin, *Cosmopolis: The Hidden Agenda of Modernity*, The Free Press, New York, 1990. Gill and Macmillan for: Antoinette Quinn, *Patrick Kavanagh – A Biography*, Gill and Macmillan, Dublin, 2001; Antoinette Quinn, *Patrick Kavanagh: Born Again Romantic*, Gill and Macmillan, Dublin, 1991. Goldsmith Press for Patrick Kavanagh, *The Complete Poems*, The Goldsmith Press, Newbridge, 1992. Hamish Hamilton for Kathleen Raine, *Collected Poems*, Hamish Hamilton, London, 1956. Harcourt, Brace & World for Edward Sapir, *Language: An Introduction to the Study of Speech*, Harcourt, Brace & World, New York, 1921. Harper & Row for *Selected poems of Rainer Maria Rilke: A Translation from the German and Commentary by Robert Bly*, Harper & Row, New York, 1981. Harper Collins for Anthony Cronin, *Samuel Beckett: The Last Modernist*, Harper Collins, London, 1996. William Heinemann for *Selected Poems of Gerard Manley Hopkins*, William Heinemann, London, 1953. Insel Verlag for *Rainer Maria Rilke Die Gedichte*, Insel Verlag, Frankfurt am Main, 1957, 1986, 1995. John Calder for Samuel Beckett: *Collected Poems in English and French*, John Calder, London, 1977. MacGibbon & Kee for Patrick Kavanagh, *Collected Poems*, MacGibbon & Kee, London, 1964. Macmillan for: W. B. Yeats, *The Collected Poems of W. B. Yeats*, Macmillan, London, 1965; W. B. Yeats 'Anima Hominis,' *Essays*, Macmillan, London, 1924. Macmillan Company for Rabindranath

Tagore, *The Crescent Moon*, translated from the original Bengali by the author, Macmillan Company, New York, 1913. Martin Brian & O'Keefe for Patrick Kavanagh, *The Green Fool*, Martin Brian & O'Keefe, London, 1971. Modern Haiku Press for Billy Collins, *She was Just Seventeen*, Lincoln, Illinois, 2006. Modern Library for *Complete Poems and Selected Letters of John Keats*, The Modern Library, New York, 2001. New Directions for *The Collected Poems of Denise Levertov*, eds. Paul A. Lacey & Anne Dewey, New Directions, New York, 2013. New Island for Mary O'Donnell, *The Place of Miracles: new and selected poems*, New Island, Dublin, 2005. Nonesuch Press for *John Donne: Complete Poetry & Selected Prose*, ed. John Hayward, The Nonesuch Press, London, 1990. Oifig an tSoláthair for Seán de Búrca, *Dafydd ap Gwilym*, Baile Átha Cliath, 1974. Oxford University Press for: *The New Oxford Book of Light Verse*, ed. Kingsley Amis, Oxford, 1978; *The Oxford Book of Seventeenth Century Verse*, Grierson and Bulloch, Oxford, 1934; *Chaucer Complete Works*, ed. Walter W. Skeat, Oxford, 1912; Janet Martin Soskice, *Metaphor and Religious Language*, Clarendon Press, Oxford, 1985. Penguin for: *The Comedy of Dante Alighieri the Florentine, Cantica III Paradise <Il Paradiso>*, translated by Dorothy L. Sayers and Barbara Reynolds, Penguin Classics, Harmondsworth, 1962; Dante Alighieri, *The Divine Comedy 1: Inferno*, translated by Robin Kirkpatrick, Penguin Classics, London, 2006; François Villon, *Selected Poems*, Chosen and translated by Peter Dale, Penguin, Harmondsworth, 1978; *William Blake*, edited with an introduction by J. Bronowski, Penguin, Harmondsworth, 1958; Gerard Manley Hopkins, *Poems and Prose of Gerard Manley Hopkins*, Penguin, Harmondsworth, 1953; George Eliot, *Middlemarch*, Penguin, Harmondsworth, Middlesex, 1965; *The Penguin Book of German Verse*, introduced and edited by Leonard Forster, Harmondsworth, 1957, 1959. Pennsylvania State University for http://www2.hn.psu.edu/faculty/jmanis/dante/norton-hell.pdf C E Norton. Phoenix for *The Dylan Thomas Omnibus*, Phoenix, London, 2000. Salmon for: Mary O'Donnell, *Reading the Sunflowers in September*, Salmon, Galway, 1990; Mary O'Donnell, *Spiderwoman's Third Avenue Rhapsody*, Salmon, Swords, 1993; Mary O'Donnell, *Unlegendary Heroes*, Salmon, Cliffs of Moher, 1998. *Studies* for: *Studies*, Autumn 2012, vol. 101; *Studies*, volume 102, number 405. *Theology* for David F. Ford, 'Reading texts, seeking wisdom: A Gospel, a system and a poem', *Theology* 114: 173–179, 2011. Twayne for John Nemo, *Patrick Kavanagh*, Twayne Publishers, New York, 1979. University of Chicago

Press for: Paul Ricoeur, *Oneself as Another*, University of Chicago Press, 1992; Paul Ricoeur, *Time and Narrative*, 3 vols, University of Chicago Press, 1985. Wahlström & Widstrand for Edith Södergran, *Samlade Dikter*, Wahlström & Widstrand, Stockholm, 1985. Warne for *The Poetical Works of Percy Bysshe Shelley*, London, Frederick Warne & Co, no date. wikiquote for en.wikiquote.org/wiki/Dafydd_ap_Gwilym. Wipf and Stock for David C. Mahan, *An Unexpected Light: Theology and Witness in the Poetry and Thought of Charles Williams, Micheal O'Siadhail and Geoffrey Hill*, Wipf and Stock Publishers, Eugene, 2009. www.gutenberg.org for Sir Thomas Wyatt, *Unstable Dream* at http://www.gutenberg.org/files/27450/27450-h/27450-h.htm#CHAPTER_I. www.gutenberg.org for http://www.gutenberg.org/cache/epub/1008/ pg1008.html. www.luminarium.org for www.luminarium.org/renascence-editions/sidpsalms.html#psalmes. www.operone.de for John Ciardi at http://www.operone.de/dante/inf01ciardi.html. www.samuel-beckett.net for http://www.samuel-beckett.net/whatistheword.html.

Editorial Notes

It has been a delight to edit this book, mainly because of the essays and addresses themselves, but especially because of the collaboration of two people. Micheal O'Siadhail, having been persuaded by us that a selection of his prose writings should be published, went to immense trouble to provide us with texts, information and advice. Ross Hinds has been a dream publisher, devoting a huge amount of time and expertise to the design and detail of the book, and making a stream of valuable suggestions.

Some sections in this collection were originally published as articles or given as lectures. Occasionally there are biographical details which reflect the time of writing. In a very few cases an idea or an explanation occurs more than once where it is germane to the argument in different contexts.

DFF and MMT

Introduction

Speaking at the Dublin launch of Micheal O'Siadhail's *Collected Poems*[1] in September 2013, Mary McAleese, the former President of Ireland, said that he is 'quite simply outstanding, a man whose genius with words is the warp and whose genius for life is the weft of that "fabric stitched and toughened in its darn"; toughened, not coarsened, made stronger through its encounter with weakness, softened by love, coloured by the mysteries of joy and grief, outrage and desire, hope and faith.' In his poetry she found that 'so many facets and situations, challenges and concerns that are part of the deeply grooved personal human condition, are captured and explored here with a cavernous curiosity and wisdom that is put at the service of the reader, not just so he or she can wonder at the gifts of insight and wordcraft but so he or she can trust life more, trust love more, care more about being careless with life and love.'

Life and Work

McAleese looked back over more than forty years to 'the outset when he first committed to this insistent vocation of poet'.

O'Siadhail was born in 1947 in Dublin, where he still lives, though with many involvements elsewhere in the world, built up over a lifetime that has included learning many languages.[2] His education in Clongowes Wood College and Trinity College Dublin was marked by distinctions in studies, sport, debating and the arts. In 1961 he visited the Aran Islands off the coast of Galway in the west of Ireland, and returned many times – a transformative encounter, living in a completely Irish-speaking community that had changed little in many centuries. The Irish language has continued to be deeply formative for him, as in different ways have other small or threatened languages in which at various times in his life he has become fluent, such as Welsh, Icelandic, Norwegian, Catalan and Latvian. He later studied in the University of Oslo, and Norway became a second homeland for the rest of his life, with Scandinavian literature a continuing influence. He then lectured in Celtic languages for a time in Trinity College Dublin, and

---

[1] Micheal O'Siadhail, *Collected Poems,* Bloodaxe, Tarset, 2013
[2] For a fuller biography and account of literature about O'Siadhail's poetry than that given here see pp1–24, David F. Ford, 'Life, Work, and Reception' in Marc Caball and David F. Ford, *Musics of Belonging: The Poetry of Micheal O'Siadhail,* Carysfort Press, Dublin, 2007

became a professor at the Dublin Institute for Advanced Studies, publishing an account of the dialects of modern Irish that is still a standard reference work.[3] Among his teachers and mentors during these years were the leading Irish writer and intellectual Máirtín Ó Cadhain and the polymathic, cosmopolitan professor of Irish, David Greene.

Two decisive developments in his early decades were his marriage and his increasing dedication to poetry. In 1970 he married Bríd Ní Chearbhaill. She was born in Gweedore, a Gaeltacht (Irish-speaking) area in Co. Donegal in north-west Ireland, and came to Dublin to train as a primary teacher. In a life of many friendships, this was undoubtedly the central relationship until, after suffering from Parkinson's for over twenty years, she died in 2013. O'Siadhail has written of her a great deal, above all in *Love Life* (2005). His desire to write led him to resign his lectureship in Trinity College in 1973 and take a year off, during which his priority shifted decisively from academic work to poetry. In 1974 he was appointed to the Dublin Institute for Advanced Studies, a research centre that carried no teaching duties and allowed more time for poetry. But in 1987, aged 40, he made the crucial decision to resign from that and become a full-time poet. The collections since that time, beginning with autobiographical *The Chosen Garden* (1990), have been thematically unified, each with its distinctive architectonic, displaying in ever-new ways what Mary McAleese described as 'focus, intensity and perfection of craft'.

After that, the main collections were *Hail! Madam Jazz* (1992), *A Fragile City* (1995), *Our Double Time* (1998), *The Gossamer Wall: poems in witness to the Holocaust* (2002), *Love Life* (2005), *Globe* (2007) and *Tongues* (2011), all now gathered into the *Collected Poems* (2013). He has also produced song cycles, articles, lectures, speeches, interviews, and broadcasts, and has given readings in many countries. There is an increasing body of writing by others about O'Siadhail's poetry, and he has received several awards and honours. He has been a member of the Arts Council of the Republic of Ireland (1988–93) and of the Advisory Committee on Cultural Relations (1989–97), a founder member of Aosdána (Academy of distinguished Irish artists) and an editor of *Poetry Ireland Review*. He was the founding chairman of ILE (Ireland Literature

---

[3] Micheal O'Siadhail, *Modern Irish. Grammatical structure and dialectal variations*, Cambridge University Press, 1989

Exchange), which sponsors the translation of Irish authors into other languages.

The publication of O'Siadhail's *Collected Poems* in 2013 has inspired a new surge of interest in his work. For over four decades, one collection succeeded another, culminating in *Tongues*. Those who had followed his work were aware of its distinctive marks. These include the coherent, thematic character of each collection since *The Chosen Garden*, some of them more personal and some more public; his ways of combining historical and contemporary breadth, and strong Irish roots with deep engagement in other cultures. The remarkable technical, linguistic and formal range, using both classic forms and inventing new ones, has drawn on the resources of many languages. In uniting head, heart and imagination, he has addressed some of the most challenging issues of our world, offering prophetic wisdom for the twenty-first century.

Yet, with the collections spanning such an extended period, and some of the earlier ones out of print, it has been hard to have an overall sense of this multifaceted lifetime's work. A range of European and North American critics and commentators made the most substantial single contribution in 2007 with *Musics of Belonging: The Poetry of Micheal O'Siadhail*.[4] These essays cover his life, work and reception. There is also a bibliography of O'Siadhail's published poetry and song cycles, his literary essays, academic books and articles on linguistics, the critical studies and reviews of his work, and translations of his poetry into other languages.

Say but the Word
The publication of the *Collected Poems* has been an even more significant aid to comprehending the scale, quality and interconnectedness of O'Siadhail's *oeuvre*. But something vital has been missing, since over the years he has also written a number of prose pieces that show how he has been thinking about his own work and that of others, and how he approaches literature and life. The present collection has selected from among these what the editors consider his main prose writings, though there is a great deal we would have included had we had the luxury of more space. The title, *Say but the Word: Poetry as Vision and Voice*, indicates not only O'Siadhail's way with language but also what we have just called his challenging prophetic wisdom for our age. He has what

---

[4] Edited by Marc Caball and David F. Ford, op. cit.

xviii

he calls 'a ministry of meaning', in which form and content go together.

The first part, 'Wonder of Words', gives O'Siadhail's approach to the astonishing phenomenon of language and explores the dimensions of his vocation as a poet.

The first piece, 'For nothing but the music's sake', is O'Siadhail's Foreword to his *Collected Poems*, and offers an overview of all his work. It both traces his life as a poet, collection by collection, and reflects on the forms he uses. 'Poet as Citizen' moves through autobiography into exploring the relation of poetry to society, its niche in a healthy 'ecology' of language and consciousness, and the power of images. 'Poet in Context' suggests that the poet is a paradigm of the modern self, facing as truthfully as possible the uncertainties and lack of overview, yet sometimes able in response to touch deeply, offer new languages of trust and responsibility, and even be the 'generator of feasts'. Vivid vignettes of how poetry can move people are set within a Dantean vision of love; yet there are no short cuts – we have to grapple with the complex challenges of modernity and its radical suspicion of love and meaning.

'How about this? – Speaking in Tongues' revels in the sounds, signs and transformations of languages, and the 'unbelievable joy' of learning a new one. It is the Foreword to *Tongues*, and guides us through the sections of this engagement with language in many modes, from lullabies, key words in various languages, and the 'nugget-like intensity' of proverbs, to Japanese characters, the 'glamour of grammar', and thank-you poems addressed to those who taught him seven of the languages he speaks. 'Feasting: A Poet Hosts Linguists' culminates the first section by opening up one of the secrets of O'Siadhail's poetry that has usually been left implicit: the interplay between the poet and the linguist in him. Addressing academic linguists at a conference dinner on an American campus, this (the most recent of the pieces in this volume) celebrates through the parable of Karen Blixen's *Babette's Feast* the 'both-and' of literature and linguistics. The 'oral pleasures' of both words and foods are enjoyed and tasty illustrations from his own and others' poems are served.

The second part, 'Working the Word', gives four master classes in 'the beloved craft' of poetry.

The first class, 'The Craft of Poetry' inquires into the whole poetic 'ecology of meaning and form', beginning with the sonnet. O'Siadhail has written hundreds of sonnets and they have been the subject of

several studies, but this is the first time he has written at length about
what he calls 'the ultimate classic form'. He studies the development and
variations of the sonnet from Petrarch through Shakespeare, Donne,
Milton and Wordsworth up to the present. He also asks why the sonnet
is 'supreme'. His suggestions are that it has a classic sonata-like discipline
of beginning, middle and end; that it acts as an acid test of whether a
poet can bring together thought, feeling and technique in a jazz-like
'precision of freedom'; and that it has the capacity to help cope, through
the containment of a strict form, with good and bad overwhelmings –
he illustrates with examples of his love poetry and the central sonnet
sequence on the extermination camps in his collection on the
Holocaust. From the sonnet he moves on to consider the variety of
forms and the possibilities of endless improvisation on them. He
appreciates both the reaction against form in the 'age of authenticity',
and also the reaction against the reaction. The result – at best – is a
marriage that is voluntary rather than arranged, with the sort of
dynamic union of discipline and freedom to be found in jazz. He writes
for the first time about his own use of the Japanese forms of *haiku* and
choka and his invention of the hybrid *saiku*.

   In 'Sources of Form: Appropriation', the *haiku* is further explored,
this time going more deeply into both its Japanese origins and the ways
it has been used in English. The context is a discussion of how several
forms have been borrowed by English poets, including Dante's Italian
terza rima, Villon's French *ballade* and the Welsh *cynghanedd*, each of
which has also been used by O'Siadhail. On *terza rima* he ends with a
pointed challenge to future poetry: 'It may be that the ultimate
appropriation of *terza rima* as part of the English language would be if
it were used in a contemporary poem commensurate with Dante's
Commedia in its scope and range.'

   'Sources of Form: Translation' is the theme of the third class. Taking
Dante's *terza rima*, Villon's *ballade* and Basho's *haiku* as examples, it
distinguishes three basic approaches to translating them into English.
The non-formal does not try to reproduce the form in English, the
formal does try, and the compromise does so loosely. O'Siadhail makes
clear that he favours taking up the challenge of the formal approach.
He gives two detailed examples in which he shows the steps and gives
the reasons for his own translations of one poem from Irish and another
from Norwegian, summing up the process as a combination of
rendering and recomposing.

Say but the Word

The final master class is on 'Sources of Form: Invention'. 'All forms have been devised at some point by a practicing poet' – in other words, they have been invented. O'Siadhail here writes about his own use of borrowed forms, especially *terza rima* and *haiku*, his variations on them (such as inverted *haiku*, rhyming *haiku* and inserted *haiku*), and his inventions: various syllabic patterns, various triplets, the zigzag rhyme, and the 'melodeon' in which the first line rhymes with the last, the second with the second last, and so on. In conclusion he speculates about how themes can reach out for appropriate new forms, and illustrates the marriage of the two in his melodeon love poem 'Complementarity'.

The third part, 'Wise in Words', is more philosophic in approach, dealing with views of history and the future, spirituality, and the rich, complex terrain where poetry, philosophy and theology try to probe the mysteries of reality.

'Identity, Memory and Meaning in the Twenty-First Century: Trauma and Vision' reflects on O'Siadhail's own times, from the aftermath of the Second World War and the Holocaust to the information age and cyberspace. How might one emerge from trauma or cope with massive change? How might it be possible to have trust and vision in the face of radical suspicion, meaninglessness and despair? Drawing on analogies from biology, the history of the English and Japanese languages, and Jewish responses to the Holocaust, and on a number of thinkers such as Prigogine, Levinas, Ricoeur, Ochs and Collins, O'Siadhail thinks through an historically-informed vision for the twenty-first century. In terms of his own poetry this essay is an illuminating companion to *The Gossamer Wall: poems in witness to the Holocaust* and to *Globe*.

In *'I'd be a damn' fool if they weren't:* Art and Spirituality' O'Siadhail tries to do justice to the mystery of art and the spiritual search. He meditates on time, music, narrative, painting and poetry in an open-ended inquiry that seeks deep connections. 'Crosslight: Poetry and Mystery' pursues similar themes through a more single-minded concentration on poetry and faith. The crosslight is where different spheres of reality intersect, and the poet copes with the abundance of multiple meanings.

The final part, 'Woven in Words', is a selection of O'Siadhail's responses to fellow poets. Here he stands in 'the fellowship of poets across generations, in a community of relationships over time'.

There is a fresh interpretation of 'Patrick Kavanagh: Poet and Prophet'. He is read as responding to the polarities of modernity in his twentieth-century Irish context. His prophecy is seen as 'the ability, in the light of the past, to live utterly in the present in a way which prepares for the future', and he emerges as the most intimately and deeply influential of O'Siadhail's Irish poet predecessors. Kavanagh's statement that 'the poet is a theologian' is taken seriously, and the coherence of his vision is revealed from this angle.

Yeats is one of the main foils for the portrayal of Kavanagh, and then in 'Yeats and Rilke: Two Towering Figures' he is set alongside a very different poet, yet one with 'strange and fascinating parallels'. The differences go deeper – in tone, in response to the world, in how they coped with ageing and suffering. The intensity of Yeats is achieved rhetorically and sonorously 'along the battlements of argument'; that of Rilke 'by the firm, suggestive yet gentle tone of a friend who insists we never lose sight of ultimate meaning'. Yeats is a master of sound, yet 'remains at heart an escape artist, a lover of might-have-beens, of imagined grandeurs, of vast theories and myths'. Rilke's poetic vocation to a 'ministry of meaning' has a realism that 'is a full acceptance of life with all that goes with it, of joy, regret, celebration, grief, delight and death'. It is not hard to deduce which resonates more strongly with O'Siadhail.

His essay on 'Samuel Beckett as Poet' resonates with a period of O'Siadhail's youth. Beckett's 'potent mixture of tedium and meaninglessness somehow caught the mood of the late fifties and early sixties'. The tramps in *Waiting for Godot* 'forced me as a young man to look down into the dark pit of their obsession and to come to understand the slow paralysis of despondency, the torpor of despair'. In contrast to Rilke, Beckett's is a realism that despairs of meaning, and O'Siadhail traces contributing factors – early emotional malnutrition, 1920s Paris, two world wars and the Holocaust, Modernism, Schopenhauer, Joyce. Close reading of Beckett's poetry becomes a lens through which Beckett's life, times and dramas can be better understood.

'George Herbert: With Open Eyes' is perhaps the most personal of the essays on fellow poets. It is O'Siadhail's delight in a friend. Beyond the account of Herbert's context and of the ups and downs of his reception over the centuries, and beyond the appreciation of how he combines 'such depth and richness of thought with such dazzling subtlety of language, expression and structure', there is a fresh appropriation of Herbert for the twenty-first century. His 'inextricable mix of theological thought and beautiful form' might come into its own in a time when 'there may be a new seriousness about religion, partly due to its emergence both for good and for bad, as a major global dynamic'. At the heart of O'Siadhail's love for Herbert is the recognition of someone for whom the 'ministry of meaning' is utterly central yet also absolutely inseparable from the exquisite crafting of language, imagery and form in both classical and innovative ways. Herbert's 'precise wildness, what in patristic times was called "sober intoxication"', is an ideal for O'Siadhail, and the personal testimony is revealing: 'The more I read him the more I find in him and the more he sustains me. There is always a freshness to his poems which is astounding, and he remains rooted in what is greater than himself.'

In '*You can only take my word for it*: Denise Levertov's Poetic Witness' O'Siadhail follows Levertov's life and work from early Communism and love poetry to later Christian faith and open verse, discovering through it all the 'epic of a lifetime's vocation'. In engagement with her he articulates the crucial elements of voice and vision which we have taken as headlines for this collection. 'A voice is a tone, a pitch that speaks the truth'. His midrashes on *vox* connect it with epic, word, vocation and witness. Vision is 'the main driver of a poet. How does the poet desire the world to be? What is the poems' horizon?' The major themes of Levertov's vision are love, justice and a passion for meaning. These are fulfilled in her later poetry, above all in 'an earned wisdom of self-surrender which seems to flow naturally from the poise and generosity so apparent in her earlier love poems'. In the concluding quotation she testifies to the mystery of reality – and of God.

'Mary O'Donnell: An Arc of a Life' offers a fresh interpretation of the work of a leading contemporary poet in terms of her growth through dealing with a range of tensions, such as those between 'domestic constraints and a full sensuous flourishing of womanhood', institutions and life-force, local and global, realistic and imaginative, learned and passionate. This is a life and work set in an Ireland going through huge transformations and also engaged internationally as never before. Central to O'Siadhail's account of the open-ended 'settlement' to which O'Donnell comes is his appreciation of the passionate art of her poems of love for her husband and her daughter. He also gives a poet's analysis of her virtuosity in poetic technique.

This collection of O'Siadhail's prose places it alongside *Musics of Belonging* and his *Collected Poems* and provides an integrated understanding of his work. It also prepares both for wider reception of his poetry to date and for the poetry he is yet to publish: several essays have something of the character of a manifesto. As he prepares to publish what is likely to be his *maximum opus*, towards which he has been building up for many years, this is an appropriate time to accompany his *Collected Poems* with this prose collection.

David F. Ford and Margie M. Tolstoy

Say but the Word

Wonder of Words

Wonder of Words

Say but the Word

People love to assign poets a line of country, to pin things down and sum them up. Sometimes it is the contents, more often the form. There are the modernists, the imagists, the language poets, the new formalists and so on. I have never felt any temptation to align myself with any given school. Others have a passion for tracing a kind of poetic lineage. So-and-so is influenced by such and such a poet. Of course, I know we are all shaped by those poets we have read who have moved us. I belong to several traditions at once, so to trace a lineage would involve some complex criss-crossing.

It is forty-five years since I was a student in Oslo. Recently revisiting Norway, a friend quoted two lines to me from a poem by the Swedish language Finnish poet[5] Edith Södergran:

Jag går på sol, jag står på sol
jag vet ingenting annat än sol

'Triumf att finnas till...'

I walk on sun, I stand in sun
I know nothing else but sun.

'Triumph to exist...'

Suddenly it all came back to me – the thrilling bare honesty of those Scandinavian women Edith Södergran, Karin Böye and Halldis Moren Vesaas. Was it shaped by Scandinavia or was it as women they could risk this? I wonder are they still ringing in me when I chronicle in *The Leap Year* a growth towards daring to live[6] in the sun:

Here I am. I walk the earth,
One lovely morning in eternity.

'Mirror'

A roofer once warned me when he saw me climbing a ladder to slide my hands up the rails on each side as I took another step up on to the next rung and not just to grab the next rung up with a free hand. It's risky – you're a second or two without a grip. It is temperament, I suppose, but all my life I love the excitement of that airy moment.

I was thirty-two when I was writing[7] *Rungs of Time*:

5   Edith Södergran, *Samlade Dikter*, Wahlström & Widstrand, Stockholm, 1985
6   p38, Micheal O'Siadhail, *Collected Poems,* Bloodaxe, Tarset, 2013
7   p58, Micheal O'Siadhail, *Collected Poems,* Bloodaxe, Tarset, 2013

'A Birthday' Already that's one year you have on Schubert,
              A whole year to bloom before Christ's torture.

My age is reflected in my concerns. Like many in their early thirties I
am grappling with the first intimations of how quickly time passes, and
of the humility required for slow work and spiritual growth, reassuring
myself of the worth and sustainability of what I felt called to do. I am
mulling over the spark of delight that made any plodding stoicism seem
so dull, while conscious of how so many are tied to repetitious drudgery.
At this time too, sheer carnal joy and deepening of love[8] are held in play:

'Roofing' A living space for a separate passion.

           A roof is framing our slanted intimacy.

By *Belonging*, it seems the themes take a further societal turn. I am taken
up with relationships and reconciliations, with forebears, family, friends
new and old, children, former teachers and lovers[9], the marginalised:

'Clerk' Parts we play prepared for us
         In the grand ensemble of humanity.

The next two collections, *Springnight* and *The Image Wheel*, which
followed closely on *Belonging* continue in a similar thematic vein. But
here I think I wanted a feel of greater ordinariness, to revel in detailed
portraiture and mood. These were to be the last 'collections' inasmuch
as soon afterwards I was able to devote all my time to my work as a poet,
and from then on I wanted to write books which circled around and
meditated on aspects of a single theme.
    In *The Chosen Garden* I try to sketch the emotional trajectory from
the garden chosen for me to the garden I chose. I am forty and living in
a suburban three-up-two-down built around the same time as a similar
house a mile or so away where I spent my early childhood. I have made
the move, declared my hand as a poet and nothing else, and am working
at a window overlooking a garden. Have I come full circle, or has this
been a spiral upward? I had left for boarding school, for the exuberance
of the 1960s, the clenched fist of ideologies, the desolation of failure,

---

[8]   p94, Micheal O'Siadhail, *Collected Poems,* Bloodaxe, Tarset, 2013
[9]   p105, Micheal O'Siadhail, *Collected Poems,* Bloodaxe, Tarset, 2013

the second chance of love, and now[10] the sense of return to a witting innocence:

Double-edge of nurture, of damage.   'Child'
There's no undoing all our knowledge.
Bon voyage! Where will you choose
another garden, another innocence?

When Bloodaxe published *Hail! Madam Jazz: New and Selected Poems*, the new part was a shorter book called *The Middle Voice*. I am forty-five and conscious of being middle-aged and in all probability well into the second moiety of life. The generation ahead is fading and I am a tradition bearer, a memory passer and a welcomer. In this baton change[11] between two generations there is a poignant responsibility:

    here I am saying it's good   'Three Rock'
to stand in between, touching our coming
and our going. Hinge and middleman.
. . . .

Receiver and sender. A signal boosted
onwards. Pride and humility of a medium.

In the early 1990s my close friend, the theologian David Ford, introduced me to the work of the philosopher Emmanuel Levinas, whose emphasis on the face of the other as the ground for ethics fascinated me, and I began *A Fragile City*. I was thinking about trust as the core of all good human and societal relationships. Trust is so open-faced, but its abuses veil and mask the face. While there are necessary boundaries to maintain otherness, the great celebration of trust is the face-to-faceness of feasting and dancing[12] together:

I feed on such courtesy.   'Courtesy'
These guests keep countenancing me.
Mine always mine. This complicity
Of faces, companions, breadbreakers.
You and you and you. My fragile city.

[10] p240, Micheal O'Siadhail, *Collected Poems,* Bloodaxe, Tarset, 2013
[11] p242, Micheal O'Siadhail, *Collected Poems,* Bloodaxe, Tarset, 2013
[12] p311, Micheal O'Siadhail, *Collected Poems,* Bloodaxe, Tarset, 2013

Say but the Word

I do not know why I was for many years haunted by the idea of death. I suspect I am not alone in this. *Our Double Time* starts as an attempt to come to terms with death. Yet it is much more. In some way the whole of life is a preparation for its end. The last section is a tribute to friends. To embrace our finitude frees us from the compulsion for escapism whether through drugs, alcohol, overwork or constant entertainment, and allows us to live in the intensity of the moment. We not only taste each moment but also savour it so that time[13] is doubled:

'Our Double   A nagging unease, a thought I'd tried to shirk,
Time'   Some hazy dread. At last I think I'll dare
              To face it squarely; even to trust its work.
              Such release! To care more and not to care!
              Twin intensity of knowing that now is now.
              All time is borrowed, borrowed and double.
              Two-sided, it both belongs and transcends.

The Gossamer Wall: poems in witness to the Holocaust is structured as a mirror image, a chiasm. At the core of the book are the concentration camps. The book begins with the build-up of prejudice over almost two thousand years, and it ends with the long aftermath. Then, on either side of the core, first, the collapse of the town Northeim to Nazism and the hardening of ordinary men to violent killings in Battalion 101; and, second, the resistance of the village of Le Chambon and of brave individuals to Nazism. All of this is based on researched historical evidence.

   Why a book of poems in witness to the Holocaust? I can try to say, but the reasons may be retrospective. I was reading Etty Hillesum. A friend showed me the tattooed camp number on her arm. I was menaced by neo-Nazis in Norway. On a different level, I felt the Holocaust had not really been confronted and that my post-war generation needed to face up to it. Whatever the reason, I simply had to bear witness and see if I could come through with hope intact, still believing that to engage with the full richness of life is the only way[14] to avoid such tragedies recurring:

'Never'   A raucous glory and the whole jazz of things.
          . . . .
          We feast to keep our promise of never again.

[13]   p391, Micheal O'Siadhail, *Collected Poems,* Bloodaxe, Tarset, 2013
[14]   p467, Micheal O'Siadhail, *Collected Poems,* Bloodaxe, Tarset, 2013

Say but the Word

What a delight it was in *Love Life* to turn to pay homage to a woman I had loved then for 36 years. To re-capture after three dozen years the first flush, the courtship, the promises, the ordinariness, the intimacy and growth in commitment, the mutual transformation and ageing together.

After a reading from *Love Life* at a conference in Scotland I sat to take a breather in an alcove. Two women sat within earshot, but didn't see me. 'What did you make of that?', asked one woman. 'I hated it,' replied the second woman, 'it brought me all the places I didn't want to go.' Ah, the power of poetry. I learned to begin such a reading by saying that I know how blessed[15] I am:

The longer we long, the further on beyond,   'Caprice'
Desire homing towards where desire began

As though from its beginning a tune returns;
Glory of our music how our music yearns.

Then comes *Globe*, a meditation on history, process and vision in a time of restless change. Who shapes history? How do we remember the scars of tragedy and loss? Is there in all the crisscross of cultures with their blurred boundaries a jazz of new and endless[16] possibilities?

Shared space   'Session'
Holding what we hold and not to fear
Those bars
Where our history clashes or jars
And in lines unsymmetrical to the ear

Still hear
Deep reasonings of a different lore.
No map
Of any middle ground or overlap
Yet listening as never before –

I trained as a linguist and have always loved language. How could a poet not love language? In *Tongues* I give explicit expression to my lifelong delight in the word. Clearly every poem I had written implicitly rejoices

[15] p538, Micheal O'Siadhail, *Collected Poems,* Bloodaxe, Tarset, 2013
[16] p640, Micheal O'Siadhail, *Collected Poems,* Bloodaxe, Tarset, 2013

Say but the Word

in language, but here I want to revel in how words shift and change, how they are interrelated across languages and echo in us with the history[17] of three or four thousand years:

'Overlap'   A hidden image lurks behind each word,
            Some secret cargo stored below my mind,
            A resonance, a coloured first-time heard,
            Recalled frisson never quite defined.

I want to show in a playful way the extraordinary variety and inventiveness of the human imagination in the workings of language, in conveying meaning through visual signs, in proverbs which store wisdom. Then there is also my deep sense of gratitude to those who initiated me into other languages and their cultures.

But all this is hindsight. Collected poems are a kind of retrospective symphony. There was no grand plan. Different phases of growth, the various exigencies in the theatre of living call up the movements.

So much for the themes and movements. The classical Greek idea of the perfect marriage of content and form is probably every artist's dream. I have always tried to let a theme find its own form. Often things just fall[18] into a form:

'Caprice'   Delicious liberty of notes to rove
            Extempore
            Con amore
            As in between the lines we wove
            Inaudible noise
            Of a middle voice
            Underwrites our undersong,
            Cantus firmus
            Holding us
            In melodic progression, headstrong
            Silent tenor,
            Our rapport.

I am sure if you could scan a world of poetry somebody has used a similar form before. Who knows? But then there are many classical

---

[17]   p655, Micheal O'Siadhail, *Collected Poems,* Bloodaxe, Tarset, 2013
[18]   p537, Micheal O'Siadhail, *Collected Poems,* Bloodaxe, Tarset, 2013

forms and variations on classical forms: the sonnet, blank verse, villanelles, couplets, tercets, quatrains and many more. There is both syllabic verse and free verse.

There are combinations of classic rhyming and syllabic verse. One I like to call a saiku (which means 'craftmanship', 'a piece of work' in Japanese) and is for me a portmanteau word to describe alternating the great classical form of Japan, the *haiku*, with the great classical form of the west, the sonnet. 'Crimson Thread', the final poem in *Love Life,* is a saiku.

Another favourite is the zigzag rhyme, where a word in each line rhymes (or occasionally half-rhymes) with one word anywhere in the following line. I use this frequently in *The Gossamer Wall* to chain together a deliberately sober[19] account:

Company platoons surround the village.   'A Polish
Fugitives are shot. The others round   Village'
them up in the market. Anyone gives
trouble, gun them with infants or feeble
or any who hide. Able-bodied men
set aside for camps as 'work Jews'.

The rhymes or half-rhymes surround / round, fugitives / gives, anyone / gun, feeble / able, hide / aside bind the description with echoes.

I also love to alternate an eight syllable line with a six syllable line. I found myself tumbling towards this in *Tongues* when meditating[20] on characters:

Earlier three birds on a tree   'Collection'
But now only the one.
Imagine swoops of homing rooks
As evening tumbles in...

It is an honour to be a channel for our cries for meaning, for our desire to be part of some greater coherence. I spend my life in this 'ministry of meaning' which is poetry. I so often receive messages of response that hearten me and remind me of the privilege it is to word for others.

There are trends, fashions, pieties and politics in poetry as in all else.

[19] p424, Micheal O'Siadhail, *Collected Poems,* Bloodaxe, Tarset, 2013
[20] p749, Micheal O'Siadhail, *Collected Poems,* Bloodaxe, Tarset, 2013

I have always taken the long-term perspective on things. The Bengali poet[21] Rabindranath Tagore was on to this:

'Paper Boats' Day by day I float my paper boats one
  by one down the running stream.

  . . . .

  I hope that someone in some strange land
will find them and know who I am.

I am grateful to critics who gave time and energy to discovering who I am. The poet and novelist Mary O'Donnell ended an extraordinarily perceptive piece on *Tongues* by asking: Whither now?[22]

As I write I am coping with the most difficult circumstances in my life so far. At the same time I am trying to contemplate how the modern world of thought, imagination and action is shaped. Things personal and things societal. God only knows where all this will take me.

I am deeply grateful to my publishers, and to those who have invited me to read and to all who have supported me in so many ways. But in the end the circle of meaning is completed[23] by readers:

'Session' Guests all
At Madam Jazz's beck and call.
For nothing but the music's sake.

---

[21] p38, Rabindranath Tagore, *The Crescent Moon*, translated from the original Bengali by the author, Macmillan Company, New York, 1913

[22] pp335–341, *Studies*, Autumn 2012, vol.101, no.403, www.studiesirishreview.ie. Mary O'Donnell also contributed a chapter to *Musics of Belonging: The Poetry of Micheal O'Siadhail* eds. Marc Caball and David F. Ford (Carysfort Press, Dublin, 2007). Among a number of works, this book and David C. Mahan *An Unexpected Light: Theology and Witness in the Poetry and Thought of Charles Williams, Micheal O'Siadhail and Geoffrey Hill* (Wipf and Stock Publishers, Eugene, 2009) have been for me particular sources of insight into my own work.

[23] p640, Micheal O'Siadhail, *Collected Poems,* Bloodaxe, Tarset, 2013

Recently, Waterstones, the British bookstore chain in Ireland and the United States told us that poetry can sell as well as hardback fiction. So the old cliché that nobody reads poetry anymore just won't do. But what is the role of the poet in this society of ours? What sort of citizen is the poet? In many ways we are still the inheritors of the Byronic image of the poet as the passionate and irresponsible romantic. In an age dominated by impersonal bureaucracy, consumerism, and galloping technology, that image retains an understandable appeal. Yet, to accept that image is to marginalize the poet. Of course, the role of the despairing outsider is alluring. Sometimes, as an overreaction of a glorified outsider-ism, we want to take a loud political line, as though to demand a share in the action. When I think of the poet as worker, I suppose I have a certain vision of the *polis*, of an ecology of living – of the poet as citizen. I am not saying that, as I close the door of my study, this vision is uppermost in my mind. I understand any artist who maintains that there is far too much to do just getting the work right and that such philosophizing is best left to others. Of course, like any one else I am consumed with the desire for the true line.

In some ways, I am simply hooked on the thrill – the pulse of a phrase, and I am a boy playing again on the garden path. Two children are turning the ends of a skipping rope, and I'm nodding my head to the rhythm waiting to jump in. *Jelly on the plate, jelly on the plate, wibelty, wobelty* ... It is just as exciting and just as precarious. Or am I remembering that first self-recognition in a poem that wants to send some message of wonderment on and on? Is it the balm of release – something borne for so long at last sculptured and left in peace? I am sure, like any decision, in any commitment, there is a whole nexus of emotions, memories and compulsions – conscious and unconscious – that carries us along.

Yet, despite any dread of an intellectualization that loses its rootedness in the earth, I know that I have some vision of a poet as a citizen, a belief that an individual search for truth and understanding has a task and accountability. Of course, it is impossible to define such a viewpoint in an intellectual climate where such a thought is regarded as a subjective illusion. But I cling stubbornly to the notion of the covenant with the *polis*. There are so many tasks: to appropriate a tradition, to recharge words with mystery, to somehow find, here and now, the images to shape our meaning. I have the highest and the humblest of ambitions: to move, just a little, someone's flagging heart.

So often people ask out of a natural curiosity whether I write poetry every day. It's hard to explain. What can I say except that, for all the complex detours, every moment of my life is invested in every poem. It is an extraordinary time to be alive – all the changes, the sifting of the rubble of old certainties for new and tentative points of departure. To be there in the whirl is a lifelong venture, and I think I have been very fortunate in my background. I can't pretend there was any grand plan. Or was there? Sometimes in hindsight it looks as if there might have been. But I wasn't in control. I just stumbled there. Rightly or wrongly, some instinct kept me away from too much literary criticism. I think I have always been afraid it might jam me up, afraid that the drudgery of essays and exam answers might dim my passion.

I am glad that I was trained in linguistics. It has been such an enablement, and at so many levels. It's not just the concentrated clarity which scientific rigor imposes, although I'm grateful for that. It provided me with a model of a living organism, adapting, rearranging, growing, shedding dead skin – all the interwoven patterns of continuity and innovation. It stands me in good stead as a paradigm, no matter what field I explore in the long quest. No wonder language has been at the core of many debates in our time from philosophy to literary theory. It is such a gift to have the roots and semantic entanglements so wittingly in the foreground as I work.

Sometimes the service of my citizenship takes a more tangible form. It's a delight to be asked to give a poetry reading. The immediacy of an incarnate audience is always uplifting. I enjoy the chance that somewhere, sometime a seed may be sown. Someone suddenly remembers a long-forgotten spell cast many years ago in a classroom. Yet, I'm aware of the inherent hazards. The nature of readings may easily spawn a lightweight type of 'performance poetry', which, while it may have an instant entertainment value, ultimately serves to put people off the scent. There is also the subtler point that the open-ended quality, the multi-faced genius of a poem, which invites readers to identify their own experience, may sometimes be temporarily curtailed, during a reading, by imposing a shape on a poem the author no longer owns. But still I am happy to take the risks.

I had the privilege of serving on the last Arts Council and at present

I serve on the Advisory Committee on Cultural Relations. I am sure many people like me dream of some great and generous Renaissance patron to support and nourish us as we work. But an essential aspect of citizenship is living in the *here* and *now*. This is the age of public patronage. If it is more impersonal, by the same token, it is less arbitrary. I am pleased to have the opportunity to work with institutions to try to ensure that artists in Ireland are fostered by the government. Lofty words. In practice, it means meetings, subcommittees, reading lengthy documents and reports, attending countless events, and generally trying to inform oneself in order to make the best possible decisions.

There is never enough money for all you would like to fund. I suppose my responsibility involves selection and judgment. We can be aware of our ambivalences, of the ambiguities of any decision. But no action is possible without making a choice. And some decisions may not go the way you might personally want. It is always worthwhile, however, so long as you feel that balance of compromises is reasonable and you remain convinced that this is where a contribution, however small, can be made. Another call on my time and energy was my stint as editor of the journal *Poetry Ireland*. Once again, a maze of choices. But then it is not as if it were a regime which allowed only one journal. I recall speaking to a wiser colleague about this citizen's hesitancy at having to sit in judgment on work. 'Yes,' he said, 'it's difficult, but it's not so bad – younger people will soon be passing judgments on us as well as on their juniors'. The way of the world!

But first and last, there is the dream of the next poem. That great leveller – the blank page – waits in front of me. I raise my head to stare out the window at the garden path below. This is my chosen garden. Suddenly, it is another garden, the one chosen for childhood, and I hear the swish and tap of the skipping rope on the damp flags of the path.

If we are to take to ecology of living as a serious image, then how do we see the poet's niche in the ecosystem? I want to explore some angles of the relationship between poetry and society. Is there a genuine interaction between the two? Might poetry still be an essential strand in the weave of society? And I think we need to begin by clearing the decks. All too often, it seems to me, we are faced with a false opposition in, roughly, this form: poetry should have an immediate impact on society, therefore any poetry which is not overtly political is irrelevant. Seldom, of course, is this stated so baldly. The subtler other side of the coin is a vague suspicion that poetry with no *obvious* social critique leans

Say but the Word

towards an easy emotionalism, toward what Milan Kundera has labelled 'a lyrical relationship to the world'. In Ireland, this misleading opposition seems to be compounded by the swing from the sometimes romanticized rural ideal of earlier generations – caricatured by de Valera's 'laughter of happy maidens' – to a tough, realistic urban posture with its air of social critique. All of this is further compounded by the postmodernist shake-up of all our assumptions.

Obviously, many will dismiss any such opposition. All artists follow their own roads towards truth and there is room for a whole spectrum of adventures. There is good poetry and bad poetry. Yet, there is a danger here. If I am right that there is a certain mood abroad, which demands a societal perspective, then there is also the risk that the immediate appeal of an openly political poetry could wrongly consign the poetry of the hidden consciousness to easy emotionalism. I borrow the term 'hidden consciousness' from Vaclav Havel's description of the context of dissidence in *An Anatomy of Reticence.* 'That even something as seemingly ephemeral as the truth spoken aloud, as openly expressed concern for the humanity of humans, bears within itself a certain power and that even a word is capable of a certain radiation, of leaving a mark on the "hidden consciousness" of a community'. In other words, I am suggesting that, in the present climate, it is vital that we remind ourselves that whether there is a visible political content or not is irrelevant. At a much more fundamental level, any poet who unswervingly pursues an artistic truth, is potentially political.

How does this work? How can poetry mark the hidden consciousness of a community? Obviously, poetry works in all sorts of unpredictable ways and at many different layers of our consciousness, and it is only possible to glance at some of the niches in a complex ecosystem. And the ecological metaphor seems particularly appropriate as it implies that loss of poetry could throw the social habitat out of equilibrium. There is, of course the further implication that poet and society share in mutual responsibility. One immediately recognizable way in which a poet serves a community is by breaking down our isolation, by letting us know that we are not alone, by revealing a network of communal intimacy which cuts through our reticence and impersonality. Others share our yearnings, our loves, our forebodings: 'You are ashamed and then after years someone blabs and you find you are in the secret majority,' as Patrick Kavanagh observed. If we consider that short-circuiting of our reserve also extends into the past and into the future, then we approach the idea of a communal memory. Memory is at the core of poetry both on a personal and on a societal plane. Memory is the clue, the ball of thread unravelled back through the endless stumbling process of becoming, which is our identity. I often think madness must come when we change and can not face up to the steps and missteps along the way. Perhaps a poet is not only George Herbert's 'secretary of praise' but also our secretary of secrets. In the rush of our living, the image of poet as secretary minuting our shifting perceptions of ourselves is particularly apt.

If understanding our past is one task, what about the future? How easily we use the word 'imagination'. At a basic level, we know that, unless we can imagine, we are unable to act, unless we are able to picture ourselves doing something, we cannot do it. Yet, what precisely do I mean if I say that one of the levels at which poetry may permeate society is that of the imagination? Poetry can offer us the images, which can release us into the future. Supposing you are unable to make a choice. You know the pros and cons of all the choices and, retaining a vague sense of superiority and a consciousness of disablement you watch others make their choices. Then, someone says you are like a man wandering about in a draughty hall unable to decide to enter any room, forgetting that he is also in a room, the coldest one of all. If the images strike home, a whole framework is shaken. An image is a shaping of our future. Think of John Montague summoning up the picture of leaping over a stream when contemplating a marriage:

Leaps in the dark   'The Leap'
Returning now to steady
my mind, nourish
my courage as

No longer young
I take your hand
to face a different
more frightening task ...

Naturally, the power of images brings us to the question of language. The insight, the image and the language are interwoven. The role of poetry is often seen as that of guardian of a language. However I would like to extend this somewhat to include the more dynamic concept of

Say but the Word

an ecology, which stresses both a mutual responsibility and a continuing process of renewal. When so much of our culture demands that language is used to dissemble – 'disinformation' for 'lying'; 'tired and emotional' for 'drunk' – or when associations with our core words – 'motherhood', for example – are daily exploited and polluted to tempt us to consume, who can re-root language in genuine feeling? And by feeling I do not mean emotionality but rather a merger of mind and heart. Take away the poets' niche and how quickly we foul the habitat!

So far, in an attempt to place a poetry, which may seem at first glance to be utterly apolitical, I have alluded to poetry's workings in 'the pre-political hinterland,' to quote Vaclav Havel; of the imaginative junction of a memory and a future to its potential implications for language. Perhaps all this has wider significance? Is it too daring to speak of poetry as a cry for meaning? It is as if, suddenly in the flow of the world, we are jolted into remembering an all-consuming desire for fullness, a desire we had almost forgotten, and at this exotic moment in our daily living seems to collide with some vast longing for coherence we carry within us. And still this reawakening points us back to the flow. It is almost as if we live in and with a tension between the ongoing process of living and a realization of our smallness in the whole. The wonder of a poem comes when, for a split second, all is in balance, when, in Seamus Heaney's[24] lines:

'Song' There are the mud-flowers of dialect
And the immortelles of perfect pitch
And the moment when the bird sings very close
To the music of what happens.

If this view of poetry is true, think of the consequences. What might appear as a marginal, harmless, even self-indulgent, occupation is then a tiny mechanism functioning as our ecological fail-safe. Supposing we were to forget our fortitude? Supposing we thought ourselves infinite and capable of conquering and mastering all we survey? An entire mentality ensues. We pollute our environment and still think that by tinkering here and there we can fix everything, forgetting that we too are just a part of the household. We stockpile arms, and we forget that only mutual trust will do. So many enticing ideologies and 'isms' beguile

---

[24] p53, Seamus Heaney, *Field Work*, Faber & Faber, London, 1979

us into believing that we are conquerors and allow us escape that tension between daily living and a sense of our humble humanity. The saddest of all is that we did set out with the highest of motives. To think that an organization called 'Islamic Dawn' held hostages in chains in a six-by-ten-foot room or that a natural wish to give one's family the best chance ends in a lifetime's pursuit of status symbols! The lie for the sake of truth. We are all in danger and so much is at stake. I begin to wonder whether Osip Mandelstam did know what he was talking about when he said that he measured a civilization by the number of its poetry readers. If there is a Government of the Tongue, is poetry the Ministry of Meaning?

Say but the Word

All poetry is written in a historical context, against the backdrop of a certain mood or intellectual climate. By the end of the last century those 'masters of suspicion' Marx, Nietzsche and Freud had begun unmasking all the certainties our world had taken for granted. W. B. Yeats was to prove prophetic: 'Things fall apart; the centre cannot hold; Mere anarchy is loosed upon the world ...'[25] In Western intellectual circles, the certainties had crumbled. Then the world was riven by two world wars. Old dogmas were shored up. Only in the upsurge of the prosperous 1960s did the old mores, the absolute certainties, fall apart for the great majority of us. After the Holocaust, any romanticism was trivial. Now, the menace of nothingness and tedium loomed. Poets like T. S. Eliot[26] had been preparing our mood:

'The Hollow Men'
We whisper together
Are quiet and meaningless
As wind in dry grass
Or rats' feet over broken glass
in our dry cellar.

In our bitter reaction to the loss of a fixed and stable view of the world, a chasm of despair has opened. The fate of humanity seemed absurd. The poets responded in various ways according to their temperaments and outlooks. Like Louis MacNeice, some took a classical and stoical stance, a sort of brave and noble resignation[27] in the face of the void:

'The sunlight on the garden'
Our freedom as free lances
Advances towards its end;
The earth compels, upon it
Sonnets and birds descend;
And soon, my friend,
We shall have no time for dances.

---

[25] p210, W. B. Yeats, 'The Second Coming', *The Collected Poems of W. B. Yeats*, Macmillan, London, 1965

[26] p89, T. S. Eliot, 'The Hollow Men', *Collected Poems 1909–1962*, Faber & Faber, London, 1963

[27] p84, Louis MacNeice, *Collected Poems*, Faber & Faber, London, 1966

Others, in the Dylan Thomas mode, burnt the candle at both ends and raged 'against the dying of the light'. Whatever the response, by the 1960s, Beckett's Vladimir and Estragon had already entered into our bloodstream. Soon, even poetry's efforts at coming to grips with life would be called into question by a powerful anti-humanist movement.

I'm sure I'm not alone in remembering childhood in 1950s Dublin as a gentle garden of certainties. Then, there was the Victorian regime of school: the medals, the prizes, proof of the existence of God – proof by design, proof by reason. Imagine the shock when 'the masters of suspicion' undermined our lives. In the smoky early hours after the party in someone's flat we drank cheap wine and talked of Freud. The huge exhilaration – we knew and we knew. Such freedom. Many of our century who speak with deep authority – such as Solzhenitsyn, Havel, or even the recent hostage Brian Keenan – have had their freedom curtailed. Yet, strange to say, for us the crucible was affluence and freedom – an overwhelming liberation from the burdens of belief. Sometimes, I think, with Charles Péguy, that freedom is the hardest challenge of all:

Nous arrivons vers Vous de Paris capitale –
C'est là que nous avons nôtre gouvernement
Et nôtre temps perdu dans le lanternement
Et nôtre liberté décevant et totale

'Présentation de la Beauce à Notre-Dame de Chartres'

We come towards You from Paris city,
There were we have our government
And our time lost dawdling idly
In a freedom so delusive and absolute.

The trouble with our freedom was that it was always *from* something – from all those illusions 'the masters of suspicion' had exposed. We knew the price of all our options. It was as if, in the name of intellectual purity, we were paralyzed. We were that figure pacing the pure corridor unable to decide to enter any room and all the while forgetting that the corridor was also a choice – a cold choice. What if our freedom was a freedom for something?

Yet no matter what the choice, there can never again be certainty. Our answer is always in the interrogative mood, tentative, probing, and in the knowledge that truth has many faces. Yet, somehow we can only

Say but the Word

evaluate any truth existentially at its personal, local and particular level. All real knowledge is inhabited. This is where the testimony of an individual poet's journey may have its validity. As the individual burrows deeper and deeper into his own narrative, only time will tell if in any sense it is a soundboard for others of a generation. Perhaps Kavanagh, with his 'local row' and his 'Gods make their own importance' was also preparing our mood. Was he also prophetic?[28]

'Canal Bank Walk'

For this soul needs to be honoured with a new dress woven
From green and blue things and arguments that cannot be proven.

Over the last three decades our intellectual picture had begun to shift again by subtly reinterpreting itself in a fundamental way. Strangely, it is the sciences, which we associate with the Enlightenment's smothering of an earlier more humanist and pluralistic phase of the Renaissance and with industrialization, that provide us with key images. With its principles of uncertainty and complementarities, physics points us towards our human limitation and our inherent diversity. Only out of such profusion, slowly and humbly, we learn that, for all our technology and weapons and consumerism, we are not masters of the universe and can never have a monopoly on truth. Somehow we have to restore what George Steiner has called 'the covenant of trust'. Have we a responsibility to something, which is beyond us? So much of our insight is dominated by that fundamental picture of the universe as a vast cooperative household, of which we are only keepers. With this insight of interdependence, comes the corollary of responsibility towards the whole. The survival of the fittest has become the survival of the fittest system.

    The journey of my generation – or should I simply say my journey? – is inexorably interwoven with the shift in mood over those thirty years. It is not that we planned the journey but, as Heisenberg would tell us, we and what we observe are inextricably connected. Brendan Kennelly[29] hints at this in 'The Limerick Train':

'The Limerick Train'

We have travelled far, the journey has been
Costly, tormented odyssey through night;
And now, noting the unmistakable green ...

[28] p150, Patrick Kavanagh, 'Canal Bank Walk', *Collected Poems*, MacGibbon & Kee, London, 1964
[29] p30, Brendan Kennelly, 'The Limerick Train', *Selected Poems*, Allen Figgis, Dublin, 1969

Say but the Word

It is impossible to say how much of our story is that of any generation and how much is particular to the theatre of our times. Yet, that tiny journey has all the elements of the classic adventure: setting out, challenging the world, endeavour and failure, the underworld, achievement, the return …

What eventually allows some of us to take the choice, responsibility implies, what can remake the 'covenant of trust' with life? Our imperfect answer has a sort of circularity. Perhaps the only answer can be to experience trust in the daily round, to have had the luck to grow again in a network of trusting relationships, or to feel responsibility for others in a grid of trust. Again, the ecological image is in place; there is a sense of interdependence. And all this leaves room for diversity and pluralism. Various ecosystems may share the same habitat. For me, the central image is the garden. We set out from that garden of certainties our parents chose for us, and return to a garden we choose. The garden is never ultimately achieved. Its growth is nursed and tended and it endures all the moods of seasons. It is always in the making.

There is little new in all of this. In some respects, if it is truthful, it is the simple story of our humanity and it courts universality. If that truth is vivid enough, it may have more than a contemporary pertinence. Still, it has the particularity of our time and place. One of the positive sides of our times, this 'post-modern' era, is that we are thrown back to the local and the particular. Only by holding up the single prism do we catch the spectrum of colours. We have no need to apologize for anything and are released from any post-colonial feelings of inferiority, as poets here on an island off an island off the European mainland. Our grain of sand is big enough to contain the universe. We are all cut down to size. Dante Alighieri, a man banished to the political wilderness, had time to think[30] that through:

In that abyss I saw how love held bound   Canto XXXIII
Into one volume all the leaves whose flight   lines 85–87
Is scattered through the universe around;

'Scattered through the universe …' Recently, as the plane broke for a moment through the clouds, I caught a frail glimpse of a city below. I

---

[30] p345, *The Comedy of Dante Alighieri the Florentine, Cantica III Paradise <Il Paradiso>*, translated by Dorothy L. Sayers and Barbara Reynolds, Penguin Classics, Harmondsworth, 1962

Say but the Word

thought again of Dante in fourteenth-century Florence grappling with choice and all its implications for city and self. I remember those diagrams of Dante's universe: 'Section-Map of Hell' with its nether regions of panderers, seducers, flatterers, or 'General View of Paradise' with its seventh heaven for contemplatives. I suppose one of the things that is fascinating about Dante is how he took on the cosmos of his time. And what a different cosmos we inhabit with our chaos theory, black holes and fuzzy logic! But it is easy to think of the past as something steady, diagrammatic and confined. Our era may resemble Dante's more than strikes us at first glance. His exploration of good and evil speaks of our time. The great Enlightenment dream of progress has been undermined. Whether it is the Holocaust, Rwanda, or Belfast, we know the struggle with the dark is always with us. We have learned yet again that the problem of power and evil is still at the core of our living. We see more acutely than ever before what Dorothy Sayers termed 'the ease with which our most God-like imaginings are betrayed by what is false within'.

The other feature of Dante that intrigues is his approach through the particulars of his time and place. His hell and heaven have real people, each with a unique face and history: Francesca da Rimini and Beatrice. Francesca was the wife of Gianciotto da Verruchio and she had an affair with her brother-in-law Paulo. And Beatrice Dante met at a party at the home of Folco Portinari in Florence and she made his heart tremble. And all this against the background of independent, feuding city-states and a power struggle between the Guelfs and the Ghibellines.

For all that our own turbulent and shifting times prepare us for Dante, there is a fundamental difference. It seems that the basic insight of our period is that there is no 'section-map' or 'general view' of our cosmos. Our world is made of each particular encounter after the next. This Francesca. That Beatrice. This chance meeting and this parting. We are immersed in something over which we have no final control. It is as though we have the particular without an overarching universal, the faces but no map. I mentioned earlier the poet's responsibility to society and about the way the potential of memory and image affect us. Our cities are so different from Dante's. There is no longer a community of one epic, one Dante. Nobody understands this better than the contemporary poet. In many ways, a poet is an intensification of the modern self. Think of the chances involved? One small book on a crowded bookshelf. Which bookshops may stock the book and for how long? Who happens into the shop or browses in that particular section?

Say but the Word

Nowhere more than at poetry readings is this serendipity apparent. Someone saw a poster or heard a radio interview. Someone had a friend who knew someone else who said she enjoyed a previous book. It's all so fragmented and haphazard. So much randomness. But it is real, and I can see those faces. I know all the risks as I read. I preface a love poem by saying that I've been so fortunate and still I wonder if there is someone in the audience struggling with a failing relationship. Or is someone suffering from loneliness? For an American audience I am reading a poem about jazz and how the extraordinary story of Black America threw up a music whose mode of surprise and improvisation, of adaptation and unpredictability, seems somehow to suggest how our cosmos works. Could that face at the back feel that I am condescending? Everything I say is poured out of a male experience, while women are more than half of my audience.

What is strange in all of this is that I know I do not own a poem. I have always felt that I have never created anything. The term 'creative writing' still frightens me; it seems to have an air of presumption about it. The most I can hope to achieve is to allow a poem to pass through me. I can shape it in the way an instrument shapes a sound. I can try to keep the instrument pure and in tune. Not only do I not own it in its making, I certainly have no rights in how it is listened to. Imagine all the various experiences, the richness of joy and sorrow, all the lives and stories being brought to bear on that listening. Good listening scotches modern correspondence theories of truth. There can be no one meaning among the endless resonances. Each member of an audience is radically different. Who has any command over the complete otherness of response?

'All the leaves whose flight is scattered through the universe'. In spite of, or maybe even on account of randomness, there is still the community of a book. I have often noticed that trait of Irish people who meet abroad to set about immediately finding someone they both know before the conversation proceeds on *terra firma*. This is how it is when I discover that the blank stranger of a moment ago admires a book that I love. Say it is *Middlemarch* and we are off talking about Casaubon. Which is the worse fate, to be a Casaubon or to be a Lydgate? Remember that scene with Dorothea at the cemetery? It is amazing that somehow Mary Garth has gifts that Dorothea had to strive for? We walk shared ground of experience, a mutual world.

Sometimes I catch glimpses. I have my precious memories of listeners – a class of convent girls I visited near Detroit. I still see those rows of beautiful, open faces. One of their young teachers had died suddenly the night before and some had obviously been crying. I read a poem in memory of a teacher of my own to channel something of their sorrow. Already recalling my own teacher, I'm overwhelmed by how time has travelled since I sat in a classroom listening to a writer. I tell them that to stand here, reading for them, is my dream come true. Then, I introduce a poem and talk about how the polyphonic music of the Renaissance seemed to allow for a plurality that Romantic music with its greater concentration on melody and accompanying chord narrowed. A glance at their names – Donovan, Fontana, Hilewsky, Roth, Young – all the spectrum of their background shines through – such blending and up-rootedness. Next day I hear from the teacher how they asked her questions they had not dared ask me. How old was he? Is he a friend of yours? Is he married? Were the love poems he read about his wife? So young, and so openhearted. Will one of those faces stand sometimes in front of a class of seventeen-year-olds telling of a dream come true?

Once in a theatre in the West of Ireland a woman bought a ticket and stood looking confused explaining she has never been in a theatre before. When she spoke to me after the reading, she told me how her alcoholic husband had drowned some months previously. She was lying in bed one day when she heard a poem on the radio and said 'I'm going to be at that reading.' One delicate message along the super-highway. Among all the daily bombardment of images manipulating us, the image in a poem invites. She had driven thirty or forty miles and here she stood facing me. I think Robert Bly's rendering[31] of those final lines of Rilke's *Das Lied des Blinden*, 'Song of the Blind Man'

'Das Lied des Blinden'

Euch kommt jeden Morgen das neue Licht
warm in die offene Wohnung.
Und ihr habt ein Gefühl von Gesicht zu Gesicht,
und das verleitet zur Schonung.

'Song of the Blind Man'

Every morning new light comes
warmly into the open house,
and you have a feeling that moves from face to face,
and that leads you astray to caring.

[31] pp114–115, *Selected poems of Rainer Maria Rilke: A Translation from the German and Commentary by Robert Bly*, Harper & Row, New York, 1981

Say but the Word

I am reading to a university library hall full of professors, scholars whose reputation I know and a crowd of the pick of the brightest students. There is the inevitable threat of inadequacy, that what you stand for will not pass intellectual muster. I gloss the title of my latest collection *The Middle Voice*, speaking of the grammatical feature known to some of us from Greek or Icelandic. It is halfway between activity and passivity and gives us a metaphor for our middle years as we feel the surge of a generation behind us and watch the one ahead fade from us. Is the silence of an audience asking 'So what?' But those reputations turn to faces and there they are vulnerable, as all of us. I have a sense that among intellectuals, and maybe particularly in North America, there is a realization that in all the uncertainty and the undercutting of humanist values, there is a new mood, interrogative and tentative, seeking to find something to unite the mind and heart. Poetry moves in from the edges.

Then there was that reading in a bookshop. I am reading to the faithful in a specially arranged nook. A flicker of my eye catches casual browsers drifting around the shelves in the background. Some are impervious and float away again, apparently utterly unaware. Some stare with a mild curiosity and wander off. Then a man carrying a book or two, waltzes right around the audience, whistling loudly like somebody warding off the dark. The organizer whispers to him. He flings the books on the floor and stomps out of the area. Is poetry so threatening?

Another sidling from behind some shelf, takes his place in the back row, drawn into the spell of words. That is how it will always be. The luck of the draw. I strive to hold my concentration and keep on reading as though nothing has happened. Patrick Kavanagh knew all about responsibility: 'Someone in the streets may guide by my star ...'

It seems as if a poet is almost a paradigm of the modern self, which is never allowed to settle in an equilibrium. Always we're off-balance, involved in the criss-cross of shifting strands of complexities, a tie in a frail network. We can never have a total vision precisely because its texture is communication. In ways, the poet is an intensifier of that experience of self with all its possibilities. In the riot of communication, which is our modern living, the distortions, the puzzles, the uncertain boundaries, the disjointedness are all our business. We have to face squarely the abuses of trust – our masking of power and domination by wealth or race or gender. The corruption of the best is, as Shakespeare[32] knew, the worst:

[32] p1377, William Shakespeare, Sonnet 94, Collins Complete Works, Glasgow, 1994

'Sonnet 94'   For sweetest things turn sourest by their deeds:
              Lilies that fester smell far worse than weeds.

Any route that evades the distortions of trust and love can so easily fade
into Romanticism or an escapist Modernism in a search for sources of
riches and meaning. I know no short cut. I don't believe we can turn our
back on the objectivity the Enlightenment led us to believe in by simply
disappearing into subjectivity in any of its many attractive guises. We
must live in that tension between the objective and the subjective with
all the choices and dilemmas that brings with it. I find myself agreeing[33]
with Charles Taylor's *Sources of the Self:*

We are now in an age in which a publicly accessible cosmic order of
meanings is an impossibility. ... why it matters and what it means to
have a more deeply resonant human environment and, even more,
to have affiliations with some depth in time and commitment. These
are questions, which we can only clarify by exploring the human
predicament, the way we are set in nature and among others, as a
locus of moral sources. As our public traditions of family ecology,
even polis are undermined or swept away, we need new languages of
personal resonance to make crucial human goods alive for us again.

For all the distortions, there is a feast. As George Herbert knew, we can
all be partakers – some of us with the anxious, caring eye and inside
knowledge of a host, others with the more carefree and observing eye
of the enjoying guest. One of the best things about arriving to give a
poetry reading is knowing that I am frequently the generator of feasts.
Often a committee or a department comes together to celebrate the
occasion. Sometimes, it is people who work together but live in the
usual rush and bustle of institutions. And the talk and fun! Everything
so unpredictable as the conversations ebb and flow. News of other poets.
Mention of books. The latest on friends of friends I have met along the
way. For a moment a node in a network[34] of fragile cities:

'Love (III)'   You must sit down, sayes Love, and taste my meat:
                  So I did sit and eat.

---

[33]   p512, Charles Taylor, *Sources of the Self: The Making of the Modern Identity*, Cambridge University
       Press, 1989
[34]   p192, 'Love (III)', *The English Poems of George Herbert*, ed. C. A. Patrides, J. M. Dent, London, 1974

Say but the Word

Isn't language an extraordinary thing? And to think that everyone has a language! It is such a take-for-granted part of all our daily lives and everything we do. It is the most distinctive human gift. Not only do we all learn and know a language but a large majority of people as mothers and fathers know the joy of being language teachers, the delight of passing on their own mother tongue.

What is also amazing is how average four-year-olds, without ever being specifically taught complex rules, can not only speak grammatically but can come up with sentences they have never heard before. It seems that we have an innate facility to acquire language. There is good linguistic and even genetic evidence, that we're hardwired to work language.

Yet we never finish and never completely know even our own language. We go on learning all our lives. If we enter a trade or profession we learn the jargon. Someone uses a phrase you never heard before and you pick it up. Think of all the new words my generation absorbed in the technological revolution we're living through as we entered a new world of 'booting up', 'dropdown menus', 'taskbars' and 'spam filters'. If you take up a new sport there are 'genoas' or 'birdies'. Part of children's fascination with Tolkien's *Lord of the Rings* is the variety of languages he invents for the Middle-Earth. Any new cult or subculture we enter will teach us a whole new vocabulary whether it's the criminal underworld of 'fencing' or the 'consciousness raising' of a political subgroup. We are endless language learners.

And words are so strange. Each seems to have an aura of its own. Whole institutions split over a word. The Roman Catholic Church and the Eastern Orthodox Church parted in 1054 over the addition of *filioque* (and the Son) to the Nicene Creed. People kill one another over words. Think of the use of 'ethnic cleansing' in Eastern Europe or how in the Rwandan genocide the Hutu branded the Tutsi as 'cockroaches'.

There are whole fields and networks of meaning. Over time meanings slide and change. When I was a boy 'adult' only meant 'grown-up'. Then it was used to convey 'suitable for adults'. Now it also means 'pornographic' as in an 'adult movie'. We are half-conscious of the transition. The shifts of sense and usage accumulate over hundreds even thousands of years within one language.

Then again languages are related. Even a quick glance at the word for 'mother' in, say, Spanish and Italian *madre*, Catalan *mare*, French *mère* and Portuguese *mãe* would lead you to think that there was something in common. On balance if we compare these various words for 'mother', we might work out what they have in common and build up a picture of what word they might all be derived from. In fact, we know that historically all of them were originally Latin and so they all come from Latin *mater*. But there again if we take a wider angle and look at the word for 'mother' in, for example, Latin *mater*, English *mother*, Irish *máthair*, Greek *mētēr* and *mātár* in the language of ancient India, by using the same comparative method, we might work out what word they should all have come from. Given the variations we reckon on a word like *mātár* as its origin. Here we do not know the history but we have to believe that in all probability this language existed. This hypothetical common ancestral language must have spread across most parts of Europe and in certain parts of India.

Scholars making use of the comparative method and what they call 'internal reconstruction', that is working out the original form within a group of closely related languages, have figured out with an extraordinary degree of precision not only the words but also the grammar of this hypothetical language, which they call 'Proto-Indo-European'. On top of this, we can get some picture of the culture, the society and environment, the economy and technology, even the religion and poetics of those who spoke this language. There is a lot of controversy as to exactly when and where this language was spoken. It is largely agreed that it probably had split into differing dialects by the third millennium BCE.

While in an example like 'mother' it is relatively easy to see the relationship, this is not always so. The nexus of rules describing the developments and connections are so well worked through that words which, on the surface seem most unlikely to be related are revealed to have a common origin. For instance, at first there seems little connection between English 'queen', the Irish word *bean* meaning woman (which has entered English as the first element in 'banshee') and the Greek word *gunē* 'woman' (which we see in the first part of 'gynecology').

Of course there are many other large families of languages besides the Indo-European. There are Sino-Tibetan, Semitic, Ural-Altaic families and so on. Some have tried to find common origins for a number of these families, but this is highly speculative.

Why am I explaining all this? I just want to give a sense of the scope of the shifts and linkages. In meditating on words, I want to allow these relationships to shine through and illuminate the intricate marvel of language.

As a poet I am utterly intrigued by the rampant imagination of human beings. I think of Wallace Stevens's famous 'Thirteen Ways of Looking at a Blackbird'. Languages have infinite ways of looking at one thing. In English there is the 'presentation' of a prize. It has all the resonances of present or gift and has its origin in the Latin for something which 'is before' someone. That seems to a speaker of English straightforward enough. But then in French it's a 'delivery' or 'handing over' (*remise*), in German it's 'hiring out' or 'loaning' (*Verleihung*), in Icelandic 'a parting with or handing over' (*afhenda*) and so on. Again to an English speaker it is clear that you can wear hats, shirts, trousers, gloves or glasses, while in Japanese there is a different verb used for all of these. Or to take the example of an idiom in English, it rains 'cats and dogs' but in French it is 'strings' (*de cordes*), in Irish 'a cobbler's knives' (*sceanna gréasaí*) and in Welsh 'old women and sticks' (*hen wragedd a fyn*). Here are just four ways of looking at rain. But of course it is endless.

The great linguist Edward Sapir[35] once said 'Every language is itself a collective art of expression... An artist must utilise the native esthetic resources of his speech. He may be thankful if the given palette of colours is rich, if the springboard is light. But he deserves no special credit for felicities that are the language's own.' For a while in the first half of the 20th century, Sapir and another linguist Benjamin Whorf propounded the view that the language a person speaks affects the way that he or she thinks, meaning that the structure of the language itself affects cognition. The standard example was the number of words (later shown to be somewhat exaggerated) Eskimos have for snow. This view, though no doubt it has some validity, is too deterministic. Life is more porous and clearly we can acquire other languages.

This brings me to that unbelievable joy of learning a new language. There is a special delight in discovering how things can be said differently. The feeling of becoming a child again and being the butt of everybody else's knowledge. Yet being an adult you are able to be guided by a tradition of grammar and rules. You are trying to get your tongue and head to chime. There is a rollercoaster of feelings of elation and despair, of progress and shortfall. Sometimes there is a sense of *déjà entendu* as if some latent part of your personality is waking. And you are not just

---

[35] p225, Edward Sapir, *Language: An Introduction to the Study of Speech*, New York, 1921.

Say but the Word

learning words but also a history, a geography, an entire culture. Then a whole new world of friendships is growing.

I mentioned the word grammar. This is in some ways an astounding phenomenon. We have here the basic patterns on which we can turn endless variations. It is a way of keeping the 'ecology' of the personal innovation and the possibility of community in play. It is the genetic code that allows for infinite mutations. Or to put it another way, it is the tune on which we can riff to our heart's content.

For many children of my generation the word conjures up hours of parsing and analysis and learning declensions and conjugations off by heart. I began Latin at primary school where we learned our verbs off by heart as we learned our tables. *Amo, amas, amat.* But looking back on the wealth of terms we used 'the ablative absolute', 'the prolative infinitive', 'the sequences of tenses' and 'final clauses', I am amazed at how as children we just drank in these mysterious expressions. I was not surprised when I discovered years later that the word 'glamour' was originally 'grammar'. It was apparently a Scottish variant of the word 'grammar', which because it was associated with learning came to mean 'magic'. And so the meanings 'charm', 'allure', 'excitement', though often with a connotation of the ephemeral. But little did I as a schoolboy think ... I want now to return, to make these terms my own, to enjoy the strange enchantment: 'verbs of hoping, promising, threatening, swearing are usually followed by the future infinitive ... '

Some years ago when my books started to appear in Japanese translation, with the help of my translator and friend Professor Shigeo Shimizu, I started to try to tackle Japanese. I was fascinated by the fantastic 'characters' or signs. You know the way, you have so often seen, what seems just a blur of eastern squiggles on a restaurant or shop front, but you could not for the life of you distinguish one from the other, not to mention remembering them or imagine how they could convey meaning. It began to dawn on me that we use such signs here in Europe too. We all know how a stylised figure of a man or woman signs which toilet we head for. Or how a knife and fork sign in a list of hotels tells us there is a restaurant. Again a stylised figure in a wheelchair indicates facilities for the disabled. But what may at first appear to us as squiggles is a whole system of such signs that has evolved over something like four millennia and which can be read by about a sixth of the world's population. But what grabs me is that these 'characters' can express abstract thought. One thing is to draw some picture of a concrete object but how do you illustrate concepts like 'worry', 'meaning' 'experience'?

These signs or characters derive from ones that originated between 2000 and 1500 BCE in the Yellow River region of China. The earliest were inscribed on bones and tortoise shells. Starting as simple they grew abstract, complex and highly stylised. They were brought to Japan by Chinese and Korean migrants in the third or fourth century CE. In Japanese, these signs can be read as Chinese loanwords or as native Japanese words. For example 言 can be read as *gen* if taken as a Chinese borrowed word or as *koto* if read as the native Japanese word. To take another example 聖 can be read as *sei-*, if taken as a Chinese borrowed word or as *hijiri* if read as a native Japanese word.

Normally the Japanese are only conscious of the origin of the most transparent characters. Otherwise they are largely unaware, just as English speakers do not know the roots of most words they use daily. I am by no means the first western poet to meditate on these signs. Probably the most famous example in English is Ezra Pound's *Cantos*. He had been introduced to them through Ernest Fenollosa's work. Fenollosa spent long periods in Japan and contributed greatly to Japanese culture. At one point he travelled through America with a magic lantern lecturing on these signs. The *Cantos* were written between about 1915 and 1956. But there is also the earlier French language tradition with figures such as the Belgian Henri Michaux and later, such works as Paul Claudel's *Connaissance de l'Est* (1900) and Victor Segalen's *Stèles* (1912). And yet we have gone beyond any simple 'Orientalia' and in a culture bombarded by visual images, these signs remain rich enough to sustain endless meditations.

We live in a new oral and visual culture. Alongside the image comes the soundbite. In any language, proverbs are a source of metaphor and wisdom. When someone says 'there is no smoke without fire', nobody looks around to find a fire. It is like the third line of a *haiku* and we know at once this is not to be taken literally. It sums up the long hard-earned experience of a community and saves it reinventing the wheel over and over again.

I find the variation in metaphors from language to language quite astonishing. Sometimes images must have spread from country to country. Other times the same image arose from a similar way of life, even though there probably was no contact. I love the nugget-like intensity of the proverbs; it is almost as if there was an economy of truth which is like gnomic Edda verse.

Say but the Word

Then too there has always been a secondary, often facetious and formulaic layer of 'Wellerism' about in many languages. A Norwegian example is: Make haste slowly, said the farmer as he ate his porridge with an awl. I believe cynical proverbs were popular in Soviet Russia. Perhaps there is some connection between the level of public trust and the frequency of these undercuttings of traditional wisdom. And they go on showing up in new circumstances or turn an old-fashioned sentiment upside down. Popular in Norway among women, for instance: 'when God created the human being, she began with a rough draft' or 'men will be men, strong and childish'.

Of course, the suspicion of language itself has been at the heart of many intellectual quandaries. Interwoven with Marxist, feminist and postcolonial critiques, language itself has been doubted. Jacques Derrida and Michel Foucault played with the Saussurean view of the sign as an arbitrary convention. Roland Barthes argued that the sign had to be seen as a sign in order not to underpin illusions of reality. Paul de Man went a stage further insisting that language is always weaving between the literal and the metaphorical which in the end renders it unreadable. And so on ...

This line of suspicion largely derives from Ferdinand de Saussure's view of language as a complete system of signs. On the other hand the French philosopher Paul Ricoeur has opened up again the whole question of the relation of the sign to reality and imagination. Clearly there is no one-to-one linkage but rather a complex interaction. Language is vital for history's narrative or for a judge's decision or for great works of fiction. According to Ricoeur 'through the capacity of language to create and recreate, we discover reality itself in the process of being re-created ... language in the making creates reality in the making'. Our sense of who we are is mediated through language.

In the end I know all the dangers and suspicion and yet I must trust. Only by keeping the whole scope and richness of words and signs in play, by feasting on the fullness of language, can we hope to allow this our unique human gift to flourish.

My friend the painter Mick O'Dea once told me how he has all his life been enthralled by paint, by the feeling of taking clay and the oils of the earth and daubing them on a canvas. As a poet I know nothing quite like the thrill of taking these organised sounds and signs we make and shaping them in sequences of rhythm and meaning. I want to hold up the wonder of words and say: How about this?

Say but the Word

Introduction

Since my childhood I had only had one dream. I wanted to write poetry. I loved language and it seemed to me that to seize thoughts and feeling in words and rhythms was a kind of magic. I chose as a student to study language and became convinced that to understand the workings and intricacies of language would enhance whatever poetry I would come to write. It always comes as a shock to me when I discover a linguist who doesn't delight in poetry or, for that matter, a poet who thinks that any systematic study of language is a hindrance to true poetic feeling.

In some ways this reflects the split between the objective and subjective approach which has permeated and indeed bedevilled so much European thought. A scientific or systematic view of language and its grammar is often thought of by poets as boring, objective and without feeling. On the other hand, for linguists all this poetry stuff is emotional, subjective and lacking in rigour.

It seems this usage of subjective as opposed to objective took root at the end of the 17th century. Besides English most major European languages such as German, French, Spanish, Italian and Russian have adopted these words to express this opposition. Some less widely spoken European languages have coined their own version. There is, for example Icelandic *huglægur* 'thought-ly' and *hlutlægur* 'thing-ly' (alongside *súbjektívur* and *objektívur*) or Welsh which employs what are basically grammatical *goddrychol* ('under' and 'aspect' with an adjectival ending) and *gwrthddrychol* ('against' and 'aspect' with an adjectival ending).

However if we move outside of Europe, it's fascinating to see how, when the Japanese came to terms with European culture during the Meiji Era (1868–1912), they came up with two extraordinarily imaginative words to express this distinction 習慣的 *shukanteki* 'seen as a host' for subjective and 客観的 *kyakukanteki* 'seen as a guest'. It's quite an image: the host is involved emotionally trying to see that all the guests are tended too; the guests are sitting back observing proceedings with dispassion. What is so intriguing about this way of conceiving the contrast is that both the host and the guest have the feast in common. This is what lies behind a short poem of mine from the second section of a collection entitled *Tongues* which celebrates language. In this section I meditate on a chain of words. Here[36] is one called 'Subjectivity':

'Subjectivity'   Was the whole world a feast for Japanese?
Europe's 'subjective' and 'objective' adapted
As either the view of host or guest.

A bird-eyed caller observes and leaves the rest
To the work of a busy host laying on a spread.
Together our life all of a piece.

The host's and the guest's perspectives may be different but they are in a mutual and complementary relationship. This brings me to Karen Blixen's *Babette's Feast.*

Babette's Feast: Both…And…

Babette's Feast is perhaps one of the most remarkable modern literary uses of feasting as a kind of parable. The novella is best known to many as a Danish film directed by Gabriel Axel in 1987. I have never seen the film. I read the book in what I took to be the original Danish only to discover afterwards that apparently Karen Blixen first both wrote and published the work in English and subsequently translated it into her native Danish. Given the beautifully nuanced and very Danish tone of the book, it's difficult to think of it as being originally written in English.

I won't attempt to summarise the plot more than to say that two sisters, daughters of the founder of an austere pious Christian sect in the extreme north of Norway and who had once been pursued by lovers, are now elderly and have a French domestic help whom they took in as a refugee from a bloody counter-revolutionary Paris. She had been a cook in a famous Paris restaurant. She wins a large sum of money in a lottery which she spends on providing a feast for the dwindling grey-haired congregation to celebrate the memory of the sisters' father. The ascetic congregation are afraid of the sensual pleasures involved and resolve not to praise the meal but they are raised by the feast to new levels of warmth, humanity and delight.

The whole novella is permeated with references to the New Testament. There are references to the New Jerusalem, to Mary and Martha and, very directly, to the Marriage Feast at Cana. Hadn't the

[36] p671, Micheal O'Siadhail, *Collected Poems*, Bloodaxe, Tarset, 2013

Lord's power chosen to reveal itself so fully, even to reveal itself in drink? There is the further suggestion of the Eucharist. The Protestant Reformation can be thought of as placing a new emphasis on the word as opposed to the greater stress laid on sacrament by the Catholic tradition. In describing the sect Blixen says that they sought out one another to read and interpret the word. The French domestic help, Babette Hersant, is clearly Catholic by background and her feast is sacramental. In many ways Blixen's novella is a parable against either/or perspectives and a plea for both/and.

So much in our society is built on such binary oppositions. So often in our universities there is little cross-fertilisation between different branches of knowledge. Various schemes try to encourage interdisciplinary study so that the university doesn't become a polyversity. Just think of how even within literature there is now a tendency to establish creative writing departments as separate from English departments. The creative writers can regard the English department as hidebound and unimaginative and the English departments return the compliment in viewing the creative writers as flabby and unschooled in the tradition of English literature. But our concern here is the divide between literature and linguistics. So I now want to invite you to a feast where we can savour the delights of both word and system, of both poetry and language.

But just before we start, it's important that that the banquet table is laid with white paper napkins. Enthusiasm, a fired up heart and mind in our age of literacy, often needs somewhere to write down an example or note a memorable phrase. I don't know if times have changed but when I was a student passionate linguists would inevitably reach for either a napkin or a coaster to demonstrate a development or a relationship between forms of words. The American linguist Eric Hamp is famous for his napkins illustrations. I know as a poet I have time and time again scribbled on a napkin a line that had been buzzing in my head or a phrase that I knew I needed. I still often find in my pockets a napkin I'd forgotten. The poet Francis Thompson (1859–1907), best known for *The Hound of Heaven*, always had lines of poems written on bits of paper. When he died a line or two were found on a scrap. Given the poverty he lived in, it was hardly a napkin. But now, provided with napkins, we can get down to the real meat of our common oral enjoyment.

Oral Pleasures: Savouring Words

What an irony that Karen Blixen, who suffered from anorexia, understood so well how both words and food are oral pleasures. The worldly wise General Löwenhielm, who had once been a suitor of one of the elderly sisters and turns up at the feast, describes how Babette was able to transform every meal at the *Café Anglais* – where she had been a cook – into a kind of love affair, a noble and romantic love relationship in which one was no longer able to distinguish between physical and spiritual appetite or satiety. The final section of a book of mine, *A Fragile City*, which is a meditation on trust, is called *Feasting.* For me sharing the pleasure of a meal is an image for full and rich relationships of trust, and I tried to catch something of this in a poem[37] entitled 'Delight':

'Delight'   Let the meal be simple. A big plate
of mussels, warm bread with garlic,
and enough mulled wine to celebrate

Being here. I open a hinged mussel
pincering a balloon of plump meat
from the blue angel wings of a shell.

A table's rising decibels of fun.
Such gossip. A story caps a story.
Banter. Then another pun on a pun.

Iced yoghurt snipes at my temples.
My tongue matches a strawberry's heart
with its rough skin of goose-pimples.

Conversations fragment. Tête-à-tête,
a confidence passes between two guests.
A munch of oatcake thickens my palate.

Juicy fumes of a mango on my breath.
(A poem with no end but delight.)
I knife to the oblong host of its pith.

---

[37]   p309, Micheal O'Siadhail, *Collected Poems,* Bloodaxe, Tarset, 2013

Wine sinks its ease to the nerve-ends.
Here are my roots. I feast on faces.
Boundless laughter. A radiance of friends.

In attempting to give some sense of that delight, which surely both poets
and linguists experience, I am of course also savouring the words 'a
hinged mussel pincering a balloon of plump meat'. There is sheer
physical pleasure in the sounds. Just feel the 'in' sound in 'hinged' and
'pincering' with the 'n' echoing again in 'balloon'. Then enjoy those
plosive 'p's in 'pincering' and 'plump' and the 'm's in 'mussel and meat'.
Then let the half-rhymes or full rhymes ricochet in your consciousness
'mango on my breath' and 'oblong host of its pith' or 'ease to the nerve-
ends and a radiance of friends'.

Even the most obdurately analytical linguist must know the charge
and taste of a word in the mouth, the oral pleasure which doesn't depend
on sense or context. This is what Lewis Carroll[38] was on about in
'Jabberwocky':

'Twas brillig, and the slithy toves   'Jabberwocky'
    Did gyre and gimble in the wabe;
All mimsy were the borogoves,
    And the mome raths outgrabe.

In my book *Tongues*, after a quarter of a century devoting my time
entirely to poetry with hardly a hint of my previous academic life as a
professor of language, I wanted, like a painter meditating on colour and
light, to celebrate the wonder of language with which I work. Here from
Tongues is a sonnet[39] from 'Grooves':

Smack and kiss of lips that spread around,   'Grooves'
Feel of tongue shaping flows of air
Knowing how to streamline any sound,
Curl and arch of oral savoir-faire.
Sheer delight before the paradigm,
Buzz of groove and tooth with z between,
Jabberwocky thrill of nonsense rhyme,

---

[38] p127, Lewis Carroll, 'Jabberwocky', *The New Oxford Book of Light Verse*, ed. Kingsley Amis,
    Oxford, 1978
[39] p660, Micheal O'Siadhail, *Collected Poems*, Bloodaxe, Tarset, 2013

Taste of words before the thing they mean.
Vowels ooze around my chortling tongue
Finding whatever curve they need to voice
Liquid music's humming jubjub bird;
Vocal chords a violin highly-strung
Freighting through my mouth a dancing voice,
Endless joy of one incarnate word.

Once sitting in a lounge at Philadelphia airport when my late-evening flight was delayed until early the following morning, I was sitting beside a mother tending an overtired infant who was growing restless. She began to repeat over and over some strange soothing phrase which the child listened to and began to settle before falling asleep. I have no idea what language this woman spoke to her child. It was clear that there is pleasure not only in speaking but also in listening. I began to think of all the words for hushaby in various languages: Irish *seoithín, seoithín, seó a leanbh*, German *aja papaya, aja papaja*, Italian *ninna nanna*, Norwegian *byssa, byssa barnet*, Icelandic *bí bí og blaka* and so on. I decided to make a kind of global cradle song. Here[40] is 'Lullaby':

'Lullaby' Stains are in, stains are in,
The instant our songs begin

To rock-a-bye my darling baby
Dreaming up worlds of maybe.

Then *byssa, byssa barnet*
Beddie byes my snowy Arne,

Quieter now and slumber-bound,
Rest in lulls of milky sound.

Ninna nanna, ninna nanna,
La mia bambina italiana.

Aja papaya, aja papaja
Doze so *meine kleine Freya*.

[40] p663, Micheal O'Siadhail, *Collected Poems*, Bloodaxe, Tarset, 2013

Say but the Word

Hushaby and *nen-nen-yo*
The moon is high in Tokyo.

Bí bí og blaka Viking Anna,
Seoithín, seoithín, seó a leanbh,

All is well I wouldn't lie,
Trust again this bye and bye.

Valleys deep and dark unruly,
Dafydd Bach, *si hei lwli.*

Kuus, kuus, kalike,
My Tallinn child, night won't stay.

Sandman fallen, lullaby sung,
Sleep my love in a mother tongue.

How deep such phrases must stain our consciousness, how profoundly our sense of being addressed by language must be rooted in such pleasurable sounds. Indeed, we are rooted by our words far into the past. Let us turn to roots.

Roots
Many of my generation were initiated into the world of philology. Though its original meaning is 'love of words', in its narrower sense it is the science of working out by comparing words in different but ultimately related languages what shape the word would have had in an original common language we reckon must have existed. Philologists then go further and again by comparison arrive at what must be the grammar of the theoretical language and can even describe social, religious and poetic aspects of the society reflected in that language. Just imagine that when we use a word like 'snow', we're using a word that was in a language spoken over five thousand years ago.

I have always loved snow. Maybe it is because I was born in January of 1947 just before the snow began in what was an extremely severe winter both in Europe and North America. For over forty-five years I have returned to Norway where I was a student and very often in midwinter to friends in a town call Raufoss when it is deep in snow.

Here[41] from *Tongues* is 'Snows':

'Snows' Here a two-hour train-ride north of Oslo
Leaden November flurries usher in
Six insisting months of snow –
Sneachta, snø, nifa, sneg or *nix* –
Swirls and wafts across
Freakish days before it layers and sticks.
Winter's falling over Raufoss.

How I love this sifting time when sap
Sinks to lull the noiseless branches down
Endless dreams that now unmap
Lines and colours autumn took for real.
Nights are ten below.
Stains of rowanberries' blood congeal,
Flaming the early snow.

Snow. Our Indo-European word,
Sniff and snivel noun of crystal flakes,
Sneaking manna blizzard,
Soundless whirlings over our cradle place.
Sneg and *sneachta*. Snow.
All our versions worlds that we retrace
Five thousand years ago.

Yet the need to say exactly where
Hazards lay, describe terrain or how
Best to be aware
Whether it could thaw or maybe slide,
Things a local knows,
Skills passed on or maybe pride,
Sheer delight in naming snows.

Fonn for drift and *gadd* for hardened snow.
Millennia and northern Europeans
Like the Eskimo

[41] p665, Micheal O'Siadhail, *Collected Poems*, Bloodaxe, Tarset, 2013

Say but the Word

Learn to label tiers and densities.
Fluffy, soft as floss,
Crusting now as layers begin to freeze.
Winter's falling over Raufoss.

Any poet will know by instinct that many words beginning with *sn* have a sneaking, snorting, snide, sniggering, sneering, snooping feel about them. Along with some other languages Greek and Latin regularly lose the initial *s* as in 'nifa' and 'nix'. Yet isn't it amazing to see this snotty, snivelling, sniffling word 'snow' shown by philologists as a word in common across most of Europe and certain parts of India for over five thousand years?

There is a scientific beauty in how the original words are reconstructed by the use of these related words known as cognates. The behaviour of these cognates reveal what is termed 'a regularity of sound correspondences.' In other words it's not just in the word for snow that the *s* disappears in Latin and Greek but it behaves in the same way in, for example, the word 'swim'. Look at the Irish word *snámh* beside Latin *natare*.

As a student I worked in the slate mines in Blaenau Ffestiniog in Wales in order to support myself while I was learning Welsh. The dust caused many ex-miners to die of silicosis, so coughing was not unusual on the job. I remember as I pushed a wagon full of chunks of uncut slate deep in the bowels of the earth how I heard for the first time *pesychu*, the Welsh word for 'coughing'. Trained in philology I knew how a certain sound known as a labiovelar becomes *c* in Irish and *p* in Welsh. The word *pesychu* was stressed on the second last syllable as is normal in Welsh. But of course, it's the same as the Irish word for 'coughing' *casacht*. To think that this was once a shared word! Scholars argue about how long ago, but we're talking about a few thousand years. I recall the thrill of that philological epiphany.

A similar sense of rootedness drives me as a poet. I often wonder how I would survive if I didn't know that others experience the same intensity of thought and feeling as I do. Without poetry it must be almost impossible to cope, to make sense of the depths of grief or of the heights of joy which are part of our humanity. How would we deal with feeling overwhelmed or abandoned, with the death of a friend, with falling in love, if we didn't know that others share what we go through? But like the rootedness of language – and indeed through language – we know that not only are we not alone in the present but that over thousands of years others have known our humanity. Every time someone quotes Psalm 18 in the Old Testament/Hebrew Bible, they are quoting in translation a poem that may be many thousand years old: 'In my distress I called upon the Lord, to my God I cried for help'. In the same way I can never read of the death of Enkidu in the Epic of Gilgamesh, written maybe four and a half thousand years ago, without tears welling up.

But let me move nearer in time and to a more allegro theme. Like many men I'm sure, I have always admired elegant women. I'm sure because Robert Herrick's *Upon Julia's Clothes* in the 17th century reassures me. Here's his extraordinary evocation[42] of a man's delight in femininity:

'Upon Julia's   When as in silks my *Julia* goes,
Clothes'   Then, then (me thinks), how sweetly flowes
         That liquefaction of her clothes.

         Next, when I cast mine eyes and see
         That brave Vibration each way free;
         O how that glittering taketh me!

Three centuries later in a book of mine, *Love Life*, I felt the need in a poem called 'Concertina' to tell someone else down the line that he[43] is not alone:

'Concertina'   1
         I know Herrick's secrets.
         Another naïve man
         I too begin to flirt

         Taken by folds of skirt
         Which like a Japanese fan
         Flicker accordion pleats,

         Sways of silk redundancy
         Whose melody's fall
         Of light and dark caprices

---

[42] p322, *The Oxford Book of Seventeenth Century Verse*, Grierson and Bulloch, Oxford, 1934
[43] p482, Micheal O'Siadhail, *Collected Poems,* Bloodaxe, Tarset, 2013

Concertina creases
To play my nerves and call
A rousing tune I fancy.

 2
The first relaxed chords
Before a tune gathers speed,
The *rallentando*
Of our toysome unswaddlings,
Switch and swop of roles,
Homo ludens make-believe
Master or mistress,
Geisha of dentelle and thong
Or Amazon queen,
Gentle games of the chamber
Licence of delight,
Time-beguiling and time out,
Our playful anything goes.

 3
Festina lente. The love-maker's paradox.
Haste made slowly, pleasures of vigilance
As *accelerando* rhythms in a squeeze-box
Now gather towards the zenith of the dance.
And we clamour for an Eden we still grieve
To let this moment eternally melodeon on;
Adam in his garden cries out to his Eve:
O do not abandon me in my abandon!
A melody peaks, evens out and mellows,
Soft cadenzas beckon childhood's sandman
And dream the pliant frame of a ballerina
Forever dancing to a tune's pleated bellows
Trembling into the narrows of a reed-organ.
Paradise squeezed in folds of a concertina.

You may notice how the folds in the concertina are 'pleated'. This echoes
the 'pl' in 'pliant' in the previous line but much more than that it
suggests a connection with the ballerina in the previous line in a more
direct way than, say, 'folded' would. We associate 'folded' more with

paper and 'pleated' more with cloth. I don't want to do this to death but a poet will often instinctively extend or slightly mix the range of meaning. You want to give the imagination a jolt, a new charge. Yet in many ways linguists are recorders of this extension of meaning which increases the nuanced vocabulary and the expressive power of a language. Linguists love telling each other how in such and such a language that word can also mean… So let us now consider the inherent ambiguity of words and the extension of their sphere of meaning.

Ambiguity and Extension of Meaning

Words are part of a sentence which has meaning in a given context. The fact that words can have more than one meaning may lead to ambiguity. This is so because if there were enough words to cover all our individual experience there would be no end to the amount of words we would require. Yet because meaning ultimately depends on the context, we can put the finite means of words to infinite use. The French philosopher Paul Ricoeur stresses how every word is latently rich with what he refers to as 'polysemy' or multiple meanings.

This is what leaves room for us to pun or play on words. One section of my collection *Tongues* takes the terms of traditional grammar as taught in the primary schools to my generation. For us it was common to learn Latin. In the primary school we learned to conjugate verbs shouting them out by rote the same way we learned our arithmetic tables, as a priest nicknamed Bulldog O'Donnell conducted the choir with a ruler. Here[44] is 'Conjugation':

'Conjugation'   After our meat and wine
Again the time, the voice and mood combine
For conjugation,
Come-hither invitation,
I can't decline.

Latin lover's tense,
Amo, amas, amat – consummate nonsense,
Charms of grammar,
Source of all glamour,
Rhythm's accidence.

[44] p707, Micheal O'Siadhail, *Collected Poems,* Bloodaxe, Tarset, 2013

A verb to x-rate –
Steady now Bulldog – don't exaggerate –
As we chant
Amamus, amatis, amant.
Let's conjugate.

Imperative but tender
Ama! Single command of either gender.
Love me.
Subject, inflect, perfect me
In my surrender.

In ordinary conversation, when we simply want to communicate, the context limits this room for ambiguity and if there is any further doubt we simply ask what the other person means and so avoid misunderstandings. In science, where the aim is to pursue an argument which is as neutral as possible rather than to communicate, we try by definitions, technical usage, symbols and axioms to eliminate the natural inherent ambiguity in language.

But what about poetry? Here, largely by use of metaphor – speaking of one thing in terms of another – we poets exploit the inherent ambiguity in words as a creative force in language by holding two things in the tension between sameness and difference. Paul Ricoeur reminds us that

This is why we may say from the likeness at work in metaphor, what we say about the genus as it is grasped in logical thought. We may say that we learn from it, that it teaches something. Aristotle once more observes that it's from metaphor we can best get hold of something fresh, for 'when Homer calls old age stubble, he teaches and informs us … for both lost their bloom …'

In other words we don't simply say that when reading Homer stubble equals old age. He is shaking up our minds to reimagine reality. By redescribing reality he is both increasing our sense of reality and our language.

This poetic use of language is of interest to linguists. It is this creative force which expands the meanings of words. Let us not forget that we are feasting together. We know from the context that I'm talking about celebrating a rich and abundant meal together. But a glance at

Chambers dictionary will tell you that feast as a noun can also mean a regularly occurring celebration commemorating a person or event, honouring a deity etc., a pleasurable abundance, (something that supplies) rich gratification of the senses (e.g. 'a feast for the eyes'), or stimulation for the mind. You see how the poetic power of the mind is expanding the range of meaning.

And what if we were to delve into its history? 'Feast' arrives in English through Old French *feste,* which is from Latin *festum* meaning 'holiday', 'festival', 'festival banquet', 'feast'. It is a neuter noun based on an adjective *festus* which means 'full of rejoicing', 'festal'. If we go further back the root of the word has religious significance and seems to be connected with the Armenian (and possibly the Greek) word for God, and with different suffixes it shows up in words such as 'fair' and 'fanatic'. And if we were to spread our net wider in Norwegian or Swedish the word *fest* can simply mean a party.

All I'm giving you here is a taste of how the poetic imagination is at the heart of language. Think of all the meanings taste can have. It again arrives through Old French *taster* from Vulgar Latin *tastare* which is taken to be from *taxiatare* which is a frequentative from *tangere* meaning 'to touch'. When you savour something you touch it often with your tongue. But to savour is yet another word that comes to English via French from Latin *sapor* which means 'taste' and is based on the verb *sapere* which means 'to taste'. However it also means in Latin 'to have sense or discernment', 'to be sensible, discreet, judicious, wise' and so is ultimately connected with the words 'sage', 'sapient' and 'savvy'.

How strange that something as basic as 'taste' should be a Latinate word. What happened to the good Germanic word we know from German *schmecken*? In English it is more limited in use. The noun 'smack' expresses a distinctive flavour, a suggestion, a trace. The verb, as sometimes happens native words, is more negatively nuanced as in 'to smack of foul play.'

But before I stray too far or run out of space on my paper napkin, I want to give you just one more example of the 'metaphoric twist' as the American philosopher of art, Monroe Beardsley, called it.

So great is the energy of metaphor in generating meaning after meaning that it can turn a full circle so that a word ends up with almost opposite meanings. It is quite extraordinary to think that the word 'guest ' and the word 'hostile' come from the same root. The English word 'guest' and the Latin word for 'enemy' *hostis* (from which the

English 'hostile' is derived) are originally the same word. Once again from *Tongues,* a three-part poem called 'Triad' which ponders this connection[45] between the guest, the enemy and the feast:

Guest   ‘Triad’
Guest had meant the one
Who stood for common
Pledges of obligation.

Hostis for alien,
Same word in Latin –
Double-edged non-citizen

Shuttling to and fro,
Inside outsider
Comes bit by bit to mean 'foe',

Why invite danger,
Guest or enemy,
The ambivalent stranger?

Host
Host once a compound:
Guest-potentate,
Lord of hospitality,

Russian *gospodin*,
Word to venerate
A foreigner as 'master'.

But treacherous guests,
Judas at the fête,
Some hostile sleepless Macbeth

Betrayed a host's trust.
The face at the gate,
Once a stranger now a foe.

[45]   p670, Micheal O'Siadhail, *Collected Poems,* Bloodaxe, Tarset, 2013

Feast
This word tapping down
Into sacred rites,
Things laid out before our gods.

Against all the odds
Again the stranger
Open to the stranger's face.

A toast and embrace
Repairing two words,
Our glasses raised, our eating

In tents of meeting,
A trust-mended pledge.
The host as guest, the guest host.

So far I've been looking at how metaphor is a creative force that expands the range of a word's meanings. As with any creative force there is constant change and rearrangement and renewal. But inherent in this concept of change and improvisation is a process which evolves over time. At some point what was once new is old. Does this mean that what has become old no longer has any relevance to the present or is there a way in which some of the past is still actively reflected in the present? When describing a language, it is possible to look at how it works now without considering the past (or the future). This is what linguists call a synchronic description. It is also possible to look at it taking the past into consideration. This is what is named a diachronic description. While this distinction is useful, it is also possible here to avoid a binary opposition and once again to combine both past and present in a subtle way.

Synchronic and Diachronic Description
As Paul Ricoeur has pointed out, viewing metaphor as the creative side of multi-meaning, as opposed to seeing it simply as a kind of coded substitution (i.e. stubble equals age in the Aristotle example we discussed previously), has one great advantage. It allows us to look at metaphor both synchronically and diachronically. This means we can now see how as time goes on what was once an enriching, expanding

metaphor becomes 'old hat' and loses its effect. This is what he refers
to as a 'dead' metaphor. On the other hand, a 'living' metaphor is one
which offers another way of seeing and thinking about something. Let
me explain this further with an example. If I use the extended metaphor
of the structure of a roof to mediate on a loving relation, it may wake
you up to thinking about a novel reality. Listen[46] to 'Roofing':

A lifelong day, a night's secrecies: 'Roofing'
Only the rafters themselves must know
The beams' strains and stresses, slow
Givings and takings, the touch and go
Of our attunements and compromise, how
We raise the roof or make our peace.

A timber's head nestles in another's,
A mitred joint, this bevelled match,
Two beams and their collar-beam which
Shape a triangle, the tie and apex
Of togetherness. So easily one forgets
Couples are a liaison of two rafters.

And always under us or in between
That dangerous breach we never close,
A zone for household gods we choose
Or need. Here, then, allow some room
For unlike memories, dreams to dream,
A living space for a separate passion.

A roof is framing our slanted intimacy.
Unless each of these matching couples
Beds snugly down into opposite walls,
The timbers sag. Somehow we're stronger
In separateness, this sloping encounter
Our braced ridge, our tie of ecstasy.

Speaking of a love in roofing terms may invite you to realize how both
intimacy and space can strengthen a relationship. A poet wants to stir

---

46   p94, Micheal O'Siadhail, *Collected Poems,* Bloodaxe, Tarset, 2013

you with a living metaphor. On the other hand if we speak of 'the leg of a chair' it doesn't open up anything new. It was once a living metaphor. It was once saying look more carefully at the supports under the chair because I talk in terms of human limbs. Over time the metaphor withers and dies. If a poet spoke of 'a chair's wobbling limbs', it might make us look afresh at the chair's legs. On the other hand, dead metaphors are still part of the present in as much as they are part of how we express ourselves. We all use 'the leg of the table' to describe what supports the table. Some poets may mock all dead metaphor as clichés, but we couldn't carry on normal communication without them. It is simply that their normality means they no longer startle us into reappraising reality.

For linguists this distinction is also a matter of importance. When I was a student the description of dialects that we studied were all synchronic. In practice this means that they described the language exactly as it is used and explained its structure as if you had no knowledge of its history. Then Noam Chomsky arrived on the scene in the late nineteen-fifties. Although there have been various theories since, I think his generative grammar was a genuine paradigm shift.

Chomsky was what Maxwell Maltz in his book *Psycho-Cybernetics* calls an impert, an expert in one field who enters another field and who, by bringing his former expertise to bear, changes his new field. Chomsky was a mathematician who turned to linguistics and altered the paradigm. He believed in universal features of language. We are so hardwired to learn language that it may even be that it is the model for how we learn everything. But a large part of his contribution was to mend the absolute split between those who describe language with no reference to its history (synchronically) and those who describe and explain language through its history (diachronically).

Let me give a simple example. As far I know there is no dialect of English where the words 'cold', 'bold', 'old' are pronounced with a short *o*-sound. This means that the current spelling with a short *o*-sound is in fact historical and so we can speak here of a diachronic view. Such words are all pronounced in Standard English with a long *o*-sound. However in certain other dialects they are pronounced with an 'au-' sound 'cauld', 'bauld', 'auld'. It is not pronounced with a short 'o' but there are advantages to keeping the short 'o' as a kind of abstract form. In one dialect there is a rule saying that a stressed short 'o' before 'ld' is pronounced with a long 'o' and in another dialect there is a rule saying that a stressed short 'o' before 'ld' is pronounced with an 'au'-sound. That abstract form with the short 'o' is called the underlying form and the actual pronunciations with a long 'o' or 'au'-sound are called surface forms. However, the point here is that the short 'o' is not retained in the underlying form because it is the historic form (which in this case it is) but rather because it is the form which allows us to generate with a minimum of rules the actual pronunciations, the surface forms.

Sometimes in fact the underlying form contradicts history. In other words it is important to note that the short *o* is retained in the underlying form not because it is historical but because it is still necessary to explain features of the living language. It is still needed to generate through a series of ordered rules the language as it is. Just as Ricoeur distinguishes between dead and living metaphor – between, say, referring to age as stubble and referring to part of a chair as a leg – Chomsky's multi-layered description differentiates between living and dead history.

We can think of the interplay of past and present as a vertical tension in both poetry and language. There is, however, also what we might call a horizontal tension, that is to say an interaction within the present itself. But here once again I use the word tension to imply that it is not a binary choice but rather two aspects which must always be kept in play. It is a tension between substance and framework. I wish to look briefly at this tension in both language and poetry.

Substance and Framework

The tension between framework and substance probably exists in any art or science. It may well be that, because I earned my living working as a linguist before being able to devote myself entirely to my poetry, I am aware of this parallel in both linguistics and poetry.

In the kind of synchronic or non-historic approach to the description of modern languages that was current in my student days, it was enough to record exactly what you heard. Much of the recording of Irish in the areas where it was still spoken was, from a linguistic point of view, rather haphazard. You might steer a conversation to certain topics, which you then recorded. Inevitably there were gaps. If you do not have a well-worked out and systematic approach as a linguist, you may not know what to look for.

Let me give one example of what I mean. The word *thuirling* which means 'descended', 'alighted', 'came down' would now be rarely used by an ordinary speaker of Irish in Galway. None of the descriptions of Irish as spoken in Galway seemed to have this word. According to a systematic account of the differences between Irish dialects you would predict that the first syllable would be pronounced with an *au*-sound, but how could you ever know? As it's now an uncommon word in normal speech in the area, anyone using it would probably be literate and influenced by the written form. Then someone turned up a tape recorded in East Galway sometime in the nineteen-fifties where the word was used in a story and yes, it was pronounced with an *au*-sound as the framework had predicted. This is the linguistic equivalent of physicists finding a boson their theory had predicted.

Any poet will know a similar tension in the classic push and pull between content and form. In some ways a poem is always the search for the perfect marriage of content and form. In the first place even the choice of form reflects what the poems intend to say. But it's a two-way process, just as the theme may dictate the form, so too the form influences the content. Take the first quatrain[47] of Shakespeare's Sonnet 47:

'Sonnet 47' Betwixt mine eye and heart a league is took,
And each doth good turns now unto the other.
When that mine eye is famish'd for a look,
Or heart in love with sighs himself doth smother;

Would Shakespeare have chosen the verb 'smother' if he didn't need to rhyme it with other? Or which line came first? And then look at the second quatrain:

With my love's picture then my eye doth feast,
And to the painted banquet bids my heart;
Another time mine eye is my heart's guest
And in his thoughts of love doth share a part:

Did the content, the desire to extend the image of the feast, demand what seems an imperfect rhyme between *feast* and *guest*?

Conclusion
I return to the feast. In the end any mutual understanding is about each

---

[47]   p1370, *Collins Complete Works of William Shakespeare*, Glasgow, 1994

Say but the Word

party being both host and guest for each other. Each is host for the other in offering the other an insight into the excitement of inhabited worlds. Each is guest to the other in being open-hearted and letting go and entering into that world. I think again of that dwindling, greying, ascetic congregation at Babette's feast and how in spite of all their misgivings, their determination not to speak of the pleasure is transformed by the feast. Karen Blixen in her Danish version uses the title *Babettes Gjæstebud*. *Gjæstebud* a lovely word which literally means a 'guest-bidding', 'bidding guests (to come).'

In bringing together poetry and linguistics I have tried to emphasise that there is no need to see the difference as a cleft between the subjective and the objective. Like Karen Blixen's word-centred sect and the more sacramentally oriented Babette, who are uplifted in feasting together, both poets and linguists savour words which are rooted in our distant past and have expressed through time our shared human thoughts and feelings. In a similar fashion the creativity of metaphor has both through language and poetry kept renewing our perception of reality. In this expansion and renewal both poetry and linguistics can hold in play the present and past in a way that distinguishes a past which is still reflected in our present from what is now moribund. Furthermore, linguists and poets work a tension between substance and framework in the sense that linguists move between theory and observation while poets juggle form and content.

As I meditated on language in *Tongues* I became more and more conscious of how, like poetry, language is both individual and societal. Both are shaped by society and, although there is scope for endless individual creativity, both retain a communal dimension that enables mutual understanding. When I learned a language I had been bidden to be a guest in another culture. I was more and more aware how grateful I was for those who hosted and nurtured me in their world. They have invited me to share a long story of lives rooted in a history, a culture, a geography, not to mention a tradition of poetry, music and painting. I have never been able to separate friendship from language. I could never simply regard a speaker of a language as an informant. Any language I speak is in the end a network of close relationships which nourish my own roots.

The final section of *Tongues* became a series of poems thanking my hosts, those who allowed me to let go, to relax, to trust and allow their world to enter in me and become partly mine. Earlier in life I learned

Say but the Word

and was parented in a new world by people older than myself. As I grew
older this changed. I was in my fifties when I began to learn Japanese; I
was fulfilling a dream I had long kept warm. So wonderful to feel even
onomatopoeic sighs, the jabberwocky words working into my being.
Here[48] to close is a poem 'Echo' from that series:

'Echo'   Into my fifties when I began –
          Too late for parent now or lover,
          This time around brother or daughter.

          First friend Shimizu-san 'Spring Water'
          Babytalking me to discover
          In myself some *déjà vu* Japan.

          Other brothers too but often young
          Women daughtering an older man,
          Nurturing some new Japanese me.

          'Peach-Tail' and 'High-up Mulberry Tree',
          Momō-san and Takakuwa-san
          Suckle me into another tongue.

          Nakamura-san sighing *yoisho*
          Or *yokkoisho* as she bent and swung
          On her chair to lift a dictionary,

          Sound of exertion 'ups-a-daisy',
          A straining creak of an effort wrung
          Out of the body, a 'yo-heave-ho'.

          Yoisho I echo and have begun
          As in second childhood to let go.
          Brothers and daughters now cradle me.

          A tongue-tied me now at last set free.
          Dream I'd given up on years ago.
          Words take wing into the rising sun.

[48] p794, Micheal O'Siadhail, *Collected Poems,* Bloodaxe, Tarset, 2013

Working the Word

Working the Word

An older poet friend of mine, John Montague, signed a book of his for me and wrote: 'For a fellow in the craft.' If asked to sign a book of my own for another poet, I like to pass on this simple message adding one further Germanic word: 'For a fellow in the beloved craft'. What a wonderful word 'craft' is! It is both Germanic and English. The German word for 'power' or 'strength' is *Kraft*. The stretching of the idea of 'power' to mean 'skill', 'art' or 'occupation' is particular to English. The meanings of 'craft' can be stretched even further but here I want to concentrate on the use of skill to give power to a poem. What do we mean when we speak of 'crafting' a poem or of a poem being 'well-crafted' and how is this craft worth loving?

Ecology of Meaning and Form

For many of us reared in a tradition imbued with certain Romantic notions about art, to stress the crafting of a poem can seem crass. The expression of feeling, the venting of emotion was what art was about. Even those of us who were young adults in the nineteen-sixties, when what Charles Taylor in his book *A Secular Age* calls 'the age of authenticity' was in full swing, may still baulk at attention to form. But even the Latinate word 'art' itself, which we borrow in English, originally meant both method and skill and is ultimately connected with the words 'order' and 'harmony'.

On the other hand, as poetry workshops and talk of 'technique' became fashionable, you could easily get the impression that poetry was all skill and no heart – just a matter of choosing the right set of words and effects. A further risk of this process is that it tends to fix one particular mode of writing as a norm. It becomes a flattening out, a sameness, which curbs the endless variety of approaches.

Both of these extremes, the over emphasis on affect and excessive attention to technique were addressed by R. G. Collingwood in his classic work, *The Principles of Art*. However, Collingwood uses somewhat different terms. He vehemently distinguishes between 'art as amusement', 'art as craft', and 'art proper'.

Art as amusement in essence is what 'is designed to stimulate a certain emotion', which is 'not intended for discharge into the occupations of ordinary life, but for enjoyment as something of value in itself'. In other words its 'function is to amuse or entertain'. There is make-believe – a cleft between art and reality.

Art as craft is where there is a fundamental split between the means and the end. In simple terms, to make a table or a basket is a craft. You use certain means so you succeed in making a table or a basket. But, clearly, you know beforehand what a table or a basket is.

On the other hand in 'art proper', artists work out for themselves, and others, in an imaginative creative act, whatever is weighing on them that they feel the urge to express. It is very much connected with reality and the particularity of lives. There is no completely preconceived end like a table or basket. Art becomes what it is in the making.

I myself have always gone for the classical combination of meaning and form. It seems to me that in the case of poetry, or indeed of any other art, the most exciting thing of all is when the meaning and the form come seamlessly together. Even the word combination falls short. I am thinking of something dynamic and interwoven where the meaning affects the form and the form in turn shapes the meaning. I opt again for ecology as my image. Ecology conjures up a shifting interdependence of meaning and form which can also, if mishandled, get out of kilter. This ecology of meaning and form is a dynamic of a particular reality which is deeply rooted in real living and only becomes what it is in the making.

Collingwood uses the word craft in the more limited and, for him, negative sense of the skill involved in making, say, a table or basket, where the end and the means are separate. I, on the other hand, use craft to speak of the skill that shapes the form of a poem which is in turn inseparable from the meaning. So now that I have so stressed the interplay of meaning and form, I am about to do something very risky. I want to go on to talk a little about form in poetry. I will begin by looking at how the history of a particular form, the sonnet, relates to a changing society.

Form and Society
It is fascinating how poetic form reflects different societies and the mood of different times. This could be an endless source of comparisons and examples but let us just glance at one form, the sonnet, and watch how, through the lens of Shakespeare, Donne and Milton, four separate forms of the sonnet resonate with four contrasting moods.

The sonnet, with two quatrains and a sestet, came to English from Italy. However, to give a 'perfect' example of the original Italian sonnet

in English, handbook writers have to resort to writing one themselves!
Sir Thomas Wyatt (1503–1542), who seems to have been the first to
introduce the sonnet into English, both studied and translated Petrarch's
sonnets. All the same, Wyatt had already begun to play around with
variations on the strict *abba* rhyme scheme in the octave of the Italian
sonnet. More significantly, he retains the sestet but instead of the slower
gradually sinking Italian *cde, cde* scheme, he ends his sonnets[49] with a
rhyming couplet:

But thus return to leap in to the fire?   'Unstable
And where it was at wish, could not remain?   Dream'
Such mocks of dreams do turn to deadly pain.

This was probably an echo of the final two rhyming lines of the
Chaucerian rime royal. One way or the other, while he still retains an
almost court Italian feel, the first big step towards the English sonnet
has been taken. The final forceful summing up couplet will become such
a characteristic of the English sonnet. The next move is to use three
quatrains instead of two. Then, if we allow the first and third, and the
second and fourth lines in each quatrain to rhyme independently, (which
some of the early Italian sonneteers had in fact also done) we have a full
English or Shakespearean sonnet. Sidney, Drayton and Shakespeare
were soon to make those two moves.

    You can hardly imagine how any other form could capture the
swagger and excitement, the danger, the explorations, the jewel and
dagger feel, the drunkenness[50] of Elizabethan England:

They that have power to hurt and will do none,   'Sonnet 94'
That do not do the thing they most do show,
Who, moving others, are themselves as stone,
Unmoved, cold, and to temptation slow –
They rightly do inherit Heaven's graces
And husband nature's riches from expense;
They are the lords and owners of their faces,
Others but stewards of their excellence.
The summer's flow'r is to the summer sweet

---

[49] Sir Thomas Wyatt, *Unstable Dream* at http://www.gutenberg.org/files/27450/27450-h/27450-
h.htm#CHAPTER_I accessed 16 September 2014
[50] p1377, *Collins Complete Works of William Shakespeare*, Glasgow, 1994

Though to itself it only live and die;
But if flow'r with base infection meet,
The basest weed outbraves his dignity.
    For sweetest things turn sourest by their deeds:
    Lilies that fester smell far worse than weeds.

A meditation on power, and what a Shakespearean sonnet! But then comes the darker, questioning, introverted Jacobean mood with its wit and complex metaphysical use of language and conceits. Donne's *Holy Sonnets* often take up again the Italian *abba* rhyme scheme in the first two quatrains but mostly follow[51] the English sonnet's *abab* in the third quatrain:

'Holy Sonnets XIV'

Batter my heart, three-person'd God; for, you
As yet but knocke, breathe, shine, and seeke to mend;
That I may rise and stand, o'erthrow mee, and bend
Your force, to breake, blowe, burn, and make me new.
I, like an usurpt towne, to'another due,
Labour to'admit you, but Oh, to no end,
Reason your viceroy in mee, mee should defend,
but is captiv'd, and proves weake or untrue.
Yet dearly 'I love you,' and would be loved fain,
But am betrothed unto your enemy:
Divorce mee,'untie or breake that knot againe;
Take mee to you, imprison mee, for I,
Except you'enthrall me, never shall be free,
Nor even chast, except you ravish mee.

By the time we reach John Milton the sonnet yet again has re-adapted. Gone the airborne, drunken Elizabethan excitement or the complex witty Jacobean temper. Now it is the sober, Puritan, reasonable mindset. The Miltonic sonnet[52] has reverted to the Italian sonnet with its octave and sestet but marks the rational age by allowing the traditional break between the octave and the sestet to occur anywhere between the middle of the eighth line to the end of the ninth line. This lent a sense of weight to the argument:

[51] *John Donne: Complete Poetry & Selected Prose,* ed. John Hayward, The Nonesuch Press, London, 1990
[52] p501, 'Sonnet xvi', John Milton, *The Oxford Book of Seventeenth Century Verse,* Grierson & Bullough, Oxford, 1934

When I consider how my light is spent   'Sonnet xvi'
Ere half my days, in this dark world and wide,
And that one Talent which is death to hide
Lodg'd with me useless, though my Soul more bent
To serve therewith my Maker, and present
My true account, lest he returning chide,
Doth God exact day-labour, light deny'd,
I fondly ask. But patience, to prevent
That murmur, soon replies, God doth not need
Either man's work or his own gifts, who best
Bear his milde yoak, they serve him best, his State
Is Kingly. Thousands at his bidding speed
And post o'er Land and Ocean without rest:
They also serve who only stand and waite.

After a gap, the Romantics returned to the sonnet. Wordsworth uses the Italian form but with almost every possible combination of rhyme scheme in the sestet, even at times allowing the final couplet to rhyme.

The tradition goes on and many great poets – right down to our day – still turn to the sonnet in various forms, even with broken rhyme. All I want to stress here is how a form can adapt so its tone resonates with different times. But now I want to ask the question; why does the sonnet as a form have such an appeal for poets?

The Appeal of the Sonnet

I have always found the sonnet an extraordinary creative instrument. Kim Bridgford in three collections *Undone, Instead of Maps* and *In the Extreme: Sonnets about World Records* is an extraordinary practitioner of the art of the sonnet. Indeed, some years ago I was very privileged to discover that she had written a chapter on my own sonnets in *Musics of Belonging*[53], a book about my work.

What is the lasting appeal of the sonnet? How can this form which thrived in Italian, French, English, Spanish and German have such a widespread and lasting attraction?

I can only answer this as best I can from my own experience and I want to come at an answer from different angles.

---

[53] *Musics of Belonging: The Poetry of Micheal O'Siadhail*, eds. Marc Caball and David F. Ford, Carysfort Press, Dublin, 2007

Firstly it seems to me that it is the ultimate classic form. I wonder do others remember the old school formula which certainly was current in my childhood? It was always trotted out when we were being taught to write essays: 'you must have a beginning, a middle and an end'! This is the core and simple reason why the sonnet is the supreme form it is. This is borne out if we ask ourselves what the equivalent in music is. Surely it is the sonata, which is fundamentally the same word as sonnet. Even though, just as in the case of the sonnet, we find many variations, in the sonata form there are basically three parts: the exposition of the theme, the developments of the theme and the recapitulation.

It is not difficult to think of a Shakespeare sonnet as a sonata. Just think of Sonnet 94, the meditation on power I quoted. The first quatrain is the exposition of the theme: 'they who have power to hurt and will do none'. The second and third quatrains can be thought of as first and second developments in the sonata. The first development is 'they rightly do inherit heaven's grace' and the second development introduces the metaphor of flowers and asks what 'if that flower with base infection meet?' The real punch is in the pithy recapitulating final couplet, which is the Shakespearian equivalent of the Latin proverb 'the corruption of the best is the worst':

'Sonnet 94'   For sweetest things turn sourest by their deeds,
          Lilies that fester smell far worse than weeds.

Another way to think of a sonnet is that it is a form, which is a kind of acid test. It is sometimes said that a poet can be so easily found out in a sonnet. No phony depth will work here. The simple logic of the form will find you out if you have nothing to say. No shimmying or dodging allowed. No clever or empty talk will wash.

Yet that is just the negative side of what I find so wonderful about the sonnet. What is so extraordinary is how the nature of the form almost ensures that, in R. G. Collingwood's terms, you work through for yourself and others the emotional pressure, which craves creative expression. The demands of the sonnet force you to think and feel in such a way that the poem becomes itself in the making. This is the jazz of creation, the surprise riff, the perpetual unexpected. By a strange irony, the form which requires so much of you, is also the one which insists on the deeper freedom of creation. But then why should that be surprising when we know from jazz the precision of freedom?

Say but the Word

A third angle for me is the effect of the sonnet form not only as a creative instrument but also as a container. There is a containment factor. What do I mean by containment? I suppose I want to say that when things go deepest in me, I feel myself overwhelmed by emotion and often unable to get any grip at all. David Ford in his book *The Shape of Living*[54], a book which makes copious use of my poetry, speaks of being 'multiply overwhelmed'. I certainly have known that feeling. It is precisely then that I reach for the sonnet to contain what is spiralling out of control.

Let me give an example or two. In *The Chosen Garden* when I reach the part I name 'Re-rooting' I know it has to be a series of love poems. How do I approach a theme, which is everywhere in our culture, longed for, stimulated, sung about, abused, sentimentalised and the core of all stories and desires? After thousands of years of love poems what possibly could I add? And yet it is *my* particular life and love that wells up and wants out. How do I harness feelings of wonder, gratitude, inadequacy, regret, sensuousness, homing and sheer joy? I find myself absolutely instinctively working in the sonnet form[55] which offers me a shape to word at least a fraction of the amazement which sweeps over me.

Nothing can explain this adventure – let's say a quirk
of fortune steered us together – we made our covenants,
began this odyssey of ours, by hunch and guesswork,
a blind date where foolish love consented in advance.
No, my beloved, neither knew what lay behind the frontiers.
You told me once you hesitated: *A needle can waver,*
Then fix on its pole; I am still after many years
baffled that the needle's gift dipped in my favour.
Should I dare to be so lucky? Is this a dream?
Suddenly in the commonplace that first amazement seizes
me all over again – a freak twist to the theme,
subtle jazz of the new familiar, trip of surprises.
Gratuitous, beyond our fathom, both binding and freeing,
This love re-invades us, shifts the boundaries of our being.

'Out of the Blue'

Then again when writing *The Gossamer Wall: poems in witness to the Holocaust*, I found myself struggling and I devoted four years to thinking

54   David Ford, *The Shape of Living,* Fount Paperbacks, London, 1997
55   p228, Micheal O'Siadhail, *Collected Poems,* Tarset, 2013

Say but the Word

and reading about it. There is such a literature about the historical background and an equally large amount on the aftermath. But at the heart of this attempt to distil the story were the concentration camps. How to enter into the belly of the beast? How to remember those who suffered when you yourself had not been there? How could I name such pain without appropriating someone else's agony, without feeding 'on another man's wounds'? Intuitively, I moved[56] into sonnets.

'Summons'   A summons to *try to look, to try to see.*
A muted dead demand their debt of memory.

Some years ago it was pointed out in an essay on my poetry that there seemed to be a thematic pattern in my published works. The poetry alternated between public concerns and intensely personal journeys. I do not think I had been aware of this when writing. Suddenly it came home to me that I had moved from *The Gossamer Wall*, where I had entirely avoided the word 'I', in so far as I never allowed my persona to enter into the story, to *Love Life*, the most vulnerable and personal of all my books where I literally put my wife and myself on the line.

Yet the sonnet had served in both books to shape some of the most deeply emotional moments. It is almost as though I had turned the early traditional use of the sonnet upside down by channelling into that form the inhumanity of the Holocaust. Yet this enriched me in a way, which permitted me to return to the sonnet to capture the intimacies of *Love Life*. In the final poem of *Love Life*, I echo again your 'lips are like a crimson thread, and your mouth is lovely' from the Song of Songs. But 'crimson' has other resonances, as Rahab in the Book of Joshua hung out a crimson thread to identify her house. A further allusion is to a previous book *Our Double Time,* where the parting crimson of the sumac's leaves signifies the completeness of a life ending. So here[57] it is:

'Crimson   Dew, spice, honey, wine and milk,
Thread'   Bone of my bone, flesh of my flesh
Wear again for me the damson silk
I take as given and still begin afresh.
Awake o north wind, come south wind....
Never enough just to have rubbed along,

[56] p432, Micheal O'Siadhail, *Collected Poems,* Tarset, 2013
[57] p552, Micheal O'Siadhail, *Collected Poems,* Tarset, 2013

Say but the Word

Promise of promises nothing can rescind.
All or nothing. All is Solomon's Song.
I come to my garden, my sister, my bride.
Eat friend, drink and be drunk with love
And every moment I think I'm satisfied
Wakes me to desires I'm dreaming of.
In Solomon's blue curtain a cord of covenant,
A crimson thread until the crimson moment.

I have been thinking about the sonnet, partly because it is one most people know and recognise and partly because of my own particular love of the form. I have been considering the sonnet as coloured by society and looking at the appeal of the sonnet.

However, clearly the sonnet is just one form. There are, of course, a myriad of forms and variations. I want to consider for a moment the endless variety of forms and variations of forms.

Variety of Forms
I have enjoyed allowing poems to find their way into all kinds of other forms with a tradition, but also yielding to the inherent inventiveness of poems that seem to fall into patterns of their own or indeed into a coherence, which shows no particular pattern.

As I have stressed, the creativity of meaning and form are inseparably interwoven. The whole poem needs to grow organically. Richard Wilbur puts this well. When asked in an interview about being traditional, he replied: 'it's undoubtedly traditional to have recourse to tetrameter and pentameter and to use rhymes. But I don't very much follow established forms such as the sonnet. I have *written* them but I don't tirelessly turn out sonnets, villanelles, *ballades*. Often the forms I choose (the stanza forms say) are arrived at rather intuitively or by luck. The line lengths will be chosen much as a free verse writer chooses his line lengths, according to the way the words want to fall. And rhymes will occur if they do occur.'[58]

I have been talking about forms which involve rhyme. It's often seen as a sophistication to eschew rhyme. Yet the delight in rhyme is deep in us from our earliest childhood:

---

[58] Richard Wilbur, *New and Collected Poems*, Faber and Faber, London, 1989

Ruba-dub-dub
Three men in a tub,
The butcher, the baker,
The candlestick maker.

It is a physical, an oral delight. There is an enjoyment of sound for its own sake. The thrill in the voiced plosion of a 'b'! And three times: ruba-dub-dub.

   Then again alongside the savouring of sounds that rhyme, there is the fascination of rhythm: 'the butcher, the baker, the candlestick maker'. At this point it is worth thinking for a moment about rhythm and metre and indeed about the connections between language and metre.

Rhythm and Metre
In some ways, maybe even deeper than the pleasure we take in the chime of words that share the same sounds is the appeal of rhythm and metre. There are all the different combinations of stressed and unstressed syllables together with variations in the order in which they occur. All those iambs, trochees, dactyls, spondees and anapaests, etc. I remember the renowned Czech harpsichordist, Stanislav Heller, demonstrating in master classes the deep connection between the language of a country and its music. There is clearly a similar relationship between language and metre. When talking about the sonnet, I take for granted the iambic metre which English, a language with a stress accent, so naturally falls into:

'Sonnet 18'   Shall I compare thee to a summer's day?
              Thou art more lovely and more temperate.

For me part of the creative variation is sometimes to keep a strict iambic beat ending with the rhymed word stressed and sometimes not. Sometimes the *donné* or given line of a poem leads to rhymes off the beat. Sometimes the rhyme brings cohesion to the poem allowing the metre to follow the rhythms which the sense of the poem dictates. Such a jazz of possibilities!

   But now look at the form in Ronsard's 'Quand vous serez bien vieille' (When you are very old), the most famous sonnet and love poem in French. As French is a language without a stress accent, the form depends on the number of syllables in the line and not on the number of stresses. The sonnet is an alexandrine which has twelve syllables per line. This reminds us that there is, as well as the accentual poetry which is so characteristic of English, a long tradition of syllabic poetry. The domination of one tradition rather than another, either accentual or syllabic, often depends on the language.

Accentual or Syllabic Poetry and Language
It is usual to divide languages into two camps. Firstly there are those like English and German, which have a so-called 'stress accent' and therefore naturally tend towards metre and rhyme. On the other hand, there are those like French or Italian, which do not have a 'stress accent' and therefore tend towards syllabic poetry. Nevertheless, a particular language and literary tradition can switch between accentual and syllabic poetry.

I suppose I am particularly aware of these sorts of shifts because they occurred in poetry in the Irish language. The oldest poetry known as *rosc* was accentual. However from the 7th to the 17th century we had a stanzaic tradition of highly intricate syllabic poetry. This syllabic poetry had complex and specific rules for ornamentation, which included full rhyme and broken rhyme used both finally and internally, and alliteration of different kinds. This was called *Dán Díreach* and was practiced by a professional class of poets who named all the variations of the stricter forms. In the seventeeth century, possibly under the influence of a shift of accent in certain dialects of Irish, which in turn may have been due to borrowings from French, this tradition gradually gave way to the *amhrán* or 'song metre'. This was a move to a richly assonated accentual stanzaic form.

It can be said that poetry, which depends on the amount of syllables, does not fit the English language. After all, it is argued, it is a modern literary import, which is ineffective in that, given the nature of English pronunciation, it is hard to be aware of the number of syllables. Yet, when you think of Dylan Thomas's well-known use of syllabic poetry, it is hard to deny that it does have a tone[59] of its own:

In my craft or sullen art
Exercised in the still night
When only the moon rages

'In my craft or sullen art'

[59] Dylan Thomas, *Collected Poems 1934–1952*, J. M. Dent & Sons Ltd, London, November 1952 (reprinted March 1962)

And the lovers lie abed
With all their griefs in their arms,
I labour by singing light
Not for ambition or bread
Or the strut and trade of charms
On the ivory stages
But for the common wages
Of their most secret heart.

Of course, the most famous example of a modern poet who wrote a great deal of syllabic poetry is Marianne Moore.

I am not sure why I have been drawn more into syllabic poetry in my more recent collections. Perhaps it is due to the interest I have taken in Japanese over the last decade. The best known Japanese form based on the number of syllables in the line is the *haiku* (俳句) with a five syllable first and third line and a second line with seven syllables.[60]

'Day'   Double-blossomed lives.
Full and by. Then, to die well.
Gently petals fall.

But there are other classic forms such as the *chōka* (長歌) meaning 'long song' which I used in a poem[61] called (of all things!) *Long Song*:

'Long Song'   Fragrance of your oils.
L'amour fou. Such sweet folly.
Your haunting presence
Distilled traces of perfume.
Resonances of voice
Dwell in my nervous body.

It is a long series of alternating five and seven syllable lines, which concludes with two seven syllable lines. But as always there is the creative jazz. I like to invent forms, nine and eight syllable lines alternating, for instance. Yet why stop there? Why not mix rhyme and syllabic verses and even stress as Dylan Thomas did? Now let me take one example of a hybrid form, which has evolved in my own work.

[60]   p549, Micheal O'Siadhail, *Collected Poems,* Tarset, 2013
[61]   p476, Micheal O'Siadhail, *Collected Poems,* Tarset, 2013

The *saiku*

First I am going to describe it and then I want to give it a name. I used this for the first time in the final poem of *Love Life* called 'Crimson Thread'. Basically it is alternating sonnets and *haiku*s. I find that some poems, which I have been working on recently, seem to demand this form. It has particular effects. Like a Greek chorus or a clown in a Shakespeare play or simply an epigraph, these interspersed *haiku*s permit another level. It allows an indirect metaphoric comment on the content of the sonnet.

But it also appeals to me because it combines the most classic form of both the East and the West. In a world where all types of music are mingling and interchanging between traditions, why not let it happen in poetry?

Let us name this mix a *saiku* – a fanciful portmanteau word for a sonnet and a *haiku* together. Yes, but there is more! *Saiku* (細工) in Japanese means 'work' or craftmanship' and has the extended meanings 'tactics', 'tricks'. In other words it moves across the same range of meaning as the word 'craft' with which we started out or the Greek word 'téchne' from which technique ultimately stems. The word 'craft' has to do with skill and workmanship but in excess, or when abused, turns to 'craftiness'.

I have been discussing the form, the appeal and variety of forms with rhyme and metre, accentual poetry and syllabic poetry. Earlier we saw how the types of sonnet reflected society. I am now about to return to the relationship between the prevailing mood of a society and the use or lack of use of form in our own time.

The Age of Authenticity and the Reaction

I mentioned earlier Charles Taylor's description of the culture of the late nineteen fifties and the nineteen-sixties as 'the age of authenticity'. This was largely a reaction to the post-war fifties. There was a new affluence which brought with it an 'expressive individualism', a whole new concentration on the 'private space' and a whole new meaning to 'the pursuit of happiness'.

I can still recall the excitement when the Irish writer Tom McIntyre, who taught me at school, gave me a copy of Lawrence Ferlinghetti's *A Coney Island of the Mind* in the early sixties. 'Sometime during eternity some guys show up' and 'Don't let that horse eat that violin' and a whole other beat world was opening up. Was this what it meant to be spontaneous? To be genuine? To be authentic? In Britain, the angry young men had had their effect and the well-made play had become a term of abuse.

I think there were a few decades, and maybe particularly in America, when any notion of formality in poetry seemed to be at best old fogeyish and at worst an attack on the new found spontaneity. Among the notable exceptions were Antony Hecht and Richard Wilbur. Yet in the interview which I quoted earlier, you can see how Richard Wilbur needed almost to justify himself when he said: 'When people are adverse on principle to formal verse of any kind they light into me. I feel that often they are prevented by their prejudice from distinguishing mere doily-making, mere fulfilment of arbitrary form, from the expressive use of form.'

The reaction to a dominant myth, particularly in North America, that formalism of any sort was simply a lack of spontaneity, was most forcibly expressed by Dana Gioia in 1987 in his *Notes on the New Formalism.* Here Gioia put it bluntly: 'The real issues presented by American poetry in the Eighties will become clearer: the debasement of poetic language; the prolixity of the lyric; the bankruptcy of the confessional mode; the inability to establish a meaningful aesthetic for new poetic narrative and the denial of a musical texture in the contemporary poem. The revival of traditional forms will be seen then as only one response to this troubling situation.' What Dana Gioia called 'the revival of traditional forms' has been called 'the new formalist movement'. He analysed it in his article in *The Atlantic Monthly* of May 1991.

Creative Expression
My own feeling is that both the howls of the Beats and the 'open field' of the Black Mountain Poets may have done us all a great service on both sides of the Atlantic. It may have been necessary for a while to move away from the perceived stuffiness of formality, to leave the stanza behind and to give free rein to a line based more on breath and utterance. But maybe their greatest gift was that the use of form is now a matter of choice. It is something a poet is allowed to do or not to do. It is like a move from an arranged marriage to a life of voluntary commitment. Their gift to us is the gift of return.

I also deeply appreciate the distinction between what Richard Wilbur called 'doily-making' and what he called 'creative expression'. It serves no purpose if formalism for the sake of formalism becomes yet another tyrannical orthodoxy. Dana Gioia was wise when he described the revival of traditional forms as 'only one response'. I share with Dana Gioia a love of jazz. I share that love of a music shaped out of suffering, the delight in the impromptu, in what will always surprise and go beyond whatever I expect. For me jazz is emblematic of the ordinary lifted beyond the ordinary, the battered tune soaring in new variations. Jazz is a wonderful mixture of freedom and form, of wildness and precision. At the core of 'my craft and sullen art' I know that Madam Jazz will always elude me and yet she demands[62] that I pursue her:

Worship, hold her a moment in thought.
Femme fatale, she shapes another face,
unveils an idol. O Never-To-Be-Caught,

O Minx beyond this mind's embrace,
Hider-Go-Seeker, Miss Unfathomable,
Demurring Lady playing at the chase.

As stars or atoms we turn, fall
towards each other's gravity. I spin
In your love's nexus, Mistress All.

Once a child of Newton's fallen
apple, I'd the measure of your ways.
My stars, my atoms, are we one?

Mischievous Strategy, Madam Jazz!
Old tunes die in metamorphosis.
Rise, fall, reawakening. I praise.

'Hail! Madam Jazz'

---

[62] p35, Micheal O'Siadhail, *Collected Poems,* Tarset, 2013

I am very much aware of the sense of tradition of form in poetry. However, the danger with any tradition is that it is all too easy to set a tradition in stone. We can sometimes tend to forget that all tradition is not only something that we receive and hand on but also something which accumulates and changes over time. In many ways any tradition is open-ended in a way which the word itself often seems to veil.

I would like to look at some of the mechanisms involved in this accumulation over time. In other words, I want to examine how certain forms and formal features enter the tradition of poetry in English. I have given these sessions the overall title 'Sources of Form'. I am sure there are all sorts of sources for forms which have become part of our repertoire but here I am going to concentrate on three particular ways in which we garner, or have garnered, new forms and formal devises. The three I have chosen are what I call 'appropriation', 'translation' and 'invention'. In all cases, I will try to choose forms to illustrate these sources. I should also stress that this division into three sections is just a matter of convenience. They are by no means watertight compartments. Appropriation and translation are especially interwoven. Let me begin with appropriation.

Meaning of Appropriation

What I mean by appropriation is acquiring new forms in a tradition from a different tradition. In the simplest case, poets in one tradition are literate in another tradition and decide to introduce a form, or feature of a form, which is well known and popular in that other tradition, into their own.

However, there are more complex cases. The borrowed form can, and often does, take on a whole new life of its own, merging with forms already existing in the tradition or spinning variations which are in time seen as intrinsic to the tradition. The sonnet is a supreme example of form, which is so deeply embedded in the English language poetic heritage with all its variations that it is almost difficult to think of it as an import that has so penetrated to the core of what we think of as English poetry. But then again there are even further complexities. The nature and stress rhythms of the English language and the already existing forms may play a large role in how pervasive an appropriated form becomes. Every language, culture and poetic tradition is porous.

The extent of that porosity in turn depends on the amount of contact. But I want to choose four other appropriated forms or formal features and look at them closely. The level of penetration of these appropriations varies greatly. By examining the origin and spread of these borrowings, I hope to heighten our awareness of the tradition before actually starting to try to put one or two of them into practice. I begin with *terza rima* (which in Italian means 'third rhyme').

Description of Terza Rima

The minute we hear *terza rima* we think of Dante. And, of course rightly so as he is credited with first inventing it for his *Divina Commedia* or Divine Comedy. Rather than describe it, I start with the opening[63] of Dante's Divine Comedy:

Nel mezzo del cammin di nostra vita (a)
mi ritrovai per una selva oscura (b)
ché la diritta via era smarrita. (a)

Ahi quanto a dir qual era è cosa dura (b)
esta selva selvaggia e aspra e forte (c)
che nel pensier rinova la paura! (b)

Tant' è amara che poco è più morte; (c)
ma per trattar del ben ch'i' vi trovai, (d)
dirò de l'altre cose ch'i' v'ho scorte. (c)

'Divina Commedia'

Below the translation[64] by Dorothy Sayers:

Midway this way of life we're bound upon,
I woke to find myself in a dark wood,
Where the right road was wholly lost and gone.

Ay me! How hard to speak of it – that rude
And rough and stubborn forest! The mere breath
Of memory stirs the old fear in the blood;

[63] p2, Dante Alighieri, *The Divine Comedy 1:Inferno*, translated by Robin Kirkpatrick, Penguin Classics, London, 2006
[64] *The Comedy of Dante Alighieri the Florentine, Cantica I Hell <L'Inferno>*, translated by Dorothy L. Sayers, Penguin Classics, Harmondsworth, 1949

It is so bitter it goes nigh to death;
That there I gained such good, that to convey
The tale, I'll write what else I found therewith.

As you can see the rhyme scheme is the pattern A-B-A, B-C-B, C-D-C, D-E-D. It is a chain or interlocked rhyme of any length you wish. Dante finishes Y-Z-Y, Z where Z is one of my favourite lines of all. Here it is again[65] in Dorothy Sayers' translation:

High fantasy lost power and here broke off;
Yet as a wheel moves smoothly, free from jars,
My will and my desire were turned by love,

The love that moves the sun and the other stars.

'Divina
Commedia' L'amor che move il sole e l'altre stelle.

Now ignore the translation here, because I am using it just to illustrate the *terza rima*. As you can see Dorothy Sayers allows herself a little latitude, a little broken or half-rhyme but it serves to show how it works.

Appropriation of *terza rima* in English

There is a long tradition of using *terza rima* in English and Geoffrey Chaucer ('Complaint to his Lady'), John Milton ('Psalm V'), Lord Byron ('Prophesy of Dante') and Percy Bysshe Shelley ('Ode to the West Wind') all used it. Among the moderns who tried their hand at the *terza rima* are W. H. Auden, William Carlos Williams, Robert Frost and Richard Wilbur.

Yet there is a fundamental difference between the depths of appropriation of *terza rima*. It is not that there are not very famous poems such as Shelley's[66] 'Ode to the West Wind':

'Ode to the
West Wind' O wild west wind, thou breath of Autumn's being,
Thou, from whose unseen presence the leaves dead
Are driven, like ghosts from an enchanter fleeing,

---

[65] *The Comedy of Dante Alighieri the Florentine, Cantica III Paradise <Il Paradiso>*, translated by
       Dorothy L. Sayers and Barbara Reynolds, Penguin Classics, Harmondsworth, 1962
[66] p453 *The Poetical Works of Percy Bysshe Shelley*, London, Frederick Warne & Co, no date

Yellow, and black, and pale, and hectic red,
Pestilence-stricken multitudes: O thou,

Who chariotest to their dark wintery bed
The winged seeds, where they lie cold and low,
Each like a corpse within its grave, until
Thine azure sister of the spring shall blow ...

This poem of Shelley's is to my mind possibly an example of where *terza rima* is most embedded in the English. For the most part I cannot help feeling that apart from translations of Dante, which are consciously attempting to reflect the original form, 'Ode to the West Wind' and Auden's usage in 'The Sea and the Mirror', *terza rima* remains what I would call an 'exhibition form' in English. By this I mean that it is a form which most poets with a sense of the inherited forms would know of and indeed might even experiment with. And yet, for the most part, it seems they merely exhibit the form. Robert Frost's poem 'Acquainted with the Night', while a very well known and much loved poem, never seems to have that quality of embeddedness, which Shelley's poem has. Somehow I am always conscious that this is an illustration of *terza rima*.

But how do we judge the degree to which a borrowed form such as *terza rima* is appropriated, how deeply it is embedded? It seems to me that there are several features, which are typical for a form which remains relatively shallow and superficially embedded.

Characteristics of Exhibition Forms
I can identify at least three features, which mark what I call exhibition forms out from a deeply embedded borrowing like, say, the sonnet.

Firstly, there are less recognised variations and outgrowths, which are practiced within English. For instance, in the case of the sonnet, we can speak of the Spenserian, the Petrarchan, the Shakespearian, the Miltonic or the Wordsworthian and there are longer forms with sequences and chains. In the case of *terza rima* there are few, if any variations, apart from the bacteriologist and poet Edward Lowbury's particular six syllable adaptation, which he called *piccolo terza rima*. There are also poems very loosely modelled on *terza rima*, such as William Carlos Williams 'Yachts'.

Secondly, there are rarely long poems written in these shallow borrowings. Aside from translations of Dante and Shelley's 'Ode to the

West Wind', most of the examples of *terza rima* that I am aware of are shortish poems.

Thirdly, it seems in the case of some poets, such as W. H. Auden and Richard Wilbur, the use of *terza rima* belongs to relatively early work. Auden's 'Antonio' in *The Sea and the Mirror* was written around the age of thirty-five. It is extraordinary how the variation from the normal regular iambic beat, the enjambment, the image of the clock, the conversational tone and the Englishness all mark his *terza rima* as so characteristically[67] audenesque:

'Antonio' As all the pigs have turned back into men
And the sky is auspicious and the sea
Calm as a clock, we can all go home again.

Yes, it undoubtedly looks as if we
Could take life as easily now as tales
Write ever-after: not only are the

Two heads silhouetted against the sails
– And kissing, of course – well-built, but the lean
Fool is quite a person, the fingernails

Of the dear old butler for once quite clean,
And the royal passengers quite as good
As rustics, perhaps better, for they mean

What they say, without, without, as a rustic would
Casting reflections on the courtly crew.
Yes, Brother Prospero, your grouping could

Not be more effective: given a few
Incomplete objects and a nice warm day,
What a lot a little music can do.

Of the four poems in *terza rima* in Richard Wilbur's oeuvre that I am aware of, 'Sun and Air', 'First Snow in Alsace', 'A Dubious Night' appear in his first collection *The Beautiful Changes and Other Poems* and the

---

[67] p410, W. H. Auden, *Collected Poems*, ed. Edward Mendelson, London, 1976

fourth 'Parable', which is a seven liner, is in his second collection *Ceremony and Other Poems.* It is almost as if it is part of a younger poet's initiation, a flexing of formal muscles. And yet I love the final lines[68] of 'First Snow in Alsace':

At children's windows, heaped, benign,
As always, winter shines the most,
And frost makes marvellous designs.

The night guard coming from his post,
Ten first-snows back in thought, walks slow
And warms him with a boyish boast:

He was the first to see the snow.

'First Snow in Alsace'

On the other hand, Robert Frost's 'Acquainted with the Night' was collected in *West-Running Brook* and published in the final years of the nineteen-twenties when Frost was about fifty-five.

When further on I will be discussing translation, I will point to the linguistic factors which militate against a deeper embedment of *terza rima* in poetry in English. However, it may be that the ultimate appropriation of *terza rima* as part of the English language would be if it were used in a contemporary poem commensurate with Dante's *Commedia* in its scope and range. But I want to move on to another appropriated form, the *ballade royal.*

The *Ballade Royal*

Once more rather than describe the rhyme scheme and metre, I want to begin with an example. Here[69] is Geoffrey Chaucer's *Good Council of Chaucer*:

Flee from the press, and dwell with soothfastness;
Suffice thee thy good, though it be small;
For hoard hath hate, and climbing tickleness,
Press hath envy, and weal is blent o'er all,
Savour no more than thee behove shall;

'Truth'

---

[68] p347, *Richard Wilbur: New and Collected Poems*, London, 1989
[69] p122, Minor Poem XIII 'Truth' Balade de bon counseyl, *Chaucer Complete Works*, ed. Walter W. Skeat, Oxford, 1912.

Read well thyself, that other folk canst read;
And truth thee shall deliver, it is no dread

Paine thee not each crooked to redress,
In trust of her that turneth as a ball;
Great rest standeth in little business:
Beware also to spurn against a nail;
Strive not as doth a crocke with a wall;
Deeme thyself that deemest others' deed,

What thee is sent, receive in buxomness;
The wrestling of this world asketh a fall;
Here is no home, here is but wilderness.
Forth, pilgrim! Forth beast, out of thy stall!
Look up on high, and thank thy God of all!
Weive thy lust, and let thy ghost thee lead,
And truth thee shall deliver, it is no dread.

The rhyme scheme is ABABBCC, where the final line is the refrain and there is often a regular metre with five stresses. It can finish with a four-lined envoi, which also has the refrain as its last line. Often the *ballade* is addressed to a patron.

In the case of this form the master is the French poet François Villon (1431–after 1463) who wrote *Le Testament* with the rhyme scheme of the *ballade royal* in each stanza. Here[70] is the first stanza:

'Le Testament' En l'an de mon trentiesme aage,
Que toutes mes hontes j'eus beues,
Ne de tout fol, ne de tout sage,
Non obstant maintes peines eues
Lesquelles j'ay toutes receues
Soubz la main Thibault d'Aussigny –
S'evesque il est, seignant les rues
Qu'il soit le mien je le regny.

And Peter Dale's translation:

[70] p40, François Villon, *Selected Poems*, Chosen and translated by Peter Dale, Penguin, Harmondsworth, 1978

Say but the Word

In the thirtieth year of my age
when I had swallowed up my shame,
not wholly foolish, nor a sage,
despite the harm and all that came
from Thibault d'Aussigny by name,
Bishop he may be, blessing streets,
but I repudiate the claim
that he is mine, for all his feats.

Although chronologically he comes a century or so after Chaucer, he is the great French model for the *ballade*. So great was his dominance that the *ballade* seems to go underground for some six centuries and is only taken up again in the nineteenth century by the like of Dante Gabriel Rossetti, Algernon Charles Swinburne and G. K. Chesterton.

Appropriation of *Ballade* in English
Swinburne uses the *ballade* with ten lines in a number of poems. Here are the first of three stanzas and the envoi from 'A Ballad of François Villon':

Bird of the bitter bright grey golden morn
Scarce risen upon the dusk of dolorous years,
First of us all and sweetest singer born
Whose far shrill note the world of new men hears
Cleave the cold shuddering shade as twilight clears;
When song new-born put off the old world's attire
And felt its tune on her changed lips expire,
Writ foremost on the roll of them that came
Fresh girt for service of the latter lyre,
Villon, our sad bad glad mad brother's name!

Prince of sweet songs made out of tears and fire,
A harlot was thy nurse, a God thy sire;
Shame soiled thy song, and song assoiled thy shame.
But from thy feet now death has washed the mire,
Love reads out first at head of all our quire,
Villon, our sad bad glad mad brother's name.

Another feature of the *ballade* is its use for semi-comic effect. You see

'A Ballad of François Villon'

Say but the Word

this in G. K. Chesterton's 'A Ballade of Theatricals'. Just the last stanza of the three and the envoi

Though all the critics' canons grow –
Far seedier than the actors' own –
Although the cottage-door's too low –
Although the fairy's twenty stone –
Although, just like the telephone,
She comes by wire and not by wings,
Though all the mechanism's known –
Believe me, there are real things.

Prince, though your hair is not your own
And half your face held on by strings,
And if you sat, you'd smash your throne –
Believe me, there are real things.

In a more flippant vein, the contemporary British poet Wendy Cope has a satire on proverbs called 'Proverbial Ballade'.

Compared with the sonnet, like *terza rima*, the *ballade* in its strict three stanzas with the same rhyme scheme plus an envoi is largely an exhibition form. Apart from Chaucer it seems to be used more as a show piece than as a deeply embedded form in English. There is a certain amount of variation and there are eight and ten line variations on the seven-liner that Chaucer and Villon used. As we will see, there are also good linguistic grounds for this shallow appropriation.

However, G. K. Chesterton took up the use of the *ballade* form in each individual stanza à la Villon in his epic poem about the Saxon King, Alfred the Great, called 'The Ballad of the White Horse', which has over two and a half thousand lines. Once more with good linguistic reason, he allows himself a fair deal of leeway in the patterns, but it is largely based on the *ballade*.

I now move to another borrowed form: the *Haiku*.

Haiku

This is a fascinating case of appropriation partly because it is an exotic borrowing, which happened in English in the twentieth century and partly because it illustrates an unusual combination of both shallow and deep appropriation.

But first let us take an example and then define what a *haiku* is. I will use what maybe one of the best known examples of all by Bashō, the dominating force in our perception of the *haiku* called *Old Pond*:

古
池
や

蛙
飛
込
む

水
の
音

furuike ya kawazu tobikomu mizu no oto
fu-ru-i-ke ya (5)
ka-wa-zu to-bi-ko-mu (7)
mi-zu no o-to (5)

old pond ...
a frog leaps in
water's sound

This example is famous and useful because it begins with the simplest case. The original Japanese is the *haiku*, where technically the translation is not. There are three lines (though they have been written vertically in Japanese!). The first has five syllables, the second seven and the third five syllables again. The *haiku* was originally a 発句 *hokku* the opening stanza of a 連歌 *renga* which was a series of collaborative *haikus*. However, there are further refinements.

The original Japanese has what is called a 切れ *kireji* which means 'a cutting word'. By convention there was a set number of these and they functioned like a caesura (which also in Latin means 'a cutting') to separate two parts or they could emphasise a preceding word like 'how' in 'how lovely!' here the *ya* at the end of the first line acts as a kind of caesura.

The original Japanese has also something called a 季語 *kigo* which means season word. In this case the frog leaping is within the culture a signal of the spring season.

One final complication is that, while in the Bashō *haiku* just quoted the Japanese has in our terms the required three lines with five, seven and then five syllables, it is always pointed out that the Japanese here do not in fact count their syllables, they count what prosodists and linguists refer to as moras. Mora is from the Latin for delay. The Japanese call it *haku* 拍 which means 'the clap of a hand'. Though a mora has various definitions, in practice it is important because in Japanese the sound 'n' counts as a mora and a double consonant in say 切手 *kitte* a stamp counts as two. Just one more example of how the

Say but the Word

distinction between a syllable has implications: 東京 Tōkyō has two moras in Japanese whereas English normally turns the name into the trisyllabic Tokyo 'Toke-ee-o'.

But why am I bothering about such subtleties? I just want to make it clear how the *haiku* which has been appropriated by the English language tradition, largely through translations of Japanese *haikus* into French and English and the work of imagist poets such as Ezra Pound and Amy Lowell, has taken on a life of its own. The complications of 切れ *kireji,* 季語 *kigo* and *haku* 拍 do not enter into the picture. What is considered the 'classic' English *haiku* is a three-liner with a five-seven-five syllable count.

Appropriation of *Haiku* in English
Apart from the interest of the imagists, we see the *haiku* enter the bloodstream of English literature with W. H. Auden. He translated the *haikus* in Dag Hammarskjöld's *Markings* and took to the form. Here are four examples from *Shorts II* written[71] between 1969 and 1971:

'Shorts II' A poet's hope: to be,
like some valley cheese,
local, but prized elsewhere.

Space was holy to
pilgrims of old, till the plane
stopped all that nonsense.

In moments of joy
all of us wish we possessed
a tail we could wag.

God never makes knots,
but is expert, if asked,
at untying them.

Richard Wilbur[72] has a *haiku* called 'Sleepless at Crown Point' which has the feel of an original Japanese *haiku* about it:

[71] p853, W. H. Auden, *Collected Poems,* ed. Edward Mendelson, Faber & Faber, London, 1976
[72] p58, Richard Wilbur: *New and Collected Poems,* London, 1989

All night this headland
Lunges into the rumpling
Capework of the wind.

'Sleepless at
Crown Point'

But just as the *haiku* was part of a longer series, this also develops in the English language tradition. Here are some *haikus* from a longer series by Billy Collins[73] called *She Was Just Seventeen*:

High cry of a hawk,
cracking ice across the lake –
enough of my talk.

'She Was Just
Seventeen'

Mid-winter evening,
alone at a sushi bar –
just me and this eel.

Awake in the dark –
so that is how rain sounds [6
on a magnolia. [6

Haiku makes you fail,
fail, fail, and fail some more – [6
then for once not fail.

Travel tomorrow,
so much I must leave behind –
this lake, this morning.

Street lights in the dark
city where I walk – [5
a man with many shadows.

But we will now look at how deep the *haiku* is in the tradition.

Embedment of *Haiku* in English

As the use of the *haiku* in English stems from the twentieth century, clearly it is not as embedded in the tradition as the sonnet. On the other

73 Billy Collins, *She Was Just Seventeen*, Lincoln, Illinois, 2006

hand, it is more pervasive than either *terza rima* or the *ballade*. It has
many home-grown variations. One of these is to combine the *haiku*
syllabic pattern with a rhyme scheme. Richard Wilbur has done this
beautifully in such poems as 'Thyme Flowering Among Rocks' and
'Alatus'. Here are the opening four stanzas of 'Alatus':

'Alatus'   Their supply-lines cut
           The leaves go down to defeat,
           Turning, flying, but

           Bravely so, the ash
           Shaking from blade and pennon
           May light's citron flash;

           And rock maple, though
           Its globed array be shivered,
           Strews its fallen so

           As to mock the cold,
           Blanketing the earth with earnest
           Of a summer's gold.

There is no shortage as to variations on the number of syllables. Look
what the beat poets like Jack Kerouac got up to in his *Book of Haikus*:

In my medicine cabinet
the winter fly
has died of old age

or

Shall I break God's commandment?
Little fly
Rubbing its back legs

The first has eight, four and five syllable lines, while the second has
seven, three and five.

However there are not many named and established variations –
though more about this later. For most poets, just like *terza rima*, it

remains on the level of an exhibition poem, something a poet tries out. Apart from a few moderately longer poems or collections of *haiku* we are dealing with once-or-twice-off single *haikus*. Yet what is strange is that the *haiku* exercises a fascination like the pursuit of chess and there is a cult of *haiku* writers at national and international levels who communicate and produce specialised journals.

But here let us turn to our fourth and final example and take a glance at another type of formal import: the usage of *cynghanedd* and *dyfalu* borrowed from Welsh language poetry.

Cynghanedd

In the previous three forms, which we looked at, the forms where taken into English, more or less as they were in the original language, though, as we saw in the case of the *haiku*, certain subtleties could not survive. When we talk of the use of *cynghanedd*, we are dealing with the taking into English of a device or technique which is the main source of ornamentation in the classic Welsh forms *awdl*, *englyn* and *cywydd*. I will not go into the differences between these forms as I want simply to concentrate on the devices, which have been borrowed.

Firstly, what is *cynghanedd*? Basically the word means harmony and describes alliteration within a line. Let us begin with a two-line example[74] from the fourteenth century poet Dafydd ap Gwilym's 'Merched Llanbadarn' (The Girls of Llanbadarn):

Plygu rhag llid yr ydwyf,
pla ar holl ferched y plwyf!

'Merched
Llanbadarn'

Kenneth Jackson's translation:[75]

I am twisted with passion –
Plague on all the girls of the parish!

Fundamentally here we are talking about alliteration between stressed consonants in a line. The second line has two stressed, beginning with 'pl' which Jackson tries to catch with a 'pl' and a 'p'.

This is a simple case of one of four types of *cynghanedd* called *cynghanedd draws* or 'crossover-harmony'. The alliteration jumps, so to

[74] p118, Seán de Búrca, *Dafydd ap Gwilym*, Baile Átha Cliath, 1974
[75] http://en.wikiquote.org/wiki/Dafydd_ap_Gwilym accessed 17th September 2014

speak, over across the line. We will look at one more complex use of what is called *cynghanedd groes* or 'crossing-harmony' where the alliteration crosses the whole line. Here is a verse from the more contemporary poet R. Williams Parry (1884–1956):

Tyner yw'r lleuad heno, – tros fawnog
Trawsfynydd yn dringo;
Tithau'n drist, a than dy ro,
Ger y ffos ddu'n gorffwyso …

Paul Carey Jones translates:

Tender is the moon tonight – over the peat
Of Trawsfynydd climbing;
You, sad, and beneath your stone,
By a dark trench resting …

In the third line 'Tithau'n drist, a than dy ro' you can see the alliterations crossing the whole line. Just one more one-line example from the more contemporary poet Dic Jones (1934–2009):

A phrancio o ffroeni y cyffro anwel

And the prancing from sniffing the invisible excitement

The pattern of consonants is quite amazing. The initial 'ph' is pronounced 'f'. This means the we have: 'ph(ff)rnc ffr n / c ffr n'.
   Now we look at this ornamentation borrowed into English.

Appropriation of Cynghanedd
Looking at such patterns of consonants the penny must have dropped. Inevitably we think[76] of Gerard Manley Hopkins:

'At the Wedding March'

God with honour hang your head,
Groom, and grace you, bride, your bed
With lissome scions, sweet scions,
Out of hallowed bodies bred.

[76]   p46, *Selected Poems of Gerard Manley Hopkins*, William Heinemann, London, 1953

Each be other's comfort kind:
Deep, deeper than divined,
Divine charity, dear charity,
Fast you ever, fast bind.

Then let the march tread our ears:
I to him turn with tears
Who to wedlock, his wonder wedlock,
Deals triumph and immortal years.

Or we might think of Dylan Thomas, whose use was probably more instinctive, maybe as much from osmosis as consciousness. The second verse[77] of 'Fern Hill'*:*

> And as I was green and carefree, famous among the barns   'Fern Hill'
> About the happy yard and singing as the farm was home,
>   In the sun that is young once only,
>   Time let me play and be
>   Golden in the mercy of his means,
> And green and golden I was huntsman and herdsman, the calves
> Sang to my horn, the foxes on the hills barked clear and cold,
>   And the sabbath rang slowly
>   In the pebbles of the holy streams.

Of course, there is nothing new about alliteration in English. Indeed Hopkin's famed 'sprung rhythm' was not new either. In essence it is simply keeping the same number of stresses in a line while allowing the off-beat sound in between the stresses. But what is absolutely intriguing is that the *cynghanedd* 'feel' marks the highly individual styles of both Hopkins and Dylan Thomas. Some have referred to this, in the case of Dylan Thomas as semi-*cynghanedd*. If we were to think of all the poets of the twentieth century writing in English it would be hard to find two poets whose style was so instantly recognisable. Both have used *cynghanedd* to such effect that their work is stamped with a quality as readily discernible as Mozart's music. In the case of Dylan Thomas, who is less influenced or less consciously using *cynghanedd* than Hopkins, he spawned a hoard of imitators through the mid-twentieth century.

[77]   p118, *The Dylan Thomas Omnibus*, Phoenix, London, 2000

Say but the Word

Whereas Hopkins was more consistently and deliberately working *cynghanedd*, Thomas was also echoing another classic Welsh tendency call *dyfalu*, which is a kind of piling up of associated personal images.

Embedment of Cynghanedd

The borrowing of this formal feature from Welsh is confined to a small number of either Welsh poets who have somehow absorbed the tradition or, in the case of Hopkins, Welsh literate poets. *Cynghanedd* differs greatly from the previous borrowed forms, which we have examined. Clearly it is more an ornamentation, a style, than a fixed stanza pattern. In some ways it resembles the loose imitation of the *haiku* by the like of Jack Kerouac or Donald Hall. There is a *cynghanedd* 'feel' just as there is a *haiku* 'feel'. The major distinction is that the *haiku* atmosphere is perceived to be vaguely Japanese but open for everyone to experiment with, while the *cynghanedd* is so highly associated with Hopkins in particular. The result is that to write in a marked *cynghanedd* style would, as yet, seem to be a form of Hopkins pastiche. I stress *as yet*, because as the years pass it may well be again possible to exploit this powerful and difficult formal feature.

Conclusion

The familiarity with form in languages other than English has been a constant source of enrichment for the tradition. It is part of the porosity between cultures, which has always engendered excitement and renewal. We must remember that this is not simply one-way traffic but rather part of the flow of cultural impulses. Goethe wrote his 'Lines on Seeing Schiller's Skull' in *terza rima*, the French alexandrine of Racine and Corneille dominated German dramatic verse, and most European languages adopted the sonnet and to a lesser extent the villanelle.

The matter of importing forms from other languages into the English language is complex. The primary source was often translations from major works in another language. The degree of penetration of the poetic inheritance varies greatly. For many poets the borrowed forms or formal features are simply something to experiment with from time to time, an opportunity to exhibit their knowledge of the form. There are many constraints involved and, as we will see further on, these have often a solid linguistic basis. On the other hand, we can never tell when a contemporary poet will renew and expand such borrowing to deal with the great themes of our times.

Say but the Word

Many of the forms and formal features, which have to differing degrees been borrowed into the English literary inheritance have arrived via translations of classic writers in other languages. In the case of *terza rima* clearly Dante's *Commedia Divina* is the model. Although Chaucer had used the *ballade* a century earlier, for all intents and purposes François Villon's *Le Testament* inspired the use of the *ballade*. By the same token translations of *haikus*, in particular those of Bashō, introduced the *haiku* to poets in English. The borrowing of *cynghanedd* is more complex in as much as translations rarely reflect the intricacies of the consonant patterns. It is largely confined to those who have absorbed the tradition either by learning or osmosis.

Translations have introduced the masters of particular imported forms to readers of English poetry. I now want to look at the various approaches that translators have made to solving the problems which reflect fundamental differences between the original language and English. Inevitably this will lead us to think a little about the mysteries of translation in a more general way. This, in turn, has a bearing on the appropriation of the forms and formal features as part of the English language inheritance.

I intend to concentrate on *terza rima* as a case study. Then, following some brief remarks on the *ballade* and *haiku*, I want to look at the problems associated with the translation of form in general and outline my own view of the best possible solutions.

Terza Rima: An Italian Invention

It is a commonplace to observe that *terza rima* is so much easier to write in Italian than in a language like English. The reason is very simply that what linguists refer to as the 'canonical form' of a word in Italian and in English is very different.

The term 'canonical form' simply means that certain combinations of sound are permitted in any given language. It is the sort of thing anyone who ever did a crossword puzzle knows. You have read the clue but cannot think of the word. If you have established from a clue you already solved that the first letter of the word is 'f' then if you have a good knowledge of English you instinctively know that in the word you are missing, the next letter must normally be a vowel or 'l' or 'r'. In other words you know intuitively that it cannot be 'fb' or 'fc' or 'fd' or 'ff' etc. The canonical form of a word only permits 'fl', 'fr', 'fa', 'fo', 'fu', 'fi', 'fe' or in very rare foreign loanwords 'fy'.

I once had a friend who never knew any other language but English. But he could do a superb imitation of several other languages using just sound and nonsense words, so his Italian was wonderful. He would string a whole lot of nonsense words together – all heavily stressed on the second last syllable – baloono, capari, portabelly and as part of his turn he interspersed them with a series of words he had picked up in Italian restaurants: mozzarella, cappuccino, espresso, spaghetti, macaroni. With the instinct of the caricaturist he had caught one important element of Italian: a fundamental rule of the canonical form.

The canonical form of Italian words permits words to end only in a vowel. What a boon for those who want to employ rhyme! All words end in 'a', 'o', 'e' or 'i'. This means that it is so much easier to find rhymes in Italian than in a language like English where the canonical form allows words to end in many different consonants and consonants clusters. Given the ability to rhyme, in some ways it is no wonder that the master of *terza rima* is Dante Alighieri. Let us now look at the opening of the *Divina Commedia*.

The Problem of Translating Dante
The opening three stanzas[78] of Dante's *Inferno* in Italian:

'Divina   Nel mezzo del cammin di nostra vita (a)
Commedia' mi ritrovai per una selva oscura (b)
ché la diritta via era smarrita. (a)

Ahi quanto a dir qual era è cosa dura (b)
esta selva selvaggia e aspra e forte (c)
che nel pensier rinova la paura! (b)

Tant' è amara che poco è più morte; (c)
ma per trattar del ben ch'i' vi trovai, (d)
dirò de l'altre cose ch'i' v'ho scorte. (c)

The first thing we notice is that already in the first three stanzas of *terza*

---

[78] p2, Dante Alighieri, *The Divine Comedy I: Inferno*, translated and edited by Robin Kirkpatrick, Penguin Classics, London, 2006

rima Dante shows us the spectrum of rhymes ending in 'a', 'e' and 'i'.

There have been many translations into English of Dante's *Commedia Divina*. The way in which the various translators tackle the question of rhyme, which lies at the heart of the translation bears on the consciousness of the possibilities of *terza rima* in English. Broadly we can group the various translations into three different approaches.

Three Broad Approaches to Translating Dante

In the first place we have those who simply make no effort to reflect the rhyme scheme in English. They simply put their hands in the air and, apart from throwing in an occasion rhyme that falls their way, trust to rhythm and stress to carry the impetus of this great epic. This school of thought simply acknowledges that the basic difference in the canonical form of words in Italian and English precludes any possibility of mirroring the rhyme scheme of Italian *terza rima* in English. It just is not possible. Any attempt to do so will sound contrived and just will not be natural in English. This is even more so in modern poetry, which aims at a syntax which follows current speech and frowns on any inversions or changes of word order which is not reckoned to be genuine. Such contortions are felt to be 'Poetic' with a big 'p' and to be avoided at all cost by a modern poet.

The avoidance of what is considered Poetic is only one aspect of the problem. It is also felt any attempt to preserve the original rhyme scheme will inevitably involve 'filling out' a line with words and thoughts not contained in the Italian. In other words you find yourself throwing in extra words or ideas just in order to achieve a neat rhyme. This for the contemporary sensibility seems to be a travesty and shows unfaithfulness to the text.

Secondly, there are those translators who feel that to lose the rhyme scheme which is so absolutely fundamental to *terza rima* invalidates the translations. Seen from this point of view, the challenge to find rhymes in English, even if it is so much more difficult than in Italian, is at the core of rendering Dante into English. I suspect also that this school of translators has fallen for the special magic of *terza rima*, the feel of two steps forward and one backward that lends both weight and momentum to Dante's argument.

The effect of translations, which give a real sense of the power of *terza rima* is to embed it deeper in the tradition as a possible vehicle for great poetry in English. Nevertheless, as we have seen, on the whole, the use of *terza rima* in English seldom goes beyond the realm of experiment. For most poets *terza rima*, this Dantean invention, is tempting only for an occasional and usually brief 'exhibition form'.

The third broad approach is a middle way, a compromise. In many ways it is thought to be a very modern compromise. In this case the two more extreme views combine. The objective is to have both form and readability. Yes, some reflection of *terza rima* is essential but at the same time, any un-modern or 'poetic' syntax is taboo. So what is the solution? This group attempts to achieve, with varying degrees of strictness, the rhymes of *terza rima,* but is quite content to abandon aspects of *terza rima* such as the 'chain effect'. Some have a penchant for more broken rhyme.

Let us now see how some of the translators of Dante have tackled the challenge of Dante's *terza rima.*

Translators of Dante

I will take some of the well known translators of the whole of the *Commedia* and categorise them generally by the approach they take. Many more have translated parts of the work, but I do not include any of them here.

Among those who eschewed the attempt to reflect the original *terza rima* form and preferred a type of blank verse would be Henry F. Cary, Henry Wadsworth Longfellow, Charles Eliot Norton, Henry Johnson, James Finn Cotter, Arthur Butler, Charles Singleton, C. H. Sisson and the more contemporary translators Thomas Bergin, Sandow Birk and Marcus Sanders, Louis Biancolli, Mark Musa, Anthony M. Esolen, Robin Kirkpatrick, and Robert and Jean Hollander.

Charles Eliot Norton's Introduction to his translation makes a strongly worded case[79] for this approach:

So many versions of the Divine Comedy exist in English that a new one might well seem needless. But most of these translations are in verse, and the intellectual temper of our time is impatient of a transmutation in which substance is sacrificed for form's sake and the new form is in itself different from the original. The conditions of verse in different languages vary so widely as to make any versified translation of a poem but an imperfect reproduction of the archetype. It is like an imperfect mirror that renders but a partial

---

[79] http://www2.hn.psu.edu/faculty/jmanis/dante/norton-hell.pdf accessed 17th September 2014

likeness, in which essential features are blurred or distorted. Dante himself, the first modern critic, declared that 'nothing harmonised by a musical bond can be transmuted from its own speech without losing all its sweetness and harmony' and every fresh attempt at translation affords a new proof of the truth of his assertion. Each language exhibits its own special genius in its poetic forms. Even when they are closely similar in rhythmical method their poetic effect is essentially different, their individuality is distinct.

He goes on to say:

The intellectual substance is there, and if the work be good, something of the emotional quality may be conveyed, the imagination may mould the prose as it moulded the verse, – but after all 'translations are but as turn-coated things at best' as Howell said in one of his Familiar Letters.

Four translators who take the second approach which I have outlined and attempted to sustain *terza rima* throughout a complete translation of Dante's *Commedia Divina* were Laurence Binyon (1869–1943), Dorothy L. Sayers (1893–1957) and in the mid 1990s, Stephen Wentworth and Peter Dale.

   Dorothy Sayers in her introduction makes a trenchant argument for translating the work into *terza rima.* After pointing out that Dante, who so strongly disapproved of translation in the *Convivio,* relearned charity before the *Commedia Divina* and wanted his poem to be available to as many people as possible, she[80] writes:

I have stuck to *terza rima*, despite the alleged impossibility of finding sufficient rhymes in English – it is, after all, less exacting in this respect than the Spenserian stanza, which nobody dreams of calling impossible. In prose a greater verbal accuracy would of course be attainable; but for the general reader this does not, I think, compensate for the loss of speed and rhythm and the 'punch' of the rhyme.

She continues later:

[80]   pp56–57, Dorothy L. Sayers, Introduction, *The Comedy of Dante Alighieri, Cantica I Hell*, Penguin Classics, Harmondsworth, 1949

Say but the Word

Blank verse, with its insidious temptation to be literal at the expense of the verse, has little advantage over prose and, though easier to write badly, is far more difficult to write well; while the rhymed couplet, or any stanza form other than Dante's own, involves the placing of stanza-breaks at places where he did not chose to place them. I agree therefore with Maurice Hewlett that, for the translator, the choice is '*terza rima* or nothing'. I have used all the license which English poetic tradition allows in the way of half rhyme, light 'Cockney', identical and (if necessary) eccentric rhyme – and indeed, without these aids, the heavy thump of the masculine rhymes (which predominate in English) would be tiresome. I have used a liberal admixture of feminine rhyme ...

She points out that a preponderance of feminine rhyme tends to produce special effects – of sonority, elegiac lamentation or burlesque and that Dante himself does not scruple to vary his feminine endings with masculine endings when he wants to, rare as these latter are in Italian verse. She also gives a masterly explanation of the possible variation in the number of syllables both English and Italian permit in *terza rima*.

The third approach outlined above is exemplified in the translations of John Chiardi (1916–1986), Geoffrey L. Bickersteth and Allen Mandelbaum (1926–2011). Although Dorothy Sayers' claim to 'have used all the license which the English poetic tradition allows' would seem to place her in this third category, we are talking about degrees of broken rhyme and also the use of the 'chain effect', as we shall see shortly.

Examples of the First Approach: Avoidance of *Terza Rima*.
Here again are the opening three stanzas[81] of *Divina Commedia* in Dante's words:

'Divina
Commedia'

    Nel mezzo del cammin di nostra vita (a)
mi ritrovai per una selva oscura (b)
ché la diritta via era smarrita. (a)

    Ahi quanto a dir qual era è cosa dura (b)
esta selva selvaggia e aspra e forte (c)
che nel pensier rinova la paura! (b)

---

[81] p2, Dante Alighieri, *The Divine Comedy I: Inferno*, translated and edited by Robin Kirkpatrick, Penguin Classics, London, 2006

    Tant' è amara che poco è più morte; (c)
ma per trattar del ben ch'i' vi trovai, (d)
dirò de l'altre cose ch'i' v'ho scorte. (c)

Let us look at just two examples of this first approach, one older and one contemporary. Firstly, Cary's translation:[82]

In the midway of this our mortal life,
I found me in a gloomy wood, astray
Gone from the path direct: and e'en to tell,

It were no easy task, how savage wild
That forest, how robust and rough its growth,
Which to remember only, my dismay

Renews, in bitterness not far from death.
Yet to discourse of what there good befell,
All else will I relate discover'd there.

It is amazing that there is a certain momentum here but no *terza rima*. Clearly some phrases such as *e'en*, befell, do give the version a slightly dated feel but at the same time does not invalidate it.

    Here[83] is the Robin Kirkpatrick's contemporary translation:

    At one point midway on our path in life,
I came around and found myself now searching
through a dark wood, the right way blurred and lost.

    How hard it is to say what that wood was,
a wilderness, savage, brute, harsh and wild.
Only to think of it renews my fear!

    So bitter, that thought, that death is hardly worse.
But since my theme will be the good I found there,
I mean to speak of other things I saw.

[82] http://www.gutenberg.org/cache/epub/1008/pg1008.html accessed 17th September 2014
[83] p3, Dante Alighieri, *The Divine Comedy I: Inferno*, translated and edited by Robin Kirkpatrick, Penguin Classics, London, 2006

This is in some ways, a conventional beginning to a medieval visionary poem. The protagonist enters often into a dreamlike state and then tells what he subsequently experiences. Dante jumps into his theme – *in medias res.* Yet the translations have to catch, without *terza rima,* a sense of the impending scope and range of this great poem that, on the threshold of modernity, so epitomises the cosmology of its time. It seems to me that the great danger of a translation with this approach is that it so easily slips into a prosy flatness so that you miss, what Norton calls 'the intellectual substance'. Many of these freer translations run the risk of 'falling off'. The poet and Dante scholar Kirkpatrick's translation has a very contemporary rhythm yet somehow manages to maintain the necessary tone of dignity and gravitas.

But what happens, despite Norton's dire warning, when *terza rima* is used in English? After all this is crucial for the inclusion of *terza rima* in the English language's formal repertoire.

Examples of the Second Approach: Usage of Terza Rima
The best known example of this approach, and the one which I first encountered as a student, is the translation[84] by Dorothy L. Sayers:

'Canto I'   Midway this way of life we're bound upon,
        I woke to find myself in a dark wood,
        Where the right road was wholly lost and gone.

Ay me! How hard to speak of it – that rude
        And rough and stubborn forest! the mere breath
        Of memory stirs the old fear in the blood;

It is so bitter, it goes nigh to death;
        Yet there I gained such good, that, to convey
        The tale, I'll write what else I found therewith.

You can see what Dorothy Sayers meant when she spoke of using half rhyme. Take for instance *wood / rude / blood* or *breath / therewith.*

I am not sure I understand why 'our time is impatient of a transmutation in which substance is sacrificed for form's sake and the new form is in itself different'. There really is not much padding here for the sake of *terza rima.*

---

[84]   p71, *The Comedy of Dante Alighieri the Florentine Cantica I Hell <L'Inferno>*, translated by Dorothy L. Sayers, Penguin Classics, Harmondsworth, 1949

Say but the Word

The Italian says literally 'in the middle of the path of our life' and this turns into 'Midway this way of life we're bound upon'. The Italian says literally 'lost' and Dorothy Sayers has 'lost and gone'. Then the literal Italian 'that in the thought the fear renews' becomes 'The mere breath / Of memory stirs the old fear in the blood'. Yes, there is a little pleonasm but it is minimal and seems to me to be well compensated by catching something of the spirit of that *terza rima* which had such theological as well as stylistic implications for Dante. Somehow the effect of the *terza rima* heightens our sense of expectancy that a work of breadth and scope is about to unfold. When we add to that, that such a translation introduces the possibility of *terza rima* into the tradition, which is what our main focus is here, it certainly does not seem too great a price to pay.

Examples of the Third Approach: No Full Chain Effect/Some Rhyme
Perhaps the best example of this approach is John Ciardi. Here is how[85] he tackles the opening stanzas:

Midway in our life's journey, I went astray   'Canto 1'
from the straight road and woke to find myself
alone in a dark wood. How shall I say

what wood that was! I never saw so drear,
so rank, so arduous a wilderness!
Its very memory gives a shape to fear.

Death could scarce be more bitter than that place!
But since it came to good, I will recount
all that I found revealed there by God's grace.

Largely, Ciardi goes for full rhyme between the first and third line of the stanza but apart from the occasional broken or slanted rhyme between the second line and the first and third of the following stanza (*wildness / place / grace*), he abandons the 'chain effect' of *terza rima*. The 'b' in 'aba' need not be the end rhyme for first and third lines of the next stanza. The scheme becomes aba cdc efe etc. It does give a stately quality if not 'the one step forward and one back', which the chain conveys. The introduction of 'by God's grace' – which is not in the original Italian –

85 http://www.operone.de/dante/inf01ciardi.html accessed 17 September 2014

might horrify Charles Eliot Norton but would hardly shock Dante.
One other example of this approach is Allen Mandelbaum:

When I had journeyed half of our life's way
I found myself within a shadowed forest,
for I had lost the path that does not stray.

Ah, it is hard to speak of what it was,
that savage forest, dense and difficult,
which even in recall renews my fear:

so bitter death is hardly more severe!
But to retell the good discovered there,
I'll also tell the other things I saw.

Mandelbaum abandons the chain effect and takes a more relaxed view
of rhyme than Ciardi. There is a full rhyme in 'way / stray' with the
casual broken rhymes as opposed to defining rhymes of *terza rima* in
'fear / severe / there'.
Now let us glance at how Villon's *Le Testament* is translated.

Translations of Villon's *Le Testament*
I think, in general, we can say that at least two of the same three
categories apply as in the case of Dante's *Divina Commedia*: there are
those who avoid the *ballade* form in English and give a free translation,
those who try to render the *ballade* in English and those who attempt a
compromise. I will give an example or two of each category.
Here[86] is the first stanza of Villon's original:

'Le Testament' En l'an de mon trentiesme aage
Que toutes mes hontes j'eus beues
Ne de tout fol, ne du tout sage,
Non obstant maintes peines eues
Lesquelles j'ay toutes receues
Soubz la main Thibault d'Aussigny –
S'evesque il est, seignant les rues,
Qu'il soit le mien je le regny.

[86] François Villon, *Selected Poems*, translated by Peter Dale, Penguin, Harmondsworth, 1978

An example that doesn't try to give the *ballade* form is the version by Galway Kinnell:

In my thirtieth year of life
When I had drunk down all my disgrace
Neither altogether a fool nor altogether wise
Despite the many blows I had
Every one of which I took
At Thibault d'Aussigny's hand
Bishop he may be as he signs the cross
Through the streets, but I deny he is mine.

The complete translations by, among others John Lepper Herron, Anthony Bonner, Barbara Sargent-Baur would subscribe to a similar approach. Once again, as in the case of Dante's *Divina Commedia*, I will not attempt to list the many well known poets who have translated portions of Villon's *Le Testament*.

    An outstanding example of the full use of the *ballade* is Peter Dale's translation, which first appeared[87] in 1973:

In the thirteenth year of my age
when I had swallowed up my shame,
not wholly foolish, nor yet a sage,
despite the harm and all that came
from Thibault d'Aussigny by name.
Bishop he may be, blessing streets,
but I repudiate the claim
That he is mine, for all his feats.

'The
Testament'

I must admit that this was the first translation which I owned, and I was bowled over by it. There is a parallel French text so you can follow along in French. This extraordinarily accurate, skilful, rhythmic and fluent translation is sustained throughout and is truly a remarkable feat. It transcends Charles Eliot Norton's 'temper of the times' and is the best possible illustration of Dorothy Sayers' demanding challenge. Inevitably, there is an occasional word that does not occur in the French. The equivalent of 'for all his feats' is not in the original and clearly is there to

[87] p41, François Villon, *Selected Poems* translated by Peter Dale, Penguin, Harmondsworth, 1978

achieve the rhyme scheme ababacbc as required. But so what! It is very much in the spirit of Villon and in no way feels like an optional extra.

Translations of *Haiku*
Similarly to the *ballade*, in *haiku* there are at least two of the approaches we saw in the case of Dante's *Divina Commedia*: those who shun the syllabic form of the *haiku* and those who to use it in their English translations. Just as Dante is the great model for *terza rima* and Villon for the *ballade,* in the West the *haikus* of Bashō are the best known exemplar for the form. I will use just two *haikus*: the famous 'frog in the pond' *haiku* and the one thought to be his final *haiku* written on his deathbed.

Here is the first one:

古池や
蛙飛込む
水の音

Furuike ya
Kawazu tobikomu
Mizu no oto

Literally translated it is word for word: Fu-ru (old) i-ke (pond) ya, ka-wa-zu (frog) to-bi-ko-mu (jumping into) mi-zu (water) no o-to (sound).

The Dubliner Lafcadio Hearn, who was one of the first westerners to open up Japanese literature to the West and the poets Allen Ginsberg and Robert Hass stay away from the Japanese syllabic scheme;

Hearn has: Old pond — frogs jumped in — sound of water.

Ginsberg's version is:

The old pond
A frog jumped in,
Kerplunk!

Hass renders it as:

The old pond —
a frog jumps in,
sound of water.

On the other hand the poet Eli Siegel chooses to keep the original scheme of five-seven-five syllable, though he adds the idea jumping from the shore:

Pond, there, still and old!
A frog has jumped from the shore.
The splash can be heard.

The second example is Bashō's deathbed *haiku*:

旅
に
病
ん
で

夢
は
枯
れ
野
を

駆
け
巡
る

Tabi ni yande
Yume wa kareno wo
 Kakemeguru

Again Robert Hass refrains from retaining the syllabic pattern:

Sick on a journey,
my dreams wander
the withered fields.

As against that Yoel Hoffman's version successfully shows the original scheme:

On a journey, ill:
My dream goes wondering
Over withered fields.

While the freer versions have the feel of a *haiku* about them, clearly the Hoffman version, which preserves the syllabic count helps to establish the *haiku* as a part of the English literary portfolio.

Now that I have looked at how *terza rima,* the *ballade* and the *haiku* are handled in translation, I want to expand a little on my own views and experience.

Say but the Word

Personal Views and Experience of Translation

I think that in my description of the three broad approaches to highly intricate forms, I have probably implicitly shown my hand. In truth I am on the side of Dorothy Sayers rather than that that of Charles Eliot Norton. While I understand Norton's ideas about the 'temperament of the times', I am much more convinced by Sayers' understanding of the tradition. The Spenserian stanza – with its eight lines in iambic pentameter followed by a single 'alexandrine' line in iambic hexameter together with the rhyme scheme ababbcbcc – is far more difficult than *terza rima*. She is also right in her awareness that broken or imperfect rhyme is a long established tradition. Such a strict master of the heroic couplet as Dryden rhymed 'express' with 'cease', 'chin' with 'unclean' etc. and Pope, another master rhymed 'caprice' and 'nice', 'heath' with 'death' etc.

Yet it is more the technical possibility that impresses me. I think it is more the ambition and desire to convey the meaning and the original form together that fires me. To say that it simply is not possible to achieve this seems to me defeatist. It reminds me of someone starting to learn a new language who does not believe that if one human being can master this, then surely another also can, and too easily throws in the towel. Yes, it takes endless patience, humility and endless desire, but there is something about believing that it is possible that makes it possible.

Let me share with you just one or two short examples. First a simple example, Here is a four-liner by the contemporary poet[88] in the Irish language, Cathal Ó Searcaigh:

'Éiríonn na focla'

Éiríonn na focla as mo chroí
ina n-éanacha uaigneacha trá
agus lorgaíonn dídean na hoíche
i nduilliúr craobhach do ghrá.

Here is a 'free' translation:

The words rise out of my heart,
become lonely birds of the shore
and seek shelter of the night
in the branching foliage of your love.

[88] p29, Cathal Ó Searcaigh, Gúrú i gClúidíní, Indreabhán, Conamara, 2006

Say but the Word

That gives you the meaning. Now just for interest let's look at a literal or word for word translation:

Éiríonn na focla as mo chroí
Rise the words out of my heart

ina n-éanacha uaigneacha trá
in their birds lonely [of] shore

agus lorgaíonn dídean na hoíche
and seek shelter of the night

i nduilliúr craobach do ghrá.
in foliage branching [of] your love.

I have square-bracketed 'of'. The 'of' is not there in the original but I use it to show that the nouns are in a genitival relationship.

Now here is what I come up with as one suggested translation:

Out of my heart a flight
of lonely shore birds;
in your love's leafage words
seek the refuge of night.

Clearly, this is just one possible solution. My feeling is that this, though less literal, is closer to the original than the freer translation. It is a strange paradox that sometimes as you move slightly away from the literal, you move nearer the spirit of the poem. It captures the meaning and the three stresses in each line. And yes, there are some compromises! The rhyme scheme is 'abba' rather than the original 'abab'. It is not *terza rima* so it is not of real importance. Only one word gets left out, that is 'branching'. But in a strange way this is perhaps more economic, terser than the original. After all most foliage is 'branching'. The alliteration in *'love's leafage'* is an added ornament, which picks up the *'l'* of *'lonely'* in the previous line. This along with the long 'e' sound in 'lonely', 'leaf' and 'seek' tie up the four-liner in a way that the original uses the long 'e' sound throughout: in *éiríonn* (Donegal), *croí, lorgaíonn, dídean oíche* and *craobhach.*

One further example of a slightly longer poem by the Norwegian poet[89] Einar Skjæraasen called *Mazurka:*

'Mazurka'   Festen er over.
Rommet står grått.
Jenten' er borte,
spellmann' har gått.
Inni meg smyg
en gjenganger-slått:
Mazurka.

Gla har je vuri
fresk er je født.
Jenter i armen
hadde je støtt,
danse med surt
og danse med søtt
– mazurka.

E var så varm som
midtsommar-sol.
E var så kald som
vintern i fjor.
Rundt med dem! Rundt
Te hanan han gol.
Mazurka.

Guten blir gubbe.
Gubben blir grå.
Nord går det da,
og ned går det så.
Dansen je danse
gjømer je på
– mazurka.

A literal prose translation would be: 'The party is over. The room is grey. The girls are off, the fiddler is gone, inside me a ghost tune sneaks; mazurka. Glad have I been, I was born healthy. Girls by the arm I had

[89]   p77, Einar Skjæraasen, *Bumerke*, Forlagt, Oslo, 1968

always, danced with the bitter, danced with the sweet – mazurka. I was as warm as a midsummer sun. I was as cold as winter last year. Around with them! Around until the cock will crow. Mazurka. The boy becomes an old man, the old man turns grey. It goes then north and down it then goes. I dance the dance and store it away – Mazurka.'

Here in a suggested translation, I hope I catch something of the spirit. The rhyme scheme is somewhat different but once again I do not think that that variation matters here as it would in *terza rima*, which clearly would be a far greater, though not impossible challenge. In Norwegian 'to go north' can mean 'to go to hell', 'to the dogs'. In English, something that is lost 'has gone west'.

A party finished,   'Mazurka'
The room now grey,
The girls vanished,
Fiddler away.
A ghost melody
Sneaks inside me:
Mazurka.

I've been glad
All my born days,
Always had
Girls on my arm,
Danced with the sweet,
Danced with the sad
– Mazurka.

I've been warm as
Mid-summer's sun,
I've been cold as
The winter gone.
So round you go
Till the cock will crow.
Mazurka.

Boys are old men,
Old men grey.
Downhill then

And west as the day.
The dance I danced
I hoard within.
– Mazurka.

Conclusion

Translations of classic works from other languages, which reflect an original form unfamiliar in the English language tradition, have certainly helped to widen its formal scope and to embed new forms and patterns. In drawing attention to the original texts and acknowledging the near impossibility of formal translation, even translators who shy off such a reflection or only partly reflect it, raise the consciousness of the form.

A proliferation of versions seems to throw up a similar spectrum of attempted solutions to the problem of translation in the case of all elaborate and intricate poetry, irrespective of whether it is a recognised classic form or simply particular to one poet or poem. While concentrating on rhyme schemes I have identified three broad categories of translation – non-formal, formal and a compromise solution – the boundaries between these are always fluid. Many versions that I call non-formal on the basis of the absence of rhyme could well be thought of as belonging to the third category inasmuch as they preserve metrical features or the stanza length of the original poem.

Besides the ordinary words for translation, both German and French have the words *Wiedergabe* and *rendre* both of which mean to re-give or give back. The best translations do give back, or, to use the English borrowing, 'render' a poem. But the Norwegians have also a second word for translation: *gjendikting*, which means 're-composing'. The best translations both render and recompose.

For all the well known dictums about the failure of all translation, from time to time the magic happens and the meaning and form combine in English to catch the wonder and spirit of a poem.

Having considered the appropriation of form into English, I surveyed the different approaches to translation as the main mechanism by which foreign forms enter the bloodstream of the tradition. However, all forms have been devised at some point by a practising poet. As a practitioner of the trade myself, this will, of course, mean using examples from my own work, which I introduce with some comments both on the content and form.

Firstly, I want to say something about my own experience of some of the appropriated forms I have already looked at and then to discuss inventions of my own, some of which involve the use of these appropriated forms.

Terza Rima in my Work

First let me say straight out that I think *terza rima* is an extraordinary form. Apart from the marvel of rhyme, the mutual echoing of words with absolutely dissimilar meanings that fascinates the child in us all, there is the chain effect which knits each stanza into the next. I love to put it to work and have used it when appropriate from very early in my life as a poet and feel at ease with it. I mentioned poets using *terza rima* as an 'exhibition form', a poem or two which experiments with the form or declares that this is something I can do too, like a boy cycling a bicycle 'no-hands'. While as yet I have not published any long poem in *terza rima*, for me it moves beyond the 'exhibition poem'.

How better to begin than with a love poem called 'Play' from the first section of my book *Love Life* which tries to capture with the retrospect of three dozen years the walking on air, the return to Eden[90] when we first fall irrevocably in love:

You, my all in one, my one in all,   'Play'
It's still summer, will you come out to play?
Let's make love inside the orchard wall.

Coy, bold, knowing, insolent, outré
Madam, goddess, nymph, vamp, flirt;
Play each woman you know how to play.

[90]   p488, Micheal O'Siadhail, *Collected Poems,* Tarset, 2013

Strip me back to my core, tease, subvert,
Dig out, scour, clean, make me ready,
Flushing and purging any wound or hurt.

Unhead this wary head, unsentry me.
The ears of Cherubim begin to tingle
I come to my garden of myrrh and honey.

O vigilant gate-keeper wink one single
Moment, sheathe again your fiery sword.
Once angels we return. We fuse. We mingle.

Let's make love again before the Fall.

I want to bring in another poem in *terza rima*. It is called 'Praise' and is taken from the section entitled 'Adage' in my book *Tongues*. I am fascinated by proverbs. It is fashionable to simply dismiss them as clichés but I am much more interested in how they are expressed in various traditions. To use the philosopher Ricoeur's phrase – 'I want to take them up and shake them by the roots'. However overused, I want to retrieve the accumulated wisdom they sum up. In the Irish Language there is a well known proverb *Mol an óige agus tiocfaidh sí* which means 'Praise youth and it will prosper'. There is something so tragic when a stunted father stunts his own son[91] for lack of praise:

'Praise'   A youngster's smile climbed from the root
Of his being, a blossom so suddenly sprung,
Out of such clay one burgeoning offshoot.

I'd forgotten a friend's father's razor tongue
And how in turn he couldn't praise his son.
A memory stinging again as it was stung.

Everything in him wanted to say 'Well done!
Good on you, my boy! That was flawless!'
No fault to find but why was there always one

[91]   p765, Micheal O'Siadhail, *Collected Poems,* Tarset, 2013

To hamper delight he so wanted to express?
For the one stunted tree, an unseen wood.
Too long a longing for his own father's caress.

A friend's son I'd praised in all likelihood
By chance, a small thing I happened to salute
But my words sank deeper than I'd understood.

Down silent wells of generations a chute
Of praise moistened years of childhoods unsung;
A shaft of sap pushing upwards to the fruit.

Now I do play fast and loose with *terza rima*. Here is a variation, an invention if you like, with four accents to a line rather than five and some enjambment. It is a poem called 'Scruples' and after this title has a brief quotation from W. B. Yeats: 'or the day's vanity, the night's remorse'.

   In some ways all artists are broken reeds. Such a terrible need to reflect on everything and to try to make sense of it all! And yet, there is an unbelievable cost. The devotion of a lifetime. That is at least our own responsibility. But then there is the cost to those[92] who love us:

Comrade, pilot of my travels,   'Scruples'
You have given generous light –
Yet an inner voice cavils;

Prophet-poet by what right?
Self-doubt and scruples hover,
Conscience cries by night.

How can I now recover,
Redeem your years spent
Loving the bemused half-lover?

Double-mated, I never meant
To fail, to shortfall you;
The mood-changer muse has leant

[92]   p173, Micheal O'Siadhail, *Collected Poems*, Tarset, 2013

On me, squeezed more than due;
Untrue, undertakings broken,
I forfeit my claims on you.

Excuses too smooth-spoken,
Words shallow at source,
Comforts too soft to token

Divided pain or to endorse
My shame, that counter-theme
Matching your sorrow with remorse.

Can nothing I do or dream
Charge a cell of resurrection
Bring again love on stream?

Amazed at such introspection,
'Love,' you whisper, 'why remorse?
Am I not queen of my affection?'

I could go on with several more examples of both strict and less strict
terza rima but instead I want to quote some *haikus*.

Haiku in my Work

I share with many others a fascination with the *haiku*. I suppose it is the
minimalist aesthetic, what the Japanese call *wabi*. This is often
translated as 'austere beauty' or 'subdued taste' and has connotations of
pining and lonesomeness. There is something extraordinarily spare and
beautiful about the best *haiku*.

I must admit that I did not find myself being moved in the direction
of the *haiku* until about a dozen years ago when I began reading them
in Japanese and they entered deeply into my consciousness. Slowly some
poems seem to demand the form. Here is one from *Love Life*. It is the
third and final section of a poem entitled 'Ceremony' which speaks of
the moments when 'we broach the Sabbath of ourselves' and 'pirouette
in the glory of an instant', the wonderful moments of love which feed
all the ordinariness[93] in a relationship:

[93]   p527, Micheal O'Siadhail, *Collected Poems,* Tarset, 2013

Bird flight at sundown.   'Ceremony'
Afterwards the aftershine
Infinite moment.

Another from *Love Life* where I face the frightening thought that no
matter how great a love, almost inevitably, one lover will die before the
other. I turned to *haikus* in a poem[94] called 'At Sea':

Jets whine overhead.   'At Sea'
Who will be lonely for whom?
One silver gull cries.

Yoked we throw our light.
That one will be first to go.
A twin star untwinned.

And from 'Full and By', the final section of *Love Life*, a series of four
haikus with another marine metaphor named *Passage* which suggests
the infinitude of longing[95] which drives our love:

So our boat ploughs on,   'Passage'
The bows still scudding with ease,
Old homing salmon.

Off course. No pinching.
A sail full and by the breeze.
One butterfly wing.

The tune yearning plays,
A song humming in the wire,
Wind sung in our stays.

Voyage we still dream.
Long perspective of desire.
Port's fugitive gleam.

But this brings me to all the variations I have found, working with the

[94] p546, Micheal O'Siadhail, *Collected Poems,* Tarset, 2013
[95] p548, Micheal O'Siadhail, *Collected Poems,* Tarset, 2013

haiku, or if you like, new forms are growing out of the *haiku*. This may be called invention. I cannot be sure that no one else has stumbled on these forms before or found a poem falling into these shapes, but I have not seen them.

The Inverted *Haiku*

I do not know if this form is my own invention or not but it seems it shaped several poems or parts of poems in my book *Tongues*. One very perceptive critic noticed it and referred to it as an 'inverted *haiku*'. Very simply, rather than three lines with five-seven-five syllables, the order is inverted and it becomes instead five-five-seven. Here are some examples.

Firstly a poem from *Tongues* contemplating the Japanese proverb which is the equivalent to the English 'too many cooks spoil the broth'. The Japanese, like indeed the Welsh, go for a nautical metaphor. It is the wonderfully[96] surreal 船頭多くして、舟山に登る *Sendō ōku shite, fune yama ni noboru* 'Skippers increase and the boat climbs a mountain':

'Confusion' For French two bosses,
Many steer in Welsh,
In Greek surplus advisers.

Too many skippers,
A boat noses down
To Davy Jones's locker.

But not in Japan.
Here in the scramble
Sailors trip each other up,

Command, countermand,
Topsyturvy world,
Torn masts and a bow ascends

Surreal Mount Fuji;
Nightmare of seascape
Where the boat climbs a mountain.

[96] p762, Micheal O'Siadhail, *Collected Poems,* Tarset, 2013

Another example of the inverted *haiku* from *Tongues* is based on the proverb in Faroese which is the equivalent of the (Hiberno-English?) 'Live horse and you'll get grass'. In Faroese *Tann sum tíðum rør út, hann fiskar umsíðir* 'The one who often rows out catches fish in the end'[97]:

Backbone. Long-haul grit.   'Shortfall'
Fishermen oaring
Bravely out from the Faroes

And day after day
Facing a knife-edge,
The cliffhangers of failure,

Chance of tides and shoals,
Skill, hunch and hearsay,
Rowing unforgiving seas.

Again and again,
Belief in frequence,
The gleam of tomorrow's catch.

And now another *haiku* invention.

The Rhyming *Haiku*
What about a series of *haikus* that rhyme or half-rhyme? Why not? There is no reason not to combine a syllabic count with a rhyme scheme. Here is an example, from *Tongues*. It is from *Word*, the second section of *Tongues* and is called 'Feast'. I am intrigued by the word 'feast', which summons up trust[98] and hospitality:

This word tapping down   'Feast'
Into sacred rites,
Things laid out before our gods.

Against all the odds
Again the stranger
Open to the stranger's face.

---

97 p769, Micheal O'Siadhail, *Collected Poems,* Tarset, 2013
98 p671, Micheal O'Siadhail, *Collected Poems,* Tarset, 2013

A toast and embrace
Repairing two words,
Our glasses raised, our eating

In tents of meeting,
A trust-mended pledge.
The host as guest, the guest host.

As you can hear in this inverted *haiku* the third line rhymes with first line of the following *haiku*.

There are endless possible combinations. I return to my delight in proverbs. This time it is the Japanese proverb[99], 'As for tomorrow, tomorrow's wind blows', which expresses the equivalent of the English phrase 'we'll cross that bridge when we come to it'. I find it quite beautiful:

'Abandon'   明日は、明日の風が吹く
            'Ashita wa, ashita no kaze ga fuku'
            As for tomorrow, tomorrow's wind blows:

For the Japanese
Moments we borrow,
Time's arrow on loan for fun.

And so no unease,
No bridge or sorrow,
Sheer lightness of abandon.

Quivers of a breeze
Put off tomorrow,
Trusting to the rising sun.

The same rhyme occurs in all three *haikus*.

The Inserted *Haiku*
A poem has sometimes demanded of me that it cadence with the high density of a *haiku*. In some cases, however, I happened on what I call

---

[99]   p783, Micheal O'Siadhail, *Collected Poems,* Tarset, 2013

the 'inserted *haiku*'. Here a *haiku* is inserted regularly between stanzas written in a different form. There are a number of these in the 'Under the Sign' section of *Tongues*. Several of the poems intersperse *haikus* between stanzas with a syllabic pattern of eight syllables alternating with six syllables. All the poems in this section are meditations on characters used in Japanese. These are signs borrowed from Chinese and are understood by over one sixth of the world's population and they are utterly fascinating. The sign, which means 'collection' is now a bird in a tree. As a friend of mine would say 'think about that!' Here is the poem[100] called 集 Shū 'Collection':

Earlier three birds on a tree   'Collection'
But now only the one.
Imagine swoops of homing rooks
As evening tumbles in
Cawing and wheeling to gather
In skeleton branches
With nodes of old nests blackening
Into the roosting night.

Treetop colony.
A rookery congregates.
Dusky assemblage.

Whatever instinct makes us hoard,
A desire to amass,
Toys, dolls, marbles, bird's-nests and eggs
We fondle and brood on
Or how we'd swoop like rooks to nab
Spiky windfalls, stamping
Open their milky husks to touch,
Smooth marvels of chestnut.

The collector's dream
To feel, to caress, to keep.
A bird in the hand.

[100] p749, Micheal O'Siadhail, *Collected Poems,* Tarset, 2013

Say but the Word

This is what I would like to name the eight/six syllabic with inserted *haiku*. Another type of inserted *haiku* I have named a *saiku* – a fanciful portmanteau word for a sonnet (sonnets are one of my absolutely favourite forms and I have written hundreds of them) and a *haiku* together. *Saiku* (細工) in Japanese means 'work' or 'craftsmanship' and has the extended meanings; 'tactics', 'tricks'. My example of a *saiku* is the final love poem in *Love Life* called 'Crimson Thread'. It clearly alludes in several places to *The Song of Songs* and is a summing up and a renewal of the promise[101] of love:

'Crimson Thread'
My love, my love along the slopes of Gilead,
This is our Eden before the bitter apricot.
How unimaginable now our story if we had
Never met, never shaped each other's plot.
Fracture and hurt of a once bruised youth,
Sores healed by wine and oil and spice.
Kiss of life. Shulammite's mouth-to-mouth.
My wounds bound up in second paradise.
Over and over. Season by season by season,
I'm older than my mother's crimson moment.
Our slow grown plot of risks and pardon
As father cries how things would be different,
If things were again. O heart's secret treason!
My sister, my bride…I come to your garden.

Again from under
Scarlet cords of winter fruit
A sumac burgeons.

We roved out all in our youth and prime.
Both real and unreal it seems somehow
Like reading a novel for the second time
To recall our unfolding in the light of now.
So much that fell almost as if by accident,
Twists and corners we couldn't see or gauge,
The plot gradually entangled as we went
That will have been our story page by page.

[101] p551, Micheal O'Siadhail, *Collected Poems*, Tarset, 2013

Say but the Word

Two so close. Two so utterly different.
Clash and blur become a rich repair,
Secrets held to love more open-eyed,
Lives sweet against a crimson moment.
Chalk or cheese of what we are or share.
Lived-in paradox of decades side by side.

Deep deeper yellow
Prepares a crimson moment.
A sumac's leaf falls.

At this point I want to move on and look at some other favourite forms
of mine and which I have found in order to deal with certain moods and
themes. I am sure the forms I am naming have been used here and there
by poets down through the years. They are inventions inasmuch as they
are forms which I have written poems in and are part of a repertoire
that certain themes demand. I illustrate only some of them.

Alternating Eight-Six Syllable Lines

Perhaps as I have grown again more conscious of syllabic poetry, I find
that some poems seem to move naturally into syllabic patterns. I say
again because as an undergraduate I read a lot of syllabic poetry in the
Irish language. One pattern, which has exercised a certain fascination
is a form which alternates eight and six syllable lines.

   I have some of these in the final 'Gratitude' section of *Tongues*. I was
a student in Oslo in 1968. Student years have a special kind of open-
heartedness where we make lifelong friends before the great
responsibilities of life sometimes make it less likely. A wonderful time
and with one extraordinary friend I would read Norwegian poetry deep
into the night. This is a poem of thanks. Strangely in Norwegian there
is no really natural everyday word for 'please'. You can say 'be so kind
as to' or 'friendliest do this or that' but no ordinary 'please'. Yet like other
Scandinavian languages, they thank all the time, for conversations, for
travelling alongside them and so forth. This poem is entitled
'Homeland', as Norway would become my second homeland. I quote
all three parts. The first illustrates the eight-six syllabic form, the second
is plain abca, defd, ghig etc. and it concludes[102] with a *haiku*.

[102] p786, Micheal O'Siadhail, *Collected Poems,* Tarset, 2013

'Homeland'   1
Age of open heart and talking soul,
Feverish plans of callow time out,
Suspended time of sixty-eighters

Before the routines of survival,
Our habits of settled common sense,
This aperture for livelong friendships.

Oslo of snow boots and *Pils* and trams,
City of youth and orphan stumblings
I grew up here with sibling students.

All hail those who made me one of you,
You who let me strike these other roots;
I flourish in my second homeland.

2
Bjørn, my proto-Scandinavian,
Long-legged, blond and blue-eyed gleam of charm,
Dreamy mountaineer those years adrift,
Mix of make-believe and action man.

'Noble the human, the earth is rich'
Mood by mood our nightly poems aloud,
Edelt er mennesket, jorden er rik
Nordahl Grieg's *To Youth* at fever pitch.

'Dance my lyric, weep my song'
Skjæraasen and Herman Wildenvey
'Life's desire so strong and near and new'
Danse mi vise, gråte min sang.

Me a poet, you now glacialist,
Every time we meet in two score years,
Quoting Gunnar's words you'd quoted me,
Ghostly Rudin I once more insist:

Say but the Word

'Don't forget the one you've never met,
She's the one you love in her you love'
Action man remember now your dream?
Lines of mine move daily in your debt.

3
Gratitude's language.
For food. For today. For now.
A tongue to thank in.

The Linked Triplet
This is a form I love. Basically the last line of a triplet rhymes with the
first line of the following triplet. So the rhyme scheme is abc cde, efg
etc. Just to illustrate this here from 'Shadow-Marks' in the first section
of *Globe* is a poem called 'Sputnik'. It is strange to remember at the age
of ten hearing for the first time the word 'sputnik'. These were the days
that the space age started as we played ring-a-ring-a-rosie in the orbit
of our childhood garden. Soon our world would become the fragile
planet we now know it is and the process[103] of globalisation was
inevitable:

Was it make-believe of childhood   'Sputnik'
That made the garden chosen seem
A time when our lives stayed still

Before the half-remembered thrill
At how a Russian sputnik hurtled
Ring-a-ring-a-rosie around an earth.

We didn't know they put a girth
On a patchwork fractious planet.
Tischa, Tischa, walls fall down.

A world that was a collective noun
Snapped from there outside itself,
A whirling clod once photographed

---

[103] p557, Micheal O'Siadhail, *Collected Poems,* Tarset, 2013

For good a delicate spinning craft,
Pocketful of posies we relearn
To tend, this fragile raft in space.

Everywhere becomes everyplace.
No man is an island Donne knew
Before the instant image wheel

Relayed the tube's mute appeal.
Hungry or broken, the wallfallen
Commands seen in Abel's face.

But now for two other kinds of triplet. First the triplet with constant rhyme.

Constant Rhyme Triplet

Again I am sure that others have fallen into this form, whether they have named it or not. It has a peculiar mesmeric effect. There are three line stanzas and the rhyme scheme is *abc, abc, abc* etc. The second part of the poem 'Crying Out' in the 'Wounded Memory' section of *Globe* is an example. I think we all try to shy away from tragedies because they are all so hard to bear. Yet in not suppressing them, can we free ourselves to celebrate genuinely what is good and wonderful[104] in our world:

'Crying Out'   The long mute pleas of the dead
For us to remember things
So beyond our ken we barely control

Our deepest urge to shun in dread
Their clammy-handed nobblings,
To flee the ghostly buttonhole

Of those whose testimony shocks
Too much for us to hear.
Of patterns we're destined to rehearse

---

[104] p619, Micheal O'Siadhail, *Collected Poems,* Tarset, 2013

Unless a patient listening unblocks
Such clogged up fear
Of our histories' ancient mariners,

Voyages we need to face and word,
Stories of dreams stillborn,
Tragedies that never found a voice,

Cries of agony yet to be heard.
So much we must mourn
Until our broken bones rejoice.

A second use of the constant rhymed triplet I take from the first part of
'Falling' in the 'Adage' section of *Tongues*. It is a midrash on the Latin
adage[105] which stems from Ovid: *Gutta cavat lapidem non vi sed saepe
cadendo* –'The drop hollows the stone not by force but by often falling':

Ovid's droplet on a stone,   'Falling'
A signet ring grown thin,
A plough worn down by soft clay.

The trickle most widely known,
For some a motto to underpin
Where there is a will there is a way.

Persistence. For me an undertone
Of danger. My mother in the kitchen
Warning as we went out to play

'Constant dripping wears a stone'.
Any bad company that we were in
Would whittle and whittle us away.

A ring worn near to the bone,
Ovid's epistle under the skin.
I hear you mother and I obey.

---

[105] p770, Micheal O'Siadhail, *Collected Poems,* Tarset, 2013

Now I turn to the form I call the mid-rhymed triplet.

The Mid-Rhymed Triplet
The characteristic of this form is that there are three lines to a stanza.
In the plainest version the rhyme scheme is *aba cbc dbd etc.* Here is an
example from *Tongues*. It ponders the Japanese character 心配 *shinpai*
'worry'[106] which consists of two characters, the first meaning heart, the
second dispersal:

'Worry'   1
First left: a minimalist stylisation
Of a heart, first organ in our embryo
Blood-pump and relay station.

And next to the left a jar of vino
At the right a figure on his knees
Maybe pouring it out to show

Dispersal. Together 'anxieties',
Shinpai 'worry', to undergo
A divided heart, a mind's unease.

2
Bird of my spirit gone into spin,
Round and round a rim of sanity.
Unnumbered hair. Fallen sparrow.

'Angst' and 'anguish' words for narrow.
The diffuse closes off in anxiety,
A widening out, a shrinking in.

So much caring too diluted, too thin.
This wine jar forever half-empty.
Scattered heart. Sapped marrow.

---

[106] p719, Micheal O'Siadhail, *Collected Poems,* Tarset, 2013

Say but the Word

3
A figure bent and busy at the jar
Pumping adrenalin in a worry gland.
An endless night, closed and circular.

O sandman break the ring of doubt
As surrendering again to the unplanned
A concentration broadens out.

Whole-hearted. All-embracing.
Blake's single grain of sand.
Carefree loving of one thing.

If you look carefully at the second part of the poem you will see it combines both the linked and the mid-rhymed triplet. This is again a shape many poems have fallen into. There are, of course, endless possibilities and variations. However, I want to look at three more forms which have proved significant for me.

The Zigzag Form
This is again not entirely my own invention. I have put it to use here and there. However, anywhere in *The Gossamer Wall: poems in witness to the Holocaust* where I do not have any other formal device, I have used it. It binds the whole narrative in an understated way, which manages the flat tone which I deliberately adopted in order to let the true horror of what happened take its own effect. Here is a poem called 'Remembrance' from the first part *Landscapes*. One word in every line in each stanza will rhyme with the next and often across stanzas, creating a kind of zigzag pattern. The words[107] are in bold type.

A **word** absorbed in an ease of childhood's garden   'Remembrance'
you **think** you've **heard** a million times over
suddenly will **sink** further **in**. A depth charge.

Or a piece you be**gin** learning **note** by **note**,
slow practicing by **rote**, a dreamlike repetition;
years **go** by before you re-awake to its music.

[107] p397, Micheal O'Siadhail, *Collected Poems,* Tarset, 2013

As **though** things can be too big for us close-up
and need the **slow**-down of both time and distance;
a wider angle, the gradual *adagio* of truth.

So complex, so tangled as **if** we have to wait
on some **riff** of imagination to re**fract** detail,
some fiction to shape elusive meanings of **fact**.

Time to find the chronicles be**low** the debris
of a **cleansed ghetto**, for piecemeal unearthings
to air their testimony **against** false witness.

Just quiet moves and shifts in geological **tempo**,
or the way climates **show** changes over decades
of **slow l**andscape. A long redemption of time.

In a **rest** between notes a music's bridled silence
or in our fictions those things still **best unsaid**,
a tacit crying out for the forgiveness of the **dead**.

Just one further example. This time it is from the 'Battalion 101' section
of *The Gossamer Wall*. It deals with the hardening of ordinary men to
carnage. The man in charge, known as Papa Trapp, was originally a
compassionate man but he[108] too becomes inured to slaughter. The
poem is called 'Papa Trapp':

[108] p426, Micheal O'Siadhail, *Collected Poems,* Tarset, 2013

'Papa Trapp' Iron Crossed veter**an** of World War One,
at fifty-**three** a career police**man** risen
through the ranks with his *esprit de corps*
but short on the blinder **zeal** of **two** captains
Wohlauf and Hoffman who **can't** now con**ceal**
young, arro**gant** contempt for their commander.
Yet Papa Trapp is popular a**mong** his men.

God, **why** *did I have to be given these orders?*
That day at Józefów he'd **cry** for the bloodshed;
a**loof** and riven he'd **paced** his head-quarters

but not the forest. Things comman**ded** not **faced**.
In de**spair** he'd **shed** tears and confided to one
of his **men** *If ever this Jewish affair is avenged*
on earth, **then** *have mercy on us Germans.*

As the police re-board**ed** trucks at Józefów
a ten-year-old girl bleeding from the **head**
appeared, he **took** her in his arms and **said**
You shall remain alive. Horror-**struck**
he'll con**sole** troops, over**look** the truancy
of men who **stole** away or **stepped** aside.
Patron of all who flinch. A major who **wept**.

Come September a sergeant slain by ambush
and Lublin demands a mini**mum two** hundred
punish**ment** shootings to sub**due** locals. Trapp
still balks at Poles but with a mayor's con**sent**
he'll **kill** just down-and outs; instead the Jews
from a **near**by ghetto can over**fill** his quota.
And Papa Trapp has no more **tears** to shed.

The Melodeon Form
This is a form which intrigues me. Again I know many have used it
before me but it has shaped several of my poems. This is a form that
melodeons out and then back like a Chopin nocturne that climaxes and
resolves. So it is abcdefg etc. etc, gfedcba. An example from *Tongues* is
entitled 'Subjectivity'. I am amazed when the Japanese, during the Meiji
Era, found words to cover the European ideas of 'subjective' and
'objective'. They expressed them as 'from the host's point of view' and
'from the guest's point of view'. This avoids a lot of European[109]
arguments.

Was the whole world a feast for Japanese?   'Subjectivity'
Europe's 'subjective' and 'objective' adapted
As either the view of host or guest.

[109] p671, Micheal O'Siadhail, *Collected Poems,* Tarset, 2013

Say but the Word

A bird-eyed caller observes and leaves the rest
To the work of a busy host laying on a spread.
Together our life all of a piece.

So just one more example, this time from *Shadow Marks,* the first section
in *Globe.* The poem is called 'Scenario' and offers a very brief glance at
how the past shapes the present, which prepares[109.1] the future:

'Scenario' In a rim's touch and turn
Our moment's wheel of now
Already become what was.

All that's to come still jazz,
An unknown latent in know-how;
Our past a future we learn.

This melodeon form has a peculiar attraction for me as a vehicle for a
certain atmosphere and tone.

Conclusion

I could go on. Other times I work with a very ordinary abab or abba
scheme. Then again maybe it turns out to be a variation on one of these,
or even both. There are countless established forms and amazing
possibilities for invention.

   What is absolutely marvellous about forms is the almost infinite
amount of combinations and permutations that open up. There are
myriads of shapes and forms that some dynamic in a poem demands. I
never know what it is that chooses the form. Sometime it is the *donné*,
the line that comes from nowhere as a surprise and offers a rhythm and
pattern. Sometimes it is a mode that seems to suit me over a particular
period. Or is it some aspect of a theme or the intensity of what a poem
wants to say that dictates whether there is a form at all? Sometimes a
free verse approach is the only way to go. I think I reach for certain
forms to cope with overpowering feelings as though the form somehow
allows me to contain the joy or pain sufficiently for the poem to take
shape. For all the namings of forms or rhyme patterns or metres, there

---

[109.1]   p562, Micheal O'Siadhail, *Collected Poems,* Tarset, 2013 is so much which always remains a great mystery. In the end I fall back on the ancient concept of inspiration and gift.

It is wonderful when the form and theme dovetail. I want to finish with one more melodeon. Here is 'Complementarity' from the opening section of *Love Life*. How desire searches and aims at love! Then, the love-making. Look how at the dead centre a Rubicon is crossed. The climax and then[110] the resolution:

Golden halo of early lust,   'Complementarity'
Arrow that trembles and aches
In a looped bow of suspense

And still delights in anticipation,
Part an aiming and part
A relished moment loth

To let go the silk string.
So, the Rubicon.
Yield and quiver of returning

Until we two are each and both
Wave and fired dart,
A misty integration.

Soft combat. Honeyed violence.
My female being awakes
Dewy-eyed with trust.

[110] p478, Micheal O'Siadhail, *Collected Poems,* Tarset, 2013

Wise in Words

Wise in Words

**Identity, Memory and Meaning in the
Twenty-First Century: Trauma and Vision**

Lecture delivered to The Institute for Humanities at University College
Dublin November 16th 2007

Introductory Remarks

Dr. Caball, Director of this Humanities Institute of Ireland together
with Professor David Ford of Cambridge University published a book
of critical essays about my work early this year. By a strange coincidence,
I owe to Professor Ford's own article in that book the insight that for
some years my poetry collections seem to have alternated between
public and more personal concerns. When Dr. Marc Caball asked me
to give this lecture, I gladly accepted his invitation because 'Identity,
Memory and Meaning in the Twenty-First Century' has long been one
of the themes central to my more public poetry. When I received a
request for a more precise title for my particular contribution I chose
'Trauma and Vision' as it seems best to crystallise my angle on the
broader theme. I hope to deal with this topic under three headings.

Firstly, I want to discuss my own background, the cultural ambience
of our times and the role of testimony in bringing together identity,
memory and meaning. Secondly, I would like to look at various images
and insights into the relation between trauma and the possibilities of
conciliation, growth and vision. Thirdly, I intend to explore and ask
some questions about the actual processes of historical change.

But before I attempt to broach all of this, I want to say that I am sure
that there are many of you who are historians or sociologists or
philosophers or economists or literary critics or academically involved
with the history of ideas and maybe much better qualified to talk on
some of these subjects. I approach all of these topics as a poet. Mind you
I use poet in the fullest meaning of the word. The poet Richard Murphy
once told me that the word poet in Sri Lanka means 'the one who sees
the connections between things' and I have since been told that this is
also true in Hindi. So in that spirit I'll try to contribute some insights
from my perspective.

One difficulty that I have is that sometimes, where I have previously
expressed an idea in poetry, I would like to quote some lines of my own
to gain the advantages of the heightened intensity and precision which
poetry offers. As Anthony Storr, the British psychologist explained in

his book *The Integrity of the Personality*, you quote yourself not out of arrogance but rather to save yourself saying it all over again. However, I am afraid I have never quite mastered the art of speaking in inverted commas! So if you notice a sudden change in the linguistic register, you will know that I have gone into poetic mode!

Background and Cultural Climate

Personal background

Anyone born as I was in the late nineteen-forties and who grew up in the fifties and went to university during the mid-sixties will know the huge cultural turmoil of that era. After two world wars, though some prefer to speak of another Thirty Years War with a lull, the intellectual critique of humanism, which had begun at the outset of the twentieth century, took hold among the educated general public.

I have just returned from Japan, where, among other things, I gave a lecture to a select research group of Japanese professors on Beckett. It was fascinating to recall how startling a play like *Waiting for Godot* was for a young undergraduate around 1965. The break with any traditional plot or development was mind-blowing. Then there was the message. Was there any point at all to existence? Did mothers give birth astride a grave? After the pieties of an enclosed and sheltered middle class upbringing in the fifties, this sent a *frisson* down our spines. So was life entirely meaningless and any hope a delusion? We had that youthful thrill of flirting with the emptiness of despair.

Those intellectual students a year or two older at Trinity College all talked of Existentialism. It was a strange idea and took a while to grasp. We learnt how existence was prior to essence, about angst and embracing freedom, how meaning did not depend on rationality but on choices taken and so on. It was fashionable to read Jean-Paul Sartre and Albert Camus. I am not sure there was any thoroughgoing coherence in all of this but there was a general sense in the air that meaning was subjective and much talk of alienation and absurdity.

It was years later when I came on *Sansibar oder der letzte Grund* by Alfred Andersch (1957) and in Norwegian *Lillelord* (1955) by Johan Borgen that it became clearer that the intellectual climate of student days in the sixties in Ireland was the reaction to the Second World War reaching us from Europe. So great was the effect of the Holocaust and the unspeakable evil of the elimination of six million Jews together with the Gypsies, homosexuals and politicos, alongside the scale of the overall loss of life, that Europe was reeling. The realisation that such violence could be initiated by Germany, the very heart of civilised Europe, the land of Bach and Beethoven, of Goethe and Schiller and the most scientifically advanced country, broke our faith in humanity. How could rationality ever be trusted? The dream of linear progress and the great story of the evolution of humanity were shattered. The result was a general atmosphere of ennui and the loss of nerve in the humanist enterprise that found expression in the guarded and minimalist meaning of existentialism or in the theatre of the absurd.

Masters of Suspicion
Of course, the questioning of what had previously been cultural certainties had been initiated by Marx, Nietzsche and Freud since the nineteenth century but there can be little doubt that it was immeasurably exacerbated by the Holocaust. The posture of mistrust which pervaded the nineteen-sixties, would continue into the nineteen-seventies and eighties. While Marx, Nietzsche and Freud had unveiled class, societal and sexual motives, the focus now shifted to language.

It came in waves. Derrida and Foucault and the deconstructionists emphasised the Saussurean understanding of a sign as an arbitrary convention. Subsequently Barthes insisted that the sign should draw attention to itself in order not to encourage an illusion of reality. He in turn was followed by de Man who proclaimed that all language is metaphorical and suspended irrevocably between literal and figurative meaning so that it becomes unreadable. With each wave of deconstruction it seemed to grow more and more esoteric.

Alongside all this interrogation of language, came the challenge of hidden ideologies and power. The Marxist and feminist critiques suggested that so much of our culture, wittingly or even worse unwittingly, shore up unfairness in our society's distribution of wealth and its treatment of women. Another viewpoint, pioneered by Edward Said, is the interpretation of power through the lens of colonial exploitation.

While all of these various insights have merit, one thing is certain, that the undergirding presumption asks the questions: What are you trying to put over on us? Who is trying to gain at someone else's expense? Who is taking some form of exploitation knowingly or unknowingly for granted? The underlying mode of intellectual thought is one of suspicion. However, ironically, the only position which seems to remain immune from such suspicion is the mode of suspicion itself.

Artistic Approach

How then does a poet address questions of identity, memory and history against this pervasive intellectual background of suspicion? Often the reply of the artist is simply to get on with it. There is some truth in this. Yet this would narrow my options. There are, at least, two stock responses. One is to opt for irony, which is indeed the dominant mode in much contemporary literature. The other is to retreat into interiority, where the inner realm of the poet's imagination sets itself up against a world of power and exploitation. Clearly, these two approaches are not mutually exclusive and many combine them.

However, neither of these responses is a satisfactory option. Heavy irony is not my way. As a young man I took Rilke's advice concerning irony in his *Letters to a Young Poet* seriously. 'Seek out the deeps of things: irony will not penetrate so deep,' wrote Rilke, 'and if this brings you right up to the margins of great matters, then ask yourself if an ironic need is born of some inner need of your own nature.' For me irony is a useful tool but it can so easily become an abuse of playfulness and escapism. As for the withdrawal into the individual mind, while I love the personal lyric, I cannot cede the public arena and allow poetry to be reduced entirely to the domain of private enhancement. I do wish to address the questions of identity, memory and meaning on a societal level.

I have tended to follow the French philosopher Paul Ricoeur's view of the culture of suspicion. Clearly, here I only touch off one or two ideas in his wide ranging work but I do see the various 'masters of suspicion', as he tagged them, as ultimately, to use another Ricoeurian phrase, 'blessing reality'. In other words, it is a good and healthy thing to be aware of all our hidden abuse of power but in the end, we have to trust. We have to move from what he calls 'a first naïveté', through the crucible of mistrust onto 'a second naïveté'. For all the shiftiness of language, it is the polysemy, the multi-layered overlapping of meaning that allows us the gift of metaphor. Ricoeur invites us, instead of simply suspecting symbols, to retrieve them. His massive final work, *Memory, History and Forgetting*, again stresses that after weighing up all the evidence we have to use our discernment and draw our conclusions. To put it too briefly and bluntly, we need, in the light of what suspicion has revealed, to move on.

The Gossamer Wall

As the last century drew to a close, it seemed to me that the pivotal event of the century had been the Holocaust. I had no doubt that it had cast so long a shadow over the intellectual climate of our times that I needed to confront it. I do not believe our culture has ever really faced it squarely. I was sure that, in some ways, it was a natural reaction, for all the good reasons historians give us. The world was too busy getting on with recovery, as indeed were the survivors. And although the savageries of Cambodia and Rwanda have since occurred, the Holocaust remains paradigmatic. I read and thought about it over many years and decided to try to distil the story in poetry in *The Gossamer Wall*. I believe the concision and metaphor possible in poetry is the ideal medium for such a distillation.

As it happened *The Gossamer Wall* was published sixty years after the worst years of the Holocaust 1942–1943. I was conscious of the symbolic and practical significance of that sixty year period. Scott's *Waverly Novels* have the alternative title '*Tis Sixty Years Since.* It was sixty years after the Jacobite Rising of 1745. Tolstoy's *War and Peace* appeared sixty years after the Napoleonic War. It is also generally agreed among Biblical scholars that the Gospels were written between forty and eighty years after Christ. But more than the symbolism, there are the practical consequences to the sixty year gap.

I was born two years after the Second World War. The fact that another generation relates what happened in the Holocaust based on eyewitness accounts represents the pivotal point when story begins to turn into history. Clearly, someone who is emotionally involved but at the same time has the distance of a generation and the wider focus of time can catch the sweep of things in a way which is difficult for a first-hand witness. Nevertheless, at this point there are still enough eyewitnesses about to judge whether the account given rings true or not. I have had the privilege of reading from *The Gossamer Wall* in the presence of survivors who had experienced the concentration camps. I can say without hesitation that one of the most moving events for me was after a reading in London, when a woman, who had been through Auschwitz, came up to me and embraced me saying 'you have spoken for us all'.

Witness

I have just spoken of eyewitnesses. I titled the book I wrote about the

Holocaust *The Gossamer Wall: poems in witness to the Holocaust.* I did this quite consciously knowing the weight of the word witness in contemporary thought. I wanted to bear witness to what had happened in carrying the knowledge further.

The concepts of witness or testimony or attestation are crucial to the theme of identity, memory and history. What are for me two giants in twentieth century philosophy, Emmanuel Levinas and Paul Ricoeur, both stressed the importance of this key idea. Levinas, himself a Lithuanian Jew, who knew the terrors of the Holocaust and based his cry for ethics on the command of the Other's face, speaks[111] constantly of witness:

When in the presence of the Other, I say, 'Here I am!', this 'Here I am' is the place through which the Infinite enters language... It is through this testimony that the very glory of the Infinite glorifies *itself.*

Paul Ricoeur[112], in *Oneself as an Other (Soi-même comme un Autre)*, which is a monumental study of the whole question of identity at the beginning of the final decade of the twentieth century, took attestation as a vital concept. The great advantage of this concept is that it avoids any form of foundationalism. Attestation, he calls a 'veritative' mode, which 'defines the sort of certainty that hermeneutics may claim, not only in respect to the epistemic exaltation of the *cogito* in Descartes, but also with respect to its humiliation in Nietzsche and his successors.' Attestation, according to Ricoeur 'links up with testimony, inasmuch as it is the speech of the one giving testimony one believes... Vulnerability will be expressed in the permanent threat of suspicion, if we allow that suspicion is the specific contrary of attestation. The kinship between attestation and testimony is verified here: there is no "true" testimony without "false" testimony. But there is no recourse against false testimony than another which is more credible; and there is no recourse against suspicion but a more reliable attestation.' He declares that 'one can call upon no epistemic instance any greater than that of belief, or if one prefers, credence... Credence is also trust... This trust in turn will be a trust in the power to say, in the power to do, as the power to recognise oneself as a character in a narrative, finally, to

---

[111] p106, Emmanuel Levinas, *Ethics and Infinity: Conversations with Philippe Nemo*, Pittsburgh, 1985
[112] Paul Ricoeur, *Oneself as Another,* University of Chicago Press, 1992

respond to the accusation in the form of the accusative: "It's me here" (*Me Voici*), to borrow an expression dear to Levinas… At this stage attestation will be that of what is commonly called conscience… As credence without any guarantee, but also as trust greater than any suspicion, the hermeneutics of the self holds itself at an equal distance from the *cogito* exalted by Descartes and from the *cogito* that Nietzsche proclaimed forfeit.'

When I think of that phrase of Ricoeur's, 'there is no recourse against false testimony than another which is more credible', I think of how they strove in the concentration camps to be sure the real story would out. I think[113] of the strange fluke of how the truth buried underground literally came to the surface years later:

Against the odds unearthed diaries, fragments.   'Haunted'
In milk cans and tin boxes Ringelblum's blow-
By-blow journals, sudden cache of documents
Dug up out of the ruins of the Warsaw ghetto.
Planting a tree some Polish children chance
On thermos-flasked notes of Salmen Lewental,
The Greek Jew's slow-release resistance,
Birkenau *Sonderkommando*'s time capsule.
All fugitive chronicles sealed into airtight
Jars interred with rubble and sunk below
Rebuilt houses, lives still waiting on the light.
Write and record. That a world may yet know.
Dubnov's orders, *shtetlekh* and ghettos wiped
From the earth's face: *Schreibt un farschreibt.*

Images of Trauma and Vision
How do we emerge from the shadow of the trauma which even yet overshadows our confidence in the humanistic enterprise? No one in their right mind would wish for trauma. On the other hand, the aftermath of trauma may either overwhelm us or become an opportunity to rearrange our world, to find images for a new vision.

Chaos out of Order
The first image I want to offer, I take from science. I have long been

[113] p446, Micheal O'Siadhail, *Collected Poems*, Bloodaxe, Tarset, 2013

fascinated by the work of Ilya Prigogine. I cannot pretend to understand all the details but I am intrigued by the general thrust. During his lifetime he was regarded as a bridge builder between the so called 'hard sciences' and the social sciences. In the book called *Chaos out of Order* he and his co-author Isabelle Stengers offer a synthesis that brings together reversible time and irreversible, disorder and order, physics and biology and chance and necessity. What concerns us here is largely the physics and biology and more particularly disorder and order.

Firstly, only in a system which behaves in a sufficiently random way is time irreversible. In other words, if there wasn't a degree of randomness, any process could be simply spooled back or forward. When a system behaves with a minimum amount of randomness it is called an open system.

The crux of the matter is that in physics, according to the Second Law of Thermodynamics the world is running down and you cannot run it backwards to make up for entropy. On the other hand, in biology, the evolutionary process moves from simple to complex, from so-called lower forms of life to so-called higher forms[114] of life.

'Radiance' As the helix tangles and grows complex,
Our feverish sun is a purse that leaks.

A knife-edge between chaos and leap.
Our running down and our building up.

.   .   .   .   .   .

The red giants die to zinc and carbon.
I grow with ashes of stars in my bone.

In other words there seems to be a fundamental contradiction. However in Prigogine's terms there is no contradiction. According to *Order out of Chaos* all open systems contain subsystems which are continually fluctuating. At times a single fluctuation or combination of them may become so powerful, as a result of positive feedback, that it shatters the previous organisation. At this 'singular moment' or bifurcation point, you cannot predict whether the system will disintegrate into 'chaos' or

[114] p298, Micheal O'Siadhail, *Collected Poems,* Bloodaxe, Tarset, 2013

leap to a new more differentiated, higher level of order. Alongside this Prigogine and Stengers persuade us that order and organisation can actually arise out of disorder and chaos through a process of what others term *autopoesis*.

All of this means that entropy is not merely a collapse of organisation but under certain conditions it generates order.

Now I will not burden you with scientific examples, but it doesn't take a great leap to see this as model for how trauma threatens both total breakdown and also offers the chance for reorganisation.

A Linguistic Metaphor
The second image I want briefly to mention is linguistic and moves therefore away from the hard sciences and into a kind of halfway house on the way to a more overtly societal model. At least half of the vocabulary of both English and Japanese is borrowed. In the case of English it is reckoned that over 50% of the vocabulary is ultimately from Romance languages. In the case of Japanese the statistics are again that about half of the vocabulary was originally Chinese.

In these days of *Franglais* it is hard to imagine how once the open system of English was so flooded by the Romance influence of French and Latin that it must have reached the bifurcation point. This was so for the three centuries less four years between the battle of Hastings in 1066 and 1362 when the Parliament was first opened in English and the Statute of Pleading was passed ensuring that all courts from then on would be conducted in English. During those three centuries and after, all the kings of England spoke French. Henry Bolingbroke who became king in 1399 was the first English king since the conquest whose mother tongue was English. The majority of abbots could only preach in Latin and French. The nobility, ecclesiastical and lay, spoke French. This doesn't seem to be what some modern sociolinguists would call 'stable diaglossia'. Given the status of French and the extent of Romance vocabulary, this sounds like an open system that might have been overwhelmed and collapsed but did not. In fact it moved to a higher level of complexity.

When Geoffrey Chaucer, who was a young man when the Statute of Pleading was enacted, wrote his poems in English, he presumed that his readers knew French and a little over half his vocabulary is of Romance origin. Let me give just one example of the further level of complexity which this involves. The Germanic word 'answer' survives but as a result of Romance influence both 'respond', 'reply' and 'retort' are also possibilities. Indeed there is a fifth word 'replication', though it is now almost obsolete. But there are nuances. You can 'answer', 'respond' or 'reply' to a letter but you can only 'respond' to a situation. A lawyer doesn't 'answer' or 'respond' to a defendant's plea just as returned gunfire is a 'reply' and not technically an 'answer' or a 'response'. You got into trouble in school for giving smart 'answers' but not for smart 'responses' or 'replies'. A 'retort' implies a quick caustic or witty reply with perhaps some connotation of retaliation. And so on!

We needn't follow the details of the Japanese parallel, more than to say that the Yamoto or native Japanese word for answer is *kotae* but the Chinese influence allows at least four other possibilities *henji*, *outou*, *henou* and *kaitou*. There could be arguments made that this type of sophistication is elitist or that it creates intellectual class barriers in a way that a language which only exploits its native resources avoids. The only point here is that an open system which risks being overwhelmed and collapsing also has the potential to become a more complex system.

Trauma, Identity and Vision

Following that biological and linguistic detour and with these images in mind, let us now return to history. As I have suggested that the Holocaust was a pivotal event which still colours our intellectual ambiance, it is fitting that we look at how some Jews have coped with trauma. There is a massive literature about Judaism after the Holocaust but I want here to look at one particular response (rather than answer!). I want to look briefly at the work of Peter Ochs of The University of Virginia, who was in turn deeply influenced by the Talmudic scholar David Weiss Halivni, a survivor of Auschwitz and former professor at Columbia University in New York.

Peter Ochs accepts neither of the two very understandable stock reactions to the Holocaust among Jews. He rejects both separatism and assimilation. On the one hand, the advocate of separatism says if they felt they should mistrust fellow Europeans and Christians before what happened, then all the more reason to distrust them now. On the other hand, the advocate of total assimilation asks what is the point? For Ochs both of these contradictory positions only induce despair.

In Peter Ochs's own words:

The lessons of experience have pulled Judaism into the contradictory ways of separatism and assimilation.

Historians might indeed reassure us with the unhappy news that the religion as well as the society of the Jews has suffered yet survived catastrophic loss several times before: after the Babylonian Exile, for example, Israel returned with a renewed but profoundly transformed religion of the Book and of Temple Worship; after Rome destroyed the Second Temple, the religion of the Book gave way to a religion of synagogue prayer and derashah or rabbinic text study. But, as yet, no historian can tell us what new form of Rabbinic Judaism may eventually enflame our hearts after the most traumatised generations have passed. No one can say when an epoch of despair has passed and one of renewed faith will begin.

Meanwhile we study, pray, wait, and look for possible signs of a new epoch.

Ochs is also convinced that the Jews must renew their vision in co-operation with others. In the words[115] of Professor David Ford of Cambridge:

In fact Ochs himself and other Jewish philosophers and text scholars have not only been waiting, but have been trying to discern and offer signs of a new epoch. At the centre of their emerging vision is a post-critical Judaism with three distinguishing marks: rereading of and renewal through classical sources, especially scripture, Talmud and liturgy, a thorough critical and constructive engagement with Western modernity; and a new dialogical and collaborative relationship with Christians and those of other faiths, especially Muslims.

It seems to me that the thought processes of Ochs are a classic example of where an identity is set in relation to memory and the testimony of history in order to overcome the aftermath of trauma by seeking a new vision. He is looking at the trauma of a people through the lens of memory and history in the hope of finding the vision that allows an identity to flourish.

Ochs is one of the founding figures in a group called Textual Reasoning, which attempts to combine modernity's critique of texts and the pre-modern ability to acknowledge the texts' claim on truth. This is an attempt to bring together the two most significant strands of

---

[115] p148, David F. Ford, *Christian Wisdom: Desiring God and Learning in Love,* Cambridge University Press, 2007

European culture: the Hellenic and the Hebraic.

It may be that our culture, where humanism has lost its nerve, may have much to learn from the vision which Ochs and his circle offers us. By a strange, but perhaps common irony, the vision we need to escape from under the intellectual shadow of the Holocaust may be offered to us by those whose people were the victims.

Processes of History

I want now to move to looking at identity, history and meaning and the concepts of witness, trauma and vision in the light of historical processes.

A Perspective on History

It is indeed strange how our perspective on history changes with age. Part of the excitement of coming of age in the nineteen-sixties was a sense of owning the world. Apart from the angst, the existentialist taking of responsibility for yourself and the world about you, made you feel not only capable but certain that our generation would fix the world and all its problems. Four decades and an unprecedented technological revolution later, my angle of vision shifts.

I find myself in a world of cyberspace, where at the press of a button monies are moved across our planet, peoples are drifting from country to country and old boundaries blur, our values seem vulnerable and shifting, our identity seems mobile. It almost seems that a generation who once thought they owned the world have been swept along by huge social forces that we neither control nor understand. All news[116] is instant:

'Underground'   Choices. Options. Preferences. All about
Freedom to zap and channel-hop, to allow
Us our daily shop around in any event.

Cameramen fly on to break another story
Across a dimming or warming atmosphere,
A jet-stream of bulletins for fear we'd wake

To stale headlines. Our yesterday is history.
Through windows of planes beginning to near
A runway reporters stare down as though to take

---

[116] p560, Micheal O'Siadhail, *Collected Poems,* Bloodaxe, Tarset, 2013

A reading of another landscape's hints and signs
On patches of an archaeologist's aerial photo
Spreading under their vapour trailing air-bus

Shadow marks the rape's yellow outlines
Over sites of older settlements bedded below.
Underground shine of bones foreshadow us.

In my latest book *Globe* I found myself asking what these seemingly unstoppable forces are? How is a world shaped? What kind of people has a hand in altering the course of history? How should we remember the unspeakable tragedies and loss? And what sort of vision is possible?

And, of course behind all these questions a feeling that it is all happening so fast that there will be no sense of continuity between our generation[117] and the next:

O angel of history, must we forget   'Thread Mark'
those hard-earned vestiges in our clay,
sweat of heritage, arrears we owe?

The dues paid, the debt assumed,
our thread mark of owing between
those who were and those who follow.

.   .   .   .   .

In these fragmented times we wonder
will those who fit the prints we leave
remember feet that walked before them?

Middle Distance
But before we look further at some of these questions let us first introduce another concept. For me one of the most significant insights is the middle distance. I first came across this in a book by J. P. Stern called *On Realism.* Stern speaks of middle distance as the hallmark of realism.

Stern is a subtle commentator and knows that neither realism nor the middle distance can be exactly defined. Indeed it may not even be

---

[117] p565, Micheal O'Siadhail, *Collected Poems,* Bloodaxe, Tarset, 2013

appropriate to try to define them with exactitude. As he puts it; 'The shape of a fiction and its "truth to life" – coherence and correspondence: its making and matching – are joined in a fine balance. The middle distance is a scale and the point chosen depends on the effect the author desires. It can have many variations and with a switch of emphasis can tip over into symbolism, social realism, *Bildungsroman* or whatever. Examples of the extremes might be, on one hand the wide-angled perspective of Tolstoy's epilogue to *War and Peace* and, on the other hand, "the microscopic perspective and huge blow-ups" of the naturalist, *chosist* or indeed the *Roman Fleuve* of Marcel Proust.' In other words, the wide-angled perspective is when the writer steps so far back that according to Stern, 'the details of the created reality become mere trends' and he is then 'doing the historian's or philosopher's work.' The close-up can be so near that it appears as a blur and we lose the overall meaning and the whole picture.

This is also a fascinating insight in terms of history. At one extreme we have the massive sweeps of Ferdinand Braudel, who turning his back on event-based history and indeed on the earlier history of mentalities of the founders of the *Annales* School, embraced the *longue durée*, where economics, geography and climate play the major roles. This is in effect a deterministic macro-history which leaves us humans with no real role to play. At the other extreme is Italian micro-history, where there is endless detail of the dynamics of a village but where there is little action and no discernible pattern of events.

Ricoeur in *Memory, History, Forgetting*, like J. P. Stern in *On Realism*, makes a plea for a scaling of history. In other words an acknowledgement of the various possible scales on which we can view history. In history, just as in the realm of literature, we choose a point on the scale to suit our purpose. The advantage of the middle distance, however, is that human action and socio-economic or geographical forces interact. This point of intersection, it seems to me, is the perspective from which we can best integrate the human desire for identity, memory and meaning with the more impersonal forces of history.

I mention, as an interesting aside, that it may indeed be our destiny as human beings to occupy the middle ground as we walk the earth poised between the vastness of a cosmos and the similar vastness of the subatomic world. According to Ahmed Zewail, the Nobel Prize winner who invented femtochemistry, the science that studies chemical reactions on extremely short timescale, we may be in the middle not only in terms of space but also in terms of time. If he is right 'it seems that on the femtosecond to attosecond scale we are reaching the inverse of Big Bang time (12–15 billion years), with the human heart beat situated in the middle as the geometric average of two limits.'

Knot-Tying

But to return to our theme, who actually helps to shape the dynamics of history? The great majority of us play an undramatic role in the unfolding of history, though the great religious traditions would probably encourage us to remember the butterfly effect of chaos theory. However, there are few who are in the right place at the right time to pick up the strands of history and tie a knot that changes the course of history. This image of a knot or crucial node in history is a favourite of Aleksandr Solzhenitsyn and which I first came across in *August 1914*. In *Globe* there is a series of poems to portray knot-tyers in various areas of endeavour. In reading and thinking about these people, I was fascinated by their courage and perseverance.

Two major facets of their lives were brought home to me. Firstly, they had spent their lives preparing their vision so that when the strands of history fell they were ready to pick them up and tie the knot. I am thinking here of such figures as Mahatma Gandhi or Nelson Mandela or Jean Vanier. Secondly, although we speak of them being at the right place at the right time, the effect may well be delayed or remain unrecognised in their lifetime, so in practice they appear before their time. I am thinking here of Bartolomé de Las Casas who fought for the rights of native Americans or Johann Mendel, who discovered how genes could skip generations and then reappear. How ironic that Mendel's work was ignored by the world of science in his lifetime and his fame skipped over a generation or two.

The concept of nodes in the great networks of history as viewed from the middle distance is valuable in allowing us to celebrate these knot-tyers as emblems of our human ability to interact with the natural and historical forces in a way which sustains our identity and our sense of memory and meaning.

Irreversible Tragedies

The other side of insisting on the memory and meaning and of taking our human responsibility for the nodes of history seriously is that we have to face the irreversible tragedies of history. In *Globe* in a section called 'Wounded Memory' I have tried to look at a small cross section of these tragedies, including the erasure of peoples like the Bushmen in Africa and other cultures, the Armenian genocide, the Holocaust and slavery.

There is no unravelling these unspeakable tragedies. And yet if our identity as humans is at stake and memory and meaning are ultimately bound up with this identity, then we owe at the very least a debt of memory to the victims of these tragedies. There is no doubt about our duty to remember. The question is how we remember. Here I return to the idea of witness. We need to continue to tell the story of what happened. At the same time, this cannot simply become a pointing of the finger at one set of perpetrators. I have tried to underscore this in 'Wounded Memory' by placing a poem about Hiroshima beside a poem about the gradual extinction of the Ainu people in Hokkaido. Memory is not simply a game of blame. Indeed, if the delicate relation between identity, memory and meaning is to be held in play, we need to be careful not to slip into a simplistic politics of identity where we all become involved in competitive victimhood. We need to think of the victim as the other.

Vision

In the title of this series of lectures the words identity and memory are often linked to the past, whereas meaning and the twenty-first century are oriented towards the future. For all the dangers of blurring or loss of identity under the pressures of technology and globalisation, in the inevitable trauma of such rapid change as we are experiencing, I do have a vision for the coming century. I see various signs in global networks of professionals, in NGOs, in *Médicins sans Frontières*, in the potential of the internet for sharing information, the potential for a new and growing loyalty to humanity. It is not any formal international government or transnational leagues but a hotchpotch, a whole jumble of piecemeal ways in which our common identity of humankind is moving. Any famine or natural disaster is on our screen immediately. The butterfly effect is taking on an even more literal meaning.

Randal Collins, in his weighty book *The Sociologies of Philosophies* traces rather than individual knot-tyers, hotbeds and networks of thought that spread great philosophical movements across cultures. This must be even more so in our global age. Perhaps we can even think of this series of lectures as a node in some great lattice of change.

   We cannot at the same time be naïve about it. Much of this change is market driven. The market place is a wonderful tool but it is not a value. What I have been suggesting is that part of this vision must keep faith with our past and bear witness to tragic memories in a way that out of our western intellectual trauma of suspicion, we can without retreating into false cocoons, trust our humanist values. Out of trauma vision. Yet a vision always under review, always an improvisation, an impromptu, an extempore, in the rough and tumble jazz[118] of our lived-in history:

Given riffs and breaks of our own,   'Tremolo'
Given a globe of boundless jazz,
Yet still a remembered undertone,

A quivering earthy line of soul
Crying in all diminished chords.
Our globe still trembles on its pole.

---

[118] p635, Micheal O'Siadhail, *Collected Poems,* Bloodaxe, Tarset, 2013

11   I'd be a damn' fool if they weren't: Art and Spirituality

The poet Patrick Kavanagh said that 'poetry has to do with the reality of the spirit, of faith and hope and sometimes even charity. It is a point of view. A poet is a theologian.'[119]

We are dealing here with various long and often interwoven traditions of art and religion. Where to begin? It almost seems an impertinence to approach the theme. And yet after many years of a life devoted to poetry, one thing is clear: we go on daring to break[120] the silence. So I dare.

'Hàvamál 57'   Brandr af brandi   brenn, unz brunninn er,
     funi kveykiz af funa:
maðr af manni   verðr at máli kuðr,
     en til dœlskr af dul.

Brand's lit by brand   till all is burnt,
     fire is kindled by fire;
by man's speech is set   the spark to man's wits;,
     to be mum makes a dolt of a man.[121]

That Edda stanza says it all. Yet even to speak about poetry strikes me as secondary and approximate. To make a poem is the only authority I may have. We have all been moulded by an enlightenment model of knowledge, a need to measure and quantify, to tie things down. There is a feeling in our culture that what cannot be grasped is dubious. Still, it is as if there are certain things we can only know by living them, by doing them, by being them. This is know-how earned over time, a way of life, the sort of behaviour the French sociologist Pierre Bourdieu describes as gained by apprenticeship and practice. Knowledge achieved through performance. So all I dare is a few insights dug out of my own experience of poetry.

---

[119] Patrick Kavanagh, *Self-Portrait,* Dolmen Press, Dublin, 1964
[120] p25, EDDA: *Die Lieder des Codex Regius Nebst Verwandten Denkmälern,* herausgegeben von Gustav Neckel, Heidelberg, 1927
[121] English version at p127, Bertha S. Phillpotts, *Edda and Saga,* London, 1931

Attention and Distillation

Intensity. Torch is lit by torch. Fire is kindled by fire. At the heart of poetry is this stretching towards life, utter concentration on the density of the moment. Attention[122] and distillation.

Tyger! Tyger! burning bright   'The Tyger'
In the forests of the night,
What immortal hand or eye
Could frame thy fearful symmetry?

In what distant deeps or skies
Burnt the fire of thine eyes?
On what wings dare he aspire?
What the hand dare seize the fire?

Of all people William Blake would know what is meant by intensity. An acceleration of experience, of expression, of a whole life. I think there is something so hard won in his line 'What the hand dare seize the fire?' He had his fingers burnt often enough. To seize the fire, to expose your whole self to experience is a hazardous business. But then prophets seemed always to live at and on the giddy edge. Even the word 'giddy' meant originally possessed by a god, mad. To live *accelerando*, on speed, *ar mire*. The absolute dedication to the call and the acceptance[123] of its gift.

It came slowly,   'The Gift'
Afraid of insufficient self-content
Or some inherent weakness in itself
Small and hesitant
Like children at the top of stairs
It came through shops, rooms, temples,
Streets, places that were badly lit.
It was a gift that took me unawares
And I accepted it

First the surprise and then, as Brendan Kennelly's poem 'The Gift' suggests, the wager of acceptance. There are no guarantees. A

[122] p49, *William Blake*, edited with an introduction by J. Bronowski, Penguin, Harmondsworth, 1958
[123] Brendan Kennelly, *A Time for Voices: Selected Poems 1960–1990*, Bloodaxe, 1990

Say but the Word

nakedness to experience is a gamble. Yet it is an obsession. Some childhood happening which we harken back to as a touchstone. Everything renews or falls short of that event. Once that Beatrice has been sighted all our desire[124] is shaped:

'If This Love Ends'

A young girl strokes the tight braids
of her hair and thinks she is one memory.
A little eye gleams in moonlight
hoping to be freed of its love of water, of
foggy nights, of wings tangled
in the hair of celestial heads.
I would die again for that girl
who received everything the world suggested
As if each moment were an ascension.

I think I remember those shaping moments in my childhood. Those strange[125] transfigurations:

'A Short Biography'

Tell me, friend, how this began.
Was it that morning you tricycled
up the slope along the path
to the woods; wheeling around.
Pedalling frantically homewards,
snowflakes spun in the trees,
and passing through the garden gate,
you turned forever into Eden?

Or maybe one winter afternoon,
alone in the sitting room listening
to music on a radio left idling
after the news, you were staring
through the window, when suddenly
the trance-dance stirred? Then
all was transfigured. Again
you'd blundered into seventh heaven.

Or the autumn evening, carrying back

[124] p221, Tess Gallagher, *My Black Horse: New and Selected Poems*, Bloodaxe, 1995
[125] p179, Micheal O'Siadhail, *Collected Poems*, Bloodaxe, Tarset, 2013

Say but the Word

messages from the shop, you watched
a man stooping to bundle the last
sheaves? The yellow stooks ranked
sunwards, the damp seed-smell
of corn seized you; startled,
a half-dazed witness to the majesty,
you climbed over the narrow stile.

The intensity is not just in the experience but also in the expression. I never cease to be amazed at the terse Edda poems. Fire is kindled by fire. One human makes another wise in words. That extraordinary compression that word by word, syllable for syllable detonates a poem. Those beautiful alliterations in the original (which the English version tries to replicate) and the gnomic poise, which suggest an entire view of the world. That stanza, along with two others (*Hávarmál* 47 and 50), outlines a philosophy of human relationships.

Part of this intensity is a density of time. So much of our thinking about time and art seems still steeped in certain notions, which stem from some romantic notion of art as above or outside life. Whether it is music, painting, sculpture or literature, especially poetry, there is still some vague feeling that art is an oasis in time, that art is time-out from the real world, an escape from the mundane tick-tock of things.

Time and Eternity
In his work on *Theology through Music: Tavener, Time and Eternity*[126] the musician and theologian Jeremy Begbie looks at some aspects of the relationship between art, in this case music, and time. He suggests that some of the popularity of the contemporary compositions of the English composer John Tavener, the Polish composer Henryk Gorecki and the Estonian Arvo Pärt are, in some measure at least, due to their ability to create music which is striving to be above time rather than engaging with time. Begbie explains how this is achieved, particularly in the case of Tavener, namely by eschewing four typical features of traditional European tonal music, which give it its fundamentally teleological or goal-orientated nature. Firstly, there is an organic development and elaboration and secondly, there is large-scale tension

---

[126] Jeremie Begbie,'Theology through Music: Taverner, Time and Eternity' in *Essentials of Christian Community*, eds. David F. Ford and Dennis L. Stamps, T&T Clark, Edinburgh, 1996

and resolution. Thirdly, there are clearly defined beginnings and endings and, finally, there is a long-term continuity. However, Tavener often prefers not to develop themes but rather to employ various techniques such as playing them backwards or creating symmetrical structures. He does not go at all for large-scale tension and resolution and Begbie amusingly quotes Tavener as saying that 'the composer should deal with his *angst* in the composing room, not in the score'. As for clearly defined beginnings and endings, Tavener's music has endings, which are hard to predict. More often than not, the music drifts seamlessly into silence. Finally, with regard to a long-term continuity, Tavener's music seems to avoid musical argument and moves simply from block to block of self-contained internally coherent material.

What is fascinating in all of this is how this sort of music is at home in our contemporary culture, in an era where the communications revolution has collapsed certain time-space barriers, where time is a tyranny. In our crowded existence, Tavener's type of music, with its deliberate exploration of pitch, timbre and volume for their own sake rather than part of a greater whole, provides us with 'an unhurried stable cavernous arena in which we are free to breathe … and in so far as this music is to be taken as a window on eternity, it is an eternity of the negation of time'.

Yet more fundamentally is the question which Begbie poses: might it be that one of music's most valuable contributions is to enable us to come to terms with created time in a more positive and fruitful way, to demonstrate concretely that fallenness is not intrinsic to temporality? Second, taking this matter further might it be that there are other forms of music, which supply more faithful sonic parables of divine eternity and created time than those we find in Tavener? Begbie's conclusion is drawn partly from the Austrian musicologist Victor Zuckerkandl's elaboration of Augustine's basic insights in *De Musica*: 'music is a temporal art not in the barren and empty sense that its tones succeed one another "in time"; it is a temporal art in the concrete sense that it enlists the flux of time as a force to serve its ends'. We experience not an absolute time but one of physical realities, we can trust time to do its work, consistency and construction are concrete possibilities in time, change and order can go hand in hand. Begbie, then takes two features of a more structured music *recapitulation* and *premature closure* as examples of how music provides a model for interaction between time and pure duration. Both the theme and its recapitulation have an utterly distinct particularity and yet there is 'a profound interactive continuity between first and second appearances of a theme'. We are dealing here with 'non-identical repetitions'. The phenomenon of the premature closure, on the other hand, is where a composer signals a closure far in advance of the actual ending. Any of us can tease out the possible images such features can provide for our lives. As a Christian theologian, Jeremy Begbie sees in recapitulation a possible interpretative model for the Eucharist and in the premature closures eschatological implications.

I have dwelt here somewhat on music partly because I have had the benefit of Jeremy Begbie's lucid and well-thought out article and partly because I do not want to concentrate entirely on literature where, naturally, I am most at home. But clearly there are parallels. In some sense all the poems I have cited have a dual temporality. By this I mean what Paul Ricoeur might describe as the chronological and the configurative time.[127] In other words, there is the event and the story. Ricoeur was concentrating on the narrative where there is, on the one hand, the ordinary episodic and linear chain of events and, on the other hand, the power of plot to shape a story with an overall theme and with a sense of ending. In his view the poetic act mediates between the event and the story.

This mediation seems to me to correspond in some sense to how a structured music transfigures a procession of discrete and internally coherent blocks of sound into an overall development and elaboration with large-scale tensions and resolutions and long-term continuity. Perhaps there are also the parallels to what I have called 'time-out music' in the current vogue for the ironic episodic or multiple-hero deconstructed novel in that it could be interpreted as a fundamental distrust of the workings of time.

It seems to me that the same mediation rings true for lyric poetry. The compact nature of a lyric makes repetition easier so that we can read, to quote Ricoeur, 'the ending in the beginning and the beginning in the ending'. In the lyric, however, the process is so elided that it feels as if one small incident implies a lifetime. Brendan Kennelly's 'The Gift', the Edda poem quoted above or the verse from Tess Gallagher's 'If This Love Ends' all fan out into a life story.

I am sure there are analogies in the visual world; the wonder of shape

---

[127] Paul Ricoeur, *Time and Narrative, 3 vols,* University of Chicago Press, 1985

and colour. Colour has for me the immediacy of rhythm or perfume. It goes straight through the senses. Its pleasures are bodily and unabashed.

Colour, just like sound and language, is multi-layered and intricate. Strange how colour, that aspect of things that comes from the differing qualities of the light reflected or emitted, can be thought of from the perspective of the observer or from that of the light itself. From the point of view of the observer, we speak of the hue, the brilliance or of colours that are deep and strong. Thought of in terms of the characteristics of light, which strike our eyes, there are varying wavelengths, luminosity and purity. This beautiful and complex weave of subjectivity and objectivity.

Temporal Intensity

When it comes to temporal intensity, perhaps the visual is the most extraordinary. I wonder if a painting isn't the most glorious attempt by humankind to, as the poet Patrick Kavanagh[128] had it 'Snatch out of time the passionate transitory'. In music or literature we configure time. There is, so to speak, a process allowing for patterns and structures, repetition and configuration in the progress of the work. It seems to me that of all the art forms the painting seems the most splendid admission of the vastness of time, the great wheel only touching the ground and moving on. And yet, the adoration of the gaze.

One of the best known of Renoir's painting is *The Luncheon of the Boating Party*. That picture of a lunching group of friends under a yellow and red canopy at the Restaurant Fournaise at the Ile de Chateau on the river Seine. It is quite an extraordinary glorying in the conviviality of youthful friends. What moment could be so transitory and all the more wonderful even in its passing? At the centre of the picture is the still-life of the actual lunch with the colourful fruit, the glasses and wine bottles. The picture framed by those strong-armed men in their yellow and dark-banded boaters. That woman in the left foreground in her straw hat with red flowers, scarf and pursed lips as she coos at the fluffy dog she is holding up on its hind legs. In the right background the man with the bowler hat, the man with the top hat. The woman in the centre is leaning on the balustrade. All that movement of conversation and *joie de vivre* caught in the frozen second of that loving gaze. This is real intensity of time. Eternal partying youth in one split second.

[128] Patrick Kavanagh *Collected Poems,* MacGibbon & Kee, London,1964

Say but the Word

This painting intrigues me. Not only does it seem 'to snatch out of time the passionate transitory' but it captures some carefree aspect of youth. I have always been aware how none of the faces that we see are actually looking at the person who is looking at them. This seems to catch the openness of a youthful party. But what is also fascinating is that we know when Renoir began this painting in the summer of 1881 that the man in the top hat to the right in the background is Baron Barbier, the jovial and horsy regimental captain who brought this group of friends together at the Restaurant Fournaise especially to pose for the picture which Renoir wanted to make. The yachts in the distant background were arranged. Even the theme of the French Sunday afternoon was a vogue of its time. And we know who all the people in the picture are: the woman with the dog is Renoir's future wife, the man in the bowler is Lestringuez the hypnotist and the man in between is a short sighted philanderer Lhote who is flirting with an actress Jeanne Samary. The woman drinking concentratedly from her glass is one of Renoir's favourite models Angèle who had a reputation for talking non-stop while she posed. There is the proprietor Monsieur Fournaise, his daughter Alphonsine, there is an artist Gustave Caillotte, the journalist Maggiolo, the actress Ellen Andrée. There they are all in their particularity forever caught in that deliberately composed stare of the painter. All caught forever looking away from whoever is looking at them in some infinite mood of a party. Keats' glorious density of time[129] and desire:

Fair youth, beneath the trees, thou canst not leave
Thy song, nor ever can those trees be bare;
Bold Love, never, never canst thou kiss,
Though winning near the goal – yet do not grieve;
She cannot fade, though thou hast not thy bliss,
Forever wilt thou love, and she be fair!

  . . . .

More happy love! more happy, happy love!
Forever warm and still to be enjoy'd,
For ever panting and for ever young;

'Ode on a
Grecian Urn'

[129] p239, *Complete Poems and Selected Letters of John Keats*, The Modern Library, New York, 2001

Say but the Word

All breathing human passion far above,
That leaves a heart high sorrowful and cloy'd,
A burning forehead, and a parching tongue.

I think it is the same temporal density I sense when I stare at Vincent Van
Gogh's friend, the postman Joseph Poulin, in his blue and yellow-
buttoned uniform and fish-tailed beard. And what a face! This was one
of the few friends at Arles. When I look at Georges de la Tour's *Saint
Joseph Charpentier* with the faces of the older man and the boy lit by the
candle, I feel the whole trajectory of our sojourn. I think I sense the folded
lives in both those pictures and how they disclose themselves to us with
all their vulnerability and uniqueness. How they open for us the whole
design of their lives, the workings of their time[130] and surroundings:

'Disclosure'   Remember how at school we folded and unfolded
sheets from a jotter, scissored chunky *m*s and *n*s,
a saw-edge,
a clump of paper squared, melodeoned.
Then delight as it reopens
a fullness of design, transfigured wounds
unfolding in a page
berries, acorns.

The moment's contours scatter in the light.
A crossbeam gathers in pattern and fringe,
traces of passion,
hologram of thought, memory's freight
until a beam re-throws the image,
An intensity unpacking stripe and whorl;
each fraction
an implicit all.

Acorns of memories, berries of dreams.
Does every pilgrim's tale sleep in one moment?
Some inbred
whole uncodes in a tree's limbs,
spreads in slow workings of environment.

[130] p231, Micheal O'Siadhail, *Collected Poems,* Tarset, 2013

Say but the Word

Soil, air, water, sun quicken
a word in the seed.
Time thickens.

Shaping Time

And all this art is not simply leisure. A time-out. An oasis. Something much more significant is at stake. If we are gripped by the time within art, the moment of the music, the stretch of the narrative, the turning of the drama, the enfolding of the painting, we embrace and are embraced by what is great and infinite. It is as if all our time is taken up into this embrace, shaped and returned to us. Time thickens. So much of the European outlook on time must have been moulded by the monastic life with its canonical hours, its divisions of day, week and year. The rule of ordinariness set off against the feast. The basic understanding that we are not only shaped by our time but we also shape our time. Perhaps liturgy is a performance art. The year staked out in feasts. I remember how as a child I'd heard the Aran islanders would refer to events as taking place so-and-so many weeks before or after the Feast of the Assumption. Time thickens. Or I think of Sigrid Unsett's great Norwegian novel where everything happens before Candlemas or after Michaelmas or around John's Eve. A calendar time that thickens. Even our bank and public holidays try to mark time. Little wonder that so much of our art, visual, musical and literary, has such deep roots in a spiritual tradition.

Another side to the intensity of art is precisely that tradition. I mentioned earlier the long and various traditions. Clearly, what I earlier spoke of as the overwhelming quality of tradition bears on musicians and on painters and sculptors. Think in the case of music of the tonal system and scales or even the instrument. For the visual artist so much must be handed on in terms of perspective and perception, not to mention availability of the materials, colours, implements.

Language – that house of air

But in the case of literature the force of tradition is set starkly in relief by language. Before we even think about the history or the schools, the lines of descent, the trends within a tradition, the tradition itself is defined by the contours of that house of air which language is. I began by quoting a verse from the Edda. The language is strong and monotone in a beautiful Germanic way. This strength of the sharp, clear, relatively unadulterated Germanic is still part of Icelandic poetry to this day. On the other hand, those of us who write in English inherit a different house of air. A whole lore of borrowings from Norse, from Norman French, from the classical Greek and Latin elements and eventually from all the cultures the English language was to come in touch with. Already the language is involving us in a tone which is multi-layered and variegated. A different tradition challenges us with all the options and overwhelming choice. We are the builders of a house[131] with a complex design:

'The Builder's Men'

Today the builder's men are scaffolding a gable.
Mortar has weathered, the brick might be unstable
And the whole frame begin to sag. Through
An open window the boom of their voices renews
A house's dominion. They climb a crib of iron bar
And space, chisel and trowel our wear and tear.

'Look, Baba window!' prompts a mothering voice.
'Look!' he mimics and splutters arrays of noise
And wonder. 'Cooey!' calls the builder's man
Appearing and hiding at the window. 'Where's he gone?'
A little bewilderment before the sudden chortle,
Skips of delight. 'Where's the man with the trowel?'

Such amazing words! *the man, the trowel, the window* –
Namings unravelled from the past that echo and echo
Saxon serfs and Normans, the scribes, the courtiers,
Puritans and frontiersmen, all owners and heirs
To a house of meaning they built and so abandoned,
Its well-worn brick now pointed in a child's astoundment.

A playpen made of sounds, gift and encumbrance
Of the past. But look! he almost seems to dance
To rhythms of syllable and scraping trowel, to begin
A long gurgle of conversation with the self. Then
Distracted, he gazes at the window we've left ajar,
The light flushed down the builder's house of air.

[131] p 248, Micheal O'Siadhail, *Collected Poems*, Tarset, 2013

Intensity begets Intensity

In speaking of language, I am highlighting the most fundamental defining quality of literature's tradition. But then, imagine all the traditions within a tradition, poems, plays, novels, short stories and, within one genre such as poetry, the variations from syllabic to free-verse with the myriad of forms in between. And yet for all the influence of Ezra Pound, particularly on the North American tradition, with his dictum: *make it new!* I want to see an engagement with a tradition as something exhilarating. Just as I do not distrust time, I do not distrust tradition. As we shape and are shaped by time, we fashion and are fashioned by tradition. There is something wonderful about passing on the gift of a tradition. I often like to think of it as that feeling of a host bringing two of his friends[132] together:

A feeling of passivity, of handing over.   'Tradition'
All that was received I again deliver

by just being here. Available. No more.
A watch of dependence, complete exposure,

not even trying not to try to achieve.
This work is a waiting, almost as if

a host, his palms held up in supplication
between two guests, begins an introduction:

'For years I've wanted you two to meet.'
The middle voice fading as they greet

in the sweet nothingness of a go-between.

Another aspect of this intensity seems to me to be the way it is out of our control. This, of course, asks how can we devote a life to what is in so many ways beyond our power? I cannot command this moment of intensity. I am utterly at its beck and call. James Joyce liked to talk of his 'epiphanies'. That is the Greek word for the tradition of the flash of recognition, the showing, the illumination, *Erleuchtung* or *léargas*. The

---

[132] p 248, Micheal O'Siadhail, *Collected Poems,* Tarset, 2013

spirit bloweth where the spirit listeth. The Latin idea of inspiration, *inspiratio,* from *in* 'into' and *spirare* 'breathe', found in most European languages either adapted in its original form or using native elements appeals to me. I like to extend the image and to think of myself as a woodwind, maybe a saxophone, maybe a recorder? At any rate, the best I can manage is to try to keep the instrument clear and in tune. And to wait …

But still there is something about the posture of waiting clear-eyed and in tune that allows for confidence. We don't even know what we're waiting for. Doubt sets in. We are not even sure how to think of it. As sure as anything, what we imagine we're waiting for is not what comes. The fervour of waiting wells up. Intensity begets intensity.[133]

'April 5 1974' The air was soft, the ground still cold.
In the dull pasture where I strolled
Was something I could not believe.
Dead grass appeared to slide and heave
Though still too frozen flat to stir,
And rocks to twitch, and all to blur.
Was this the rippling of the land?
Was matter getting out of hand
And making free with natural law?
I stopped and blinked, and then I saw
A fact as eerie as a dream.
There was a subtle flood of stream
Moving upon the face of things.
It came from standing pools and springs
And what of snow was still around;
It came of winter's giving ground
So that the freeze was coming out,
As when a set mind, blessed by doubt,
Relaxes into mother wit.
Flowers, I said, will come of it.

Taken by surprise, by the subtle flood of stream. Richard Wilbur's 'April 5, 1974', resonates with George Herbert's marvellous 'How sweet and clean are thy returns' in *The Flower.* This resonance, the echoes, the

---

[133] Richard Wilbur, 'April 5 1974' *New and Collected Poems,* Faber & Faber, 1989

Say but the Word

taking up again of themes are all part of the tradition of overflow. I can never hear Beethoven's *Diabelli Variations* without being overawed by the infinite possibilities of transfiguration in a theme. Musician friends of mine who like to improvise speak of the latent variation, which lies waiting in a phrase. Yet there is nothing facile about the ability to release this inherent gift. All the hours of practice, all the experience of performance, all the knowledge of harmonies, all the hours of listening are a whole apprenticeship and a trained instinct brought to bear on that moment.

Making Connections
Another fundamental characteristic of poetry is how it seems to make connections between so many things. It is as though poetry is a vital nodal point in a culture where we have tended to departmentalise. It is so easy to think in terms of the intellect, the imagination, the emotions and the body as separate entities. People like to apportion the emotions and even the imagination, to the artistic domain. The intellect is thought of as belonging to the world of reasoning and science while the body is for sport and athletics. Yet strangely it seems to me that poetry is well positioned to link all of these, to allow a more holistic view. All those various roles of the poet are reflected in the different traditions with their name for the task: Greek poet 'the one who makes', Irish *file* the one who sees, Icelandic *skáld* 'the one who narrates', Welsh *bardd* 'the one who praises', and, as I have mentioned elsewhere, the poet Richard Murphy once told me that in Sri Lanka the word for poet meant 'seer of the connections between things'.

I always think of poetry as being somewhere near the middle of a spectrum, which stretches between music and prose. Poetry has many of the physical qualities of music, which satisfy the body. There is the pulse and delight of rhythm. There is the varied pitch of a sentence. Even more, there is the sheer bodily joy of the sounds made by the tongue, the lips, the palate, the throat. We breathe our vowels. Language is housed in the mouth and nose, shaped by organs, which can be such sources of sensuous pleasure. Our voluptuous words! Poetry is an oral art. Even when we read it inwardly, I think we are conscious of a physical gratification and an emotional sway. And yet, on the other hand, unlike music and like prose, there is also an intellectual or cerebral element at work. It often has a sequence of thoughts, a process of meditation even sometimes an argument or deliberate configuration.

Clearly, we need to speak of a spectrum, as some music may be programmatic and good prose can share many of the characteristics of poetry. All I want to stress is that poetry, in a special heightened way, travels the mind and body at once.

   Maybe poetry makes connections in an even more radical and profound way. Once again, making use of figures of speech are not the sole possession of poetry. It is just that it is more concise and concentrated. My favourite description of metaphor is the ability to speak of one thing in terms of another. This is subtle in that it refuses the simplistic substitution of one thing[134] for another:

‘What can I tell my bones?’ Loved heart what can I say?
When I was a lark, I sang;
When I was a worm, I devoured.

I cannot just say that the protagonist is a bird or a worm. Nor can I say that the protagonist is compared to a lark or to a worm. It is much more powerful. By speaking of a human in terms of a bird or insect, Theodore Roethke holds us in the tension between the two, as he also does in his poem[135] ‘The Young Girl’:

‘The Young Girl’ What can the spirit believe? –
It takes in the whole body;
I, on coming to love,
Make that my study.

We are one, and yet we are more,
I am told by those who know, –
At times content to be two,
Today I skipped on the shore,
My eyes neither here nor there,
My thin arms to and fro,
A bird my body,
My bird-blood ready.

Perhaps, the most astonishing and enduring impulse at the core of artistic endeavour is that of overcoming the desire to cry out at the

---

[134] p165, Theodore Roethke, *Collected Poems*, Faber & Faber, London, 1968
[135] p200, Theodore Roethke, *Collected Poems*, Faber & Faber, London, 1968

beauty and majesty of the world. Sheer joy. The magnificence of it all! It is Cézanne relishing the cylinder, sphere and cone of fruits in a still life or gazing at *The Card Players*. Or is it Schubert beyond the exquisite *adagio* and the third movement, attacking the final *Allegretto* of his posthumous *String Quintet*? 'My cup runneth over ...'[136] That ancient urge: 'therefore my heart is glad, and my glory rejoiceth ... in thy presence is fullness of joy, at thy right hand there are pleasures for ever more'[137]. I love the absolute lack of reserve. The complete giving over. Yielding to an overflow. A taking up of everything into thanks and delight; succumbing to an invitation:

Anywhere and always just as you expect it least,   'Invitation'
Welling or oozing from nowhere a desire to feast.

At Auschwitz Wolf hums Brahms' rhapsody by heart
As Eddy, thief turned juggler, rehearses his art.

Fling and abandon, gaieties colourful and porous.
The Mexican beggar's skirt, an Araner's *crios*.

Irresistible laughter, hiss and giggle of overflow.
That black engine-driver crooning his life's motto:

'Paint or tell a story, sing or shovel coal,
You gotta get a glory or the job lacks soul.'

Abundance of joy bubbling some underground jazz.
A voice whispers: Be with me tonight in paradise.[138]

And so often our first world is frightened by this surrender to wonder. As if in the luxury of our welfare we're afraid to give in. Perhaps, there are good reasons. The sombre existentialism of a post-Holocaust culture dreaded the *rausch,* the romantic intoxication of overarching world-views which had paved the way for the Shoah. Then, with the questioning and doubting of ourselves and the suspicion of the foundations of all culture à la Michel Foucault, we so frequently turned

[136] Psalm 23
[137] Psalm 16
[138] p307, Micheal O'Siadhail, *Collected Poems,* Tarset, 2013

towards the one remove of irony. It is so strange to think of the extraordinary gaiety of that Dutch witness to the Desolation, Etty Hillesum. That postcard which she flung out of a train on her way to a death camp and found by a farmer, who sent it on: 'We have left the camp singing'.

Yet I know and understand our cultural reserve, our reluctance. That fear of celebration was part of the intellectual milieu I was formed by. It was intellectually *de rigueur* to adopt a pose of diehard, devil-take-the-hindmost despair. I deeply appreciate its roots and its caution and even its desperation. I had to grow through it and out of it. I had to make my painful way to abandon, to the chosen garden of second innocence. And now as the years pass, I keep hearing at the heart of that joy without reserve some endless desire, those strange longings of the psalmist: 'Turn again our captivity, O Lord, as the streams in the south. They that sow in tears shall reap in joy. He that goeth forth and weepeth, bearing precious seed, shall doubtless come again with rejoicing, bringing his sheaves with him.'[139]

Is it another stage in our lives that allows a joy to be counterpointed with a wistfulness, that enriches rather than menaces? Is there a tone of yearning that deepens[140] the desire?

'Ageing'   It wasn't the devil-may-care bit or even the folly
Of so much of what we did, but more the way
We just espoused a kind of cavalier melancholy:
And does it all mean nothing? One long decay.
But broken down, backed up against nothing,
Emptied, then came that shock of second sight.
That all might be well? How hard I had to cling
To a rumour, a desire, a single welling delight.
And now it's both. Almost as if I'm possessed
By a strange northern rhythm that sways the heart,
One of those long wistful folk-tunes from Sweden
When you imagine low-lit miles of spruce forest
Where darker joys absorb a wishful counterpart
And you know you've begun a slow return to Eden.[141]

---

[139] Psalm 126
[140] p335, Micheal O'Siadhail, *Collected Poems,* Bloodaxe Tarset, 2013
[141] Micheal O'Siadhail, *Our Double Time,* Bloodaxe Tarset, 1998

All I do here is to touch off a few aspects of the mystery, which is art. I am intrigued by the intensity and the concentration. I am obsessed by the interconnectedness of all things. I yearn to shape a silence. I am time and time again overcome by the need to celebrate. I have to confess anytime I ever tried to read a description of a spiritual search I kept recognising the pursuit of the muse. I wonder if the reverse is true?

Clearly I do not wish to idolise art. It is all too easy in our society to seek to turn the artist into some form of secular priest. It remains somehow acceptable in a society, which claims to be secular to speak of artists as being spiritual. This comes as no surprise. There is a fundamental connection. In some ways the danger is more for the artist who may be tempted to take over the mantle of priest. Indeed, perhaps the greatest temptation for an artist is to try to play at being God.

The Artistic Enterprise
There is probably an element in the artistic personality, which involves a certain standing aside, a separateness, some compulsion to make sense of it all. This separation, even loneliness, is captured in a beautiful and well-loved poem of Patrick Kavanagh[142] founded in his own small-farmer background in County Monaghan:

The bicycles go by in twos and threes –
There's a dance in Billy Brennan's barn tonight,
And there's the half-talk code of mysteries
And the wink-and-elbow language of delight.
Half-past eight and there is not a spot
Upon a mile of road, no shadow thrown
That might turn out a man or woman, not
A footfall tapping secrecies of stone.

'Inniskeen Road: July Evening'

I have what every poet hates in spite
Of all the solemn talk of contemplation.
Oh, Alexander Selkirk knew the plight
Of being king and government and nation.
A road, a mile of kingdom, I am king
Of banks and stones and every blooming thing.

---

[142] p19, Patrick Kavanagh, *Collected Poems*, MacGibbon & Kee, London, 1964

To live with all the intensities is a gamble. There is a school of thought that describes the work of art in terms of an attempt by artists to create a world of their own, to see art as a talented psychosis. According to Freud's contemporary Otto Rank: 'No wonder that historically art and psychosis have had such an intimate relationship, that the road to creativity passes so close to the madhouse and often detours or ends there. The artist and the madman are trapped in their own fabrications ...'[143] The drift of what Rank understood is absolutely clear. I'm sure any artist knows the hazards of the intensity, the concentration, the celebration, the yearning and feeling of living at the node of so much connectedness. John Dryden's famous couplet[144] rings ominously:

'Shaftesbury'   Great Wits are sure to Madness near alli'd
And thin partitions do their Bounds divide.

But then, for all the risks, who would want it any other way? It is counter-pointed by Michael Drayton's[145] couplet:

'of Poets and   For that fine madness still he did retain
Poesy'   Which rightly should possess a poet's brain.

Of course, there may be an element of counter-world building in any artistic enterprise. There have been the classic descriptions of a final questioning of the success of that wager. Yeats with Plato's ghost crying 'What then?' or Ibsen in *When we Dead Awaken*. There are many tragic ends.

And yet I do not think that the idea of the counter-world is my image. I fear idolatry. I have hinted earlier at how I see a connection between madness and the classical notion of inspiration. That lack of control – wild – untameable. Am I[146] a simple recorder?

'Recorder'   Some uniqueness of self I think I need to prove.
A trying too hard, some virtuoso inner strife,
The world kept at bay in musics of one remove,
A kind of holding on to Eden for dear life.

[143] Quoted in Ernest Becker, *The Denial of Death,* The Free Press, New York, 1973
[144] p843, John Dryden, 'From "Absolom and Achitophel", 1681', *The Oxford Book of Seventeenth Century Verse,* eds. Grierson & Bullough, Oxford, 1934
[145] Michael Drayton, 'To Henry Reynolds, of Poets and Poesy' (1627)
[146] p342, Micheal O'Siadhail, *Collected Poems,* Bloodaxe, Tarset, 2013

Say but the Word

Strange how that holding becomes a letting go
And sounds of a woodwind plays low and tender,
A tenor saxophone, the slow penetrating oboe
Or a recorder most myself in a self-surrender?
And the utter fragility of every passing note,
Our world of grails, things mortal and makeshift.
O my Elsa never ask from where! A Lohengrin
I too have to return in that swan-drawn boat.
All said and done, is everything love's gift?
I clean, I tune and wait until I'm blown in.

I see the role of an artist as something much humbler than a counter-world maker. I often think of Dylan Thomas' foreword to his *Collected Poems*:

I read somewhere of a shepherd who, when asked why he made, from within fairy rings, ritual observances to the moon to protect his flocks, replied: "I'd be a damn' fool if I didn't": These poems, with all their crudities, doubts, and confusions, are written for the love of Man and in praise of God, and I'd be a damn' fool if they weren't.[147]

And Dylan Thomas, for all his raging against the night, was on to something.

Shall the dust praise thee?   Psalm 30
Shall it declare thy truth?

   . . . .

Thou has turned for me my mourning into dancing

   . . . .

To the end that my glory may sing praise to thee,
and not be silent.

It is as if all art is taken up into what is greater than itself. Maybe the most we can hope to do in daring to break the silence is to be George Herbert's 'secretary of praise'.

[147] Dylan Thomas, *Collected Poems 1934–1952*, J. M. Dent and Sons, London, 1952

'Man as poet and priest of creation' is an ancient concept and what extraordinary poets and authors of the Psalms and Song of Songs[148] must have been:

'Song of Songs'

My beloved is mine, and I am his;
he feeds among the lilies.

Standing in the presence of a poem, in the tension of the images, accepting metaphors not as rhetorical devices but rather as a mode of saying. So often literary criticism veers towards trivialities of technique or show-off comparisons and misses the point of all that energy and imagination searching for 'the light supreme'. At least, Kavanagh, with his dictum that a poet is a theologian,[149] might not be too surprised! At first glance Kavanagh's remark may look easy and off-the-cuff. But there was nothing easy or unearned about his journey, he understood worship instinctively and at the deepest level[150] of his being:

'Canal Bank Walk'

Leafy-with-love banks and green waters of the canal
Pouring redemption for me, that I do
The will of God, wallow in the habitual, the banal
Grow with nature again as before I grew.
The bright stick trapped, the breeze adding a third
Party to the couple kissing on an old seat,
And a bird gathering materials for the nest for the Word
Eloquently new and abandoned to its delirious beat.
O unworn world enrapture me, enrapture me in a web
Of fabulous grass and eternal voices by a beech
Feed the gaping need of my senses, give me ad lib
To pray unselfconsciously with overflowing speech
For this soul needs to be honoured with a new dress woven
From green and blue things and arguments that cannot be proven.

---

[148] Song of Songs 2:16
[149] pp27–8, Patrick Kavanagh, *Self-Portrait,* Dolmen Press, Dublin, 1964
[150] Patrick Kavanagh, *Collected Poems,* MacGibbon & Kee, London, 1964

I thank you and I say how proud
That I have been by fate allowed
To stand here having the joyful chance
To claim my inheritance
For most have died the day before
The opening of that holy door.

Although I claim no knowledge of theology, I suspect that the temptations for a theologian are either, at one extreme, to withdraw entirely from modernity into a pure traditionalism or, at the other extreme, to reinterpret a religion in terms of modern secularity. It is fascinating the way a religious tradition and modernity in its various scientific, sociological and cultural expressions throw light on each other. Neither subsumes the other and both are richer[151] caught in the cross-light:

I wove the web of colour
Before the rainbow,
The intricacy of the flower
Before the leaf grew.

I was the buried ore,
The fossil forest,
I know the roots of things:
Before death's kingdom
I passed through the grave.

Times out of mind my journey
Circles the universe
And I remain
Before the first day

Literature and Faith
Apart from the deep and historical bonds of literature and faith, in our culture there may be parallel dilemmas. It is just that these terribly brittle worlds of word and metaphor so often face similar temptations. Poetry's reaction to any crude cultural positivism has so often been

---

[151] p111, Kathleen Raine, *Collected Poems,* Hamish Hamilton, London, 1956

either to retreat into Romanticism or to adapt to the needs of cultural consumerism until any sense of 'saying the unsayable' is lost. We often find ourselves pulled between the poles of a poetics of private piety and that of an excessive postmodernist irony. I am outlining extreme positions and there are all the gradations between. I am speaking of an ideal poetics, for as always, the corruption of the best is worst. The shadow of Foucault passes over us reminding us all too clearly that a poetics can simply serve to bolster a dominant regime. I want to stand in the crosslight, to stand where all we can grasp of the world around us, scientifically, sociologically and culturally, can still be seen and spoken of with wonder and compassion.

There are all kinds of comparisons between the world of faith and the world of art: the weight of tradition and community, the role of memory, the self-abandon, the need of apprenticeship, metaphor as a vehicle of thought and feeling, the inadequacies and longings. But I must concentrate on my own delight in poetry and let any other comparison be merely implicit; partly for fear of the charge of idolatry, partly because I reckon this cobbler should stick to his last and can only hope that revelling in the marvel of language and poetry may reflect something of the ultimate fullness.

The joy of art, it seems to me, is its invitation and its gift; its claim on us to lose our dominion and simply to behold. It has often been said that music is the purest form of contemplation. Certainly, it enters me unbidden like a perfume. But beloved poetry can have the same bodily pleasure of rhythm and metre, the moods, the precision and the silence. Then, there is the dimension of concept and metaphor which music evades. The endless intrigues, the delights, the insistences and inadequacies of language; the vagaries of words.

I remember how surprised I was, when I took lessons in classical harmony, at how mechanical and arithmetic it seemed. All those octaves, fifths and fourths, the desirable intervals, harmonics, the series of progressions by which you homed to the tonic. I know these rules and regulations were artificially distilled from one period of European music, but it is beautifully mathematical. I could feel the enthusiasm of Pythagoras halving the length of a vibrating string to raise its pitch by an octave or reducing its length by a third to raise its pitch a fifth. And so on, as the intervals work in ratios. Naturally, in taking harmony lessons I was doing it the wrong way around because my apprenticeship in culture means that at some subconscious level at least I can guess where the line of a hymn or a folksong is leading. It is precisely that subconscious level that I find so marvellous. But, of course, I should not have been so surprised at this subconscious arithmetic. After all I had trained in philology and in generative grammar and knew how one dimension of language also operates at a similar subconscious and almost mechanical[152] level:

> I have found my music in a common word,
> Trying each pleasurable throat that sings
> And every praisèd sequence of sweet strings ...

'The Alchemist in the City'

Layers of Language

It is by no means necessary for a poet to be aware of the dynamic layers of language rules and developments, no more than a musician need be a mathematician or a sculptor a geologist. Yet it fascinates. Perhaps all those laws and sound-shifts triggered and patterned subconsciously over time reflect our deep and endless desire to order and re-order, this ballet of symmetry and arrangement highlighting our universal and inherited potential for syntheses and learning. Nor is it simply in the past. It is unpredictable and it keeps on happening. I remember how when I was young, older people pronounced *garage* with the second syllable stressed (the way Americans still pronounce it, showing its French origins). I stressed it on the first syllable, which reduced the second syllable to – *idge* as in words like *cabbage* or *porridge*. It would have sounded silly for someone of my generation to pronounce it like older people. On the other hand, I was brought up stressing the first syllable in the words *primarily*, *harass* and *controversy* and now I notice people all around me accenting the second syllable. The great unpredictability of deviation and re-configuration which has over thousands of years shaped and re-shaped language into language. A model of contingency and of continuation. But I do not want to dwell too much on this constant re-arranging on the level of pronunciation and inflectional paradigms.

What is most interesting is the shifts which take place at the semantic level, how words connect and shade from one meaning to another, Just think of a word like *trust* which is borrowed from Old Norse *traustr* meaning 'confidence', 'firmness' with its origins in an Indo-European root **deru* 'to be firm', 'solid', 'steadfast'. In its more specialized sense it

[152] p5, Gerard Manley Hopkins, *Poems and Prose of Gerard Manley Hopkins*, Penguin, Harmondsworth, 1953

means 'wood', 'tree', 'truth', '(be)trow' and 'truce', and through its
cognates with Latin *durus/durare* whose English derivatives give us a
word like 'endure'. In German *trost* or in Norwegian *trost* comes to mean
consolation, 'comfort', 'solace'. Even the French *triste* is thought to be
derived from the Old Norse verbal form of the same word, so a *triste* is
'a place where one stands trustingly'. It begins to read like a meditative
poem on the theme of trust. To know that some truth endures and
stands like a tree to believe and console us and to give us somewhere we
can stand[153] with confidence:

'Affliction' Now I am here, what thou wilt do with me
None of my books will show:
I reade, and sigh, and wish I were a tree;
For sure then I should grow
To fruit or shade: at least some bird would trust
Her household to me, and I should be just.

I never cease to be amazed by this choreography of words. A lovely and
especially English word is 'worship'. As a noun it expresses the quality
of having worth (and therefore to be revered). I often think it is a pity
that its spelling does not show its almost transparent make-up: *worthship*
that is *worth* and *ship*. However I am a little late with my regrets as
Middle English had *worschipe* and we have to go back to Old English
for *weorthscipe.* What a rich and layered world! The ending *–ship* we
know from words like *horsemanship* or *scholarship* where it signifies the
state or condition of having the quality of a horseman or what pertains
to a scholar. (The ending has in itself an interesting background; it's a
collective suffix connected to the word *shape* which provides other
Germanic languages with their word for 'create', for instance,
Norwegian). But the central idea here is *worth.* This is believed to be
derived from a root **wert* which means 'to turn', 'to wind' which we see
in English '*inward*', '*toward*' etc. The verb is common in other German
languages, for instance, *werden* 'to become' (from 'to turn into') and has
a cognate in Latin *vertere* 'to turn' from whose compounds many English
words such as 'convert', 'invert', 'avert' are derived. The word 'worth'
apparently derives from *werthaz* meaning 'toward', 'opposite' and
therefore 'equivalent', 'worth' and the noun clearly associates value and

[153] p364, George Herbert, *Oxford Book of Seventeenth Century Verse*, eds. Grierson & Bulloch,
Oxford, 1934

worth with the idea of equivalence. Perhaps it is fanciful but in that sequence of subtle semantic shifts maybe there is a hint of some link between what is opposite and equivalent and what is worth. We touch here on the whole philosophical idea of accepting what is opposite, turned towards and facing us, as having the equivalent needs and rights as ourselves. The well known *Thou* of Martin Buber or less symmetrically, the command of 'the face of the other' in Emmanuel Levinas. My own associations are with the revelation of Dorothea Brooke in George Eliot's *Middlemarch*[154] that her husband Casaubon 'had an equivalent centre of self, where the lights and shadows must always fall with a certain difference'. There are all sorts of implications of worship and otherness. At any rate, the word 'worship' is a unique development in English and trust Gerard Manley Hopkins with his love of Anglo-Saxon[155] to pick it up:

To man, that needs would worship block or barren stone,
Our law says: Love what are love's worthiest, were all known;
World's loveliest – men's selves. Self flashes off frame and face.

'To What Serves Mortal Beauty'

In the Cross-light of Tonalities

All the slippage and overlapping of words. Maybe these ambiguities and finesses, these ambivalences and paradoxes reflect much about what's most captivating and mysterious in our dealings with others. There is room for change and subtlety and tension. Music holds us poised, expectant and agog, on a diminished seventh chord in the cross-light between tonalities; room for transcendence and playfulness. So much of our fun is based on double meanings, homonyms and puns. I think of John Donne at this most boisterous[156] in the virtuoso 'To his Mistris going to Bed':

Come, Madam, come, all rest my powers defie.
Until I labour, I in labour lie.
The foe oft-times having the foe in sight,
Is tir'd with standing though he never fight.
Off with that girdle, like heaven's Zone glistering,

'Elegie xix To His Mistris Going to Bed'

. . . .

[154] p243, George Eliot, *Middlemarch,* Penguin, Harmondsworth, Middlesex, 1965
[155] p58, Gerald Manley Hopkins, *Poems and Prose,* Penguin, Harmondsworth, 1953
[156] pp96–7, John Donne, *Complete Poetry and Selected Prose,* ed. John Hayward, The Nonesuch Press, London, 1990

Say but the Word

Licence my roaving hands, and let them go,
Before, behind, between, above, below,
O my America! my new-found-land,
My kingdome, safliest when with one man man'd,
My Myne of precious stones, My Emperie,
How blest as I in this discovering thee!

I do not wish to labour the word play! That rumbustious and
swaggering youth! Listening carefully you could almost guess that the
intensity of the temperament would issue in 'Ask not for whom the bell
tolls, it tolls for thee'. But there are quieter, fine-drawn uses of language's
ambiguity. Richard Wilbur's 'The Beautiful Changes' in a book of the
same title published when he was only twenty-six allows the mystery
of ambivalence to enter in to us. Does the beautiful change or are the
changes[157] beautiful? Or both?

'The Beautiful   The beautiful changes as a forest is changed
    Changes'   By a chameleon's tuning his skin to it;
As a mantis, arranged
On a green leaf, grows
Into it, makes the leaf leafier, and proves
Any greenness is deeper than anyone knows.

Your hands hold roses always in a way that says
They are not only yours; the beautiful changes
In such kind ways,
Wishing ever to sunder
Things and things' selves for a second finding, to lose
For a moment all that it touches back to wonder.

Yet I wonder if it is not this equivocal quality, the slippage and polysemy,
which sometimes drives us to despair of language. The terrible
inadequacy of words – always falling short of desire. The ungraspable
joy, the un-communicable sorrow. And even here there is another
paradox. The drift and shortcomings of language. This causes us to fail
again and again and also urges us to begin afresh, poem after poem,
generation after generation. This inexhaustible hankering after the

[157] p392, Richard Wilbur, *New and Collected Poems,* Faber &Faber, London, 1989

absent – the necessary absconding[158] of the sacred.

'A Photograph'

You are for me now
The mystery of time
i.e., of a person
Changing and the same,

Who runs in the garden
Fragrant after the rain
With a ribbon in your hair
And lives in the beyond.

You see how I try
To reach with words
What matters most
And how I fail.

Though perhaps this moment
When you are close
Is precisely your help
And an act of forgiveness.

Multiple Meanings

For all its shortfalls, the property of words to have more than one meaning is at the core of language. For reasons of economy there have to be limits to the number of sounds and words and a deal of doubling-up of meanings. This in turn makes it necessary for a word's meaning to be dependent on the context. You can often only understand what a word means from a whole sentence and context. In a poem, where you cannot question the author as you could in a conversation, there is the possibility of ambiguity and misunderstanding. Donne's word play exploits the tension between the equivocality of the word 'discover' ('uncover', 'undress', or 'explore previously unknown territory') and the unambiguous meaning in the overall context. In Wilbur's 'The Beautiful Changes' the spell is in the veiled ambiguity, which remains at the level of the sentence and context. It is the magic and power of under-determinacy. Miłosz, for his part, is coming to terms with the

---

[158] p33, Czesław Miłosz, *Provinces,* The Ecco Press, New York, 1991

fact that we must live with the mystery of the elusive otherness. In spite of our best efforts in language, at some level every human is forever a stranger. Communication without the forgiveness of love always falls short. By polysemy, this property of words to have more than one meaning, has an even more significant role. I am not thinking here of scientific language where the aim is to totally eliminate polysemy and where it employs metaphor to tie down the context to one narrow meaning in the interests of argument. Scientific language is, of course, necessary and complements the ordinary language of communication. It is in our efforts to heighten and deepen our perception, however, that the ability of words to have more than one meaning comes into its own.

We approach the use of metaphor as the exploitation of polysemy at the ever-expanding boundaries of language.

Many of us were schooled in the rhetorical tradition where we learned a long list of various figures of speech: hyperbole, oxymoron, irony, synecdoche, metonymy, simile, metaphor, and so on. Unless we have had particular cause to look them up afterwards, most of us have probably forgotten how they are defined. The most unfortunate outcome of this tradition was in fact to make you think of all of these figures of speech as ornaments, a sort of decoration to make our language high-flown. The result is especially regrettable in the case of metaphor and leads to what is called a substitution view of metaphor. Take Brendan Kennelly's short poem[159] 'Ambulance':

'Ambulance'   Shrieking on its mercy mission,
The white hysterical bully
Blows all things out of its way,
Cutting through the slack city
Like a knife through flesh.
People respect potential saviours
And immediately step aside,
Watching it pitch and scream ahead,
Ignoring the lights, breaking the rules,
Lurching on the crazy line
Between the living and the dead.

So easily we are trained to think that the poet uses 'the white hysterical

[159] p121, Brendan Kennelly, *A Time for Voices*, Bloodaxe, Newcastle upon Tyne, 1992

Say but the Word

bully' when, of course, he means the ambulance. We just need to substitute 'ambulance' for 'the white hysterical bully' and we're back to square one. Happily, there is a series of thinkers (among them I. A. Richards, Monroe Beardsley and Max Black), who have abandoned the idea of metaphor as something stylistic and devoid of content. Janet Martin Soskice's definition of metaphor as when 'we speak about one thing in terms suggestive of another' gets nearer the mark.[160] The real wonder is that metaphor blurs the usual logical boundaries and uncovers new likenesses. There is a whole spectrum from the dead metaphor, which has become an entry in the dictionary, from 'the hands of the clock' all the way to referring to 'the white hysterical bully' in a poem describing an ambulance. And indeed the so-called 'dead metaphor' may not be without its effect on our way of viewing reality as shaped by our language. To quote the philosopher, Paul Ricoeur:

Our concept of likeness as the tension between sameness and difference has the extraordinary power of re-describing reality…the strategy of discourse implied in metaphorical language is neither to improve communication nor to insure univocity in argumentation, but to shatter and to increase our sense of reality by shattering and increasing our language…With metaphor we experience the metamorphosis of both language and reality.[161]

An ambulance rushing through the city streets will never look the same again!

Our sign system is finite but the potential for growth in meaning is infinite; we stand in the cross-light of structure[162] and freedom:

Freedom. We sang of freedom   'Freedom'
(travel lightly, anything goes)
and somehow became strangers
to each other, like gabblers
at cross purposes, builders
    of Babel.

---

[160] p54, Janet Martin Soskice, *Metaphor and Religious Language,* Clarendon Press, Oxford, 1985
[161] pp132–3, Paul Ricoeur, 'Creativity in Language, Word, Polysemy, Metaphor' in *The Philosophy of Paul Ricoeur: An Anthology of His Work,* Beacon Press, Boston, 1978
[162] p221, Micheal O'Siadhail, *Collected Poems,* Tarset, 2013

Slowly I relearn a *lingua*
shared overlays of rule,
lattice of memory and meaning,
our latent images, a tongue
at large in an endlessness
    of sentences unsaid.

All Things are One

And just as in language and metaphor, tradition and innovation are held in tension, so too in literature. There is both the desire to absorb the canon and to interrupt and subvert it.

In an interview, the American poet Richard Wilbur was reminded that both he and Robert Lowell had said that all poetry of the highest quality is religious. He responded by saying that there are various ways you could argue for the position. 'You could say that all poetry, however much it may be irrational, moves towards clarity and order, that it affirms all that is clear and orderly in the world, affirms the roots of clarity in the world. Then, you might say that poetry is given not only to saying that this is like that, as in the simile; it is given also to saying that this is that, to affirming rather nervily, that prosaically unlike things are to poetry's eye identical, co-natural. I think that there is a natural disposition of the poetic mind to assert all things are one, are part of the same thing, that anything may be compared to anything else. And if anything can be compared to anything else, the ground of comparison is likely to be divine'.[163]

'Love Calls Us   The soul shrinks
to the Things
of this World'

    From all that it is about to remember,
From the punctual rape of every blessèd day,
And cries,
        "Oh let there be nothing on earth but laundry,
Nothing but rosy hands in the rising steam
And clear dances done in the sight of heaven."

    Yet, as the sun acknowledges
With a warm look the world's hunks and colours,

---

[163] pp24–5, Richard Wilbur, from 'Richard Wilbur: an interview with Robert Frank and Stephen Mitchell' in *In Conversation with Richard Wilbur*, University Press of Mississippi, Jackson and London, 1964

The soul descends once more in bitter love
To accept the waking body, saying now
In a changed voice as the man yawns and rises,

   "Bring them down from their ruddy gallows;
Let there be clean linen for the backs of thieves;
Let lovers go fresh and sweet to be undone,
And the heaviest nuns walk in a pure floating
Of dark habits,
       keeping their difficult balance."[164]

Wilbur described this poem as 'against dissociated and abstracted spirituality'. Keeping the difficult balance, indeed. And all the traditions with their names for the task; Greek poet 'the one who makes', Irish *file* 'the one who sees', Icelandic *skald* 'the one who narrates', Welsh *bardd* 'the one who praises'. The acknowledgement as to the source of the great plenitude of order, energy and life. The extraordinary strata of richness and complexity found in language, which in turn are just a glimpse of the fullness and diversities of our cosmos and our culture. Music, physics, sociology, biology, genetics. The abundance[165] of it!

O unworn world, enrapture me, enrapture me in a web ...   'Canal Bank Walk'

A source in the light around us and everything around us in the light of this source. To be a poet is to make sense of it, to be a seer, a narrator, a praiser in the cross-light. Dare I say a lover? The wonderful and bewildering paradoxes and complementarities, the constant change and becoming. The threat of chaos, the leaps to greater intricacy. And running through it all, irrepressible[166] richness.

Anywhere and always just as you expect it least,   'Invitation'
Welling and oozing from nowhere a desire to feast.

At Auschwitz Wolf hums Brahms' rhapsody by heart
As Eddy, thief turned juggler, rehearses his art.

[164] pp 233–4, Richard Wilbur, *New and Selected Poems,* Faber and Faber, London, 1988
[165] p150, Patrick Kavanagh, *Collected Poems,* MacGibbon & Kee, London, 1964
[166] p307, Micheal O'Siadhail, *Collected Poems,* Bloodaxe, Tarset, 2013

Fling and abandon, gaieties colourful and porous,
The Mexican beggar's skirt, an Araner's *crios*.

Irresistible laughter, hiss and giggle of overflow,
That black engine-driver crooning his life's motto:

'Paint or tell a story, sing or shovel coal,
You gotta get a glory or the job lacks soul.'

Abundance of joy bubbling some underground jazz.
A voice whispers: Be with me tonight in paradise.

Woven in Words

Woven in Words

13   Patrick Kavanagh: Poet and Prophet

Keynote Address for Patrick Kavanagh Weekend Inniskeen September 28th 2012.

Introduction
Poet and Prophet. This echoes the phrase 'the role is that of prophet and saviour' from the poem[167] 'After Forty Years of Age':

>   Tell us what life has taught you. Not just
>   about persons –
> Which is futile anyway in the long run – but a concrete,
>   as it were, essence.

> The role is that of prophet and saviour. To smelt in
>   passion
> The common places of life.

But before I go any further, I want to make clear what I mean by a prophet. The word can too easily conjure up an image of a long-robed, long-bearded figure with his head in the clouds forecasting the future. What I mean, and I think Patrick Kavanagh meant, either consciously or unconsciously, was someone with feet on the ground and deeply involved in the society around him. What makes someone prophetic is the ability, in the light of the past, to live utterly in the present in a way which prepares for the future. I don't think Patrick Kavanagh set out deliberately to do that. As he remarked in the Introduction[168] to the MacGibbon and Kee *Collected Poems*: 'A man (I am thinking of myself) innocently dabbles in words and rhymes and finds that it is his life.' I think that by living intensely through all the stages of his life, he stumbled towards prophecy. I don't mean, of course, that he wasn't aware of his point of view, his angle of vision. No one was more convinced of his own opinion than Patrick Kavanagh. However, the way in which I find his work prophetic may be clearer when seen over fifty years on and with a broader historical perspective. I'll try to show how I see him in this prophetic role.

---

[167] p148, Patrick Kavanagh, *Collected Poems,* MacGibbon & Kee, London, 1964
[168] pxiii, Patrick Kavanagh, *Collected Poems,* MacGibbon & Kee, London, 1964

Broad Context

I want to look very briefly at the broad context of the poet's times and sketch the intellectual hinterland.

Patrick Kavanagh was almost thirty-four and had already published *Ploughman and Other Poems* two years earlier and was just publishing[169] *The Green Fool* when Chamberlain declared that he had achieved 'peace in our times'. As the poem 'Epic' so memorably tells us 'That was the year of the Munich bother'. This wonderful phrase, in the context of the poem, throws us back to the local, to where we are and where we act – in this case Ballyrush and Gortin. However, in January of the following year Yeats died and by September the Second World War had begun.

Although, as he expressed it in 'Lough Derg', during those war years 'all Ireland… froze for want of Europe', it's extraordinary to think that somewhere between 1940 and 1942, Patrick Kavanagh wrote both his two longer poems 'The Great Hunger' and 'Lough Derg'.

The aftermath of the Second World War would see a huge loss of belief in the Enlightenment dream of continual human progress. The confidence in modernity which had been so strong throughout the 19th century was shattered. After all, Germany, which had represented the best in science and the arts, had brought to bear all the bureaucratic apparatus of a modern state to exterminate Jews as well as the disabled, the homosexuals, the gypsies and the political left. This disillusionment found expression in all kinds of ways in our culture, including the philosophies of suspicion, the plunge into despair and meaninglessness, the turn towards irony. We need only think of, say, the work of Beckett or Pinter.

It seems to me that Patrick Kavanagh's extraordinary achievement and his prophetic insight must be seen against this cultural background, this intellectual ambience of disillusionment and deep despondency.

Phase and Temptations

The work of any poet is ultimately all of a piece. Nevertheless before looking at how, and possibly why, Patrick Kavanagh points beyond the dilemmas of his times, I want to think a little about some general facets of his work.

Antoinette Quinn's comprehensive biography[170] and her critical

[169] Patrick Kavanagh, *The Green Fool*, Martin Brian & O'Keefe, London, 1971
[170] Antoinette Quinn, *Patrick Kavanagh – A Biography,* Gill and Macmillan, Dublin, 2001

study[171] take us chronologically through the poet's growth phase by phase. This makes great sense for a biographer who has to follow the ins and outs of a life. It also shows how a poet, who had to find his own way, learned his trade slowly and painfully. There is the early school-book phase, the rural-romantic, the turn to more objective description, the social-realistic stage, the confessional and satirical period and the post-operation time. I could give examples of poems from these different phases but a glance at his *Collected Poems* would show this progression.

Clearly any list of phases could be expanded and the various twists and turns explained by influences of AE or of Frank O'Connor, Sean O'Faolain, Peadar O'Donnell and *The Bell* and so on. There are, however, themes and attitudes which overlap or run right through his life and are not always amenable to chronological description.

There is perhaps another complementary way of looking at his work which doesn't follow a chronological framework. There are a number of tendencies or temptations to which he is exposed, either due to his background and personal circumstances or to the social and intellectual climate of his times. Together these point to what might be called the dynamic, one might say the DNA, of his life's work. I want to mention three elements of this dynamic in particular and, needless to say, these are not unique to Patrick Kavanagh. The first two he would always struggle with, the third he managed to overstride with greater ease.

The first of these is the temptation to play the part of the miraculous uneducated poet. Here is a small farmer in Monaghan writing about nature around him. The world of literature often looks around for simple labels. It provides a handy way of keeping a controlling overview. Of course, Robert Burns, the ploughman poet, springs to mind. Even the title *Ploughman and Other Poems* invites this comparison and categorisation. Another possible candidate is William Henry Davies famous for 'What is this life if, full of care, / We have no time to stand and stare?' While his upbringing wasn't rural, he was a self-educated poet. Yet another model, nearer home, would be Lord Dunsany's view of Francis Ledwidge. We might also think of John Clare. This was a ready made slot for Patrick Kavanagh and it would have been so easy to accept the role.

For a while Kavanagh played along with this. His walking to Dublin to visit AE (George Russell), suitably dressed in his work clothes was

---

[171] Antoinette Quinn, *Patrick Kavanagh: Born Again Romantic*, Gill and Macmillan, Dublin, 1991

certainly taking the part seriously. Indeed, as he was later to acknowledge, in many ways *The Green Fool*[172] was playing to this particular gallery. The 'green' in the title even introduces a note of paddywhackery, what Kavanagh would later refer to as 'bucklepping'. Here was the original miraculous peasant Irish poet. Later he would vehemently reject this role. In a review of Lord Dunsany's Donnellan Lectures on Francis Ledwidge, Kavanagh accuses him of regarding the poet as 'a sort of angelic moron, with none of the normal appetites or capabilities – a curse for which we have Keats, Shelley and Byron to thank.'[173] In his *Self Portrait*[174] he pillories the Celtic twilight as made up and patented by Yeats and Lady Gregory. Yet the temptation was always there to mark himself as the authentic Irishman as opposed to, on one hand the likes of Yeats who wasn't, in Kavanagh's view, the genuine article, or on the other hand the likes of Austin Clarke, Roibeard Ó Farracháin or P. J. McManus, who wanted a 'national' verse in English with use of, for example, assonance taken from the Irish tradition.

The second tendency or temptation was to adopt the role of the poet as the romantic outsider, the martyr in society. Once again this is not unique to Patrick Kavanagh and many poets in their early work take this stance. It comes and goes throughout his work, even in some of our favourite poems such as[175] 'Inniskeen Road: July Evening':

'Inniskeen Road: July Evening'

A road, a mile of kingdom. I am king
Of banks and stones and every blooming thing.

This note of the poet as outsider and martyr is more strident and bitter in his 1944 poem[176] 'Pegasus':

'Pegasus'

My soul was an old horse
Offered for sale in twenty fairs.
I offered him to the Church – the buyers
Were little men who feared his unusual airs.

---

[172] op. cit.
[173] p218, Quoted in Antoinette Quinn, *Patrick Kavanagh: A Biography*. Such a statement raises serious questions about describing Kavanagh as a Romantic. Antoinette Quinn concludes that he is 'a born-again romantic'. In view of Kavanagh's own reservations about the label Romantic, I suppose the appropriateness of this depends on the meaning one ascribes to 'born-again'.
[174] Patrick Kavanagh, *Self Portrait*, Dolmen Press, Dublin, 1964
[175] p18, Patrick Kavanagh, *The Complete Poems*, The Goldsmith Press, Newbridge, 1992
[176] p149, op. cit.

Say but the Word

While this tendency dogs him through his work, often he rises above it. Actually, as I'll go on to show, the nature of his prophecy at its most mature is not that of the martyred outsider but rather that of a seer speaking from within society and in solidarity with ordinary people. He is a prophet seeking wisdom in the mundaneness of our daily incarnate life.

The third temptation is more of a social nature. I'm thinking here of the air of post-war disillusionment, the tendency towards despondency or even meaninglessness, what Antoinette Quinn refers to in her biography[177] as discussions of the then fashionable *angst*. Though he did go through a period of what might be called social realism, ultimately this was the temptation Patrick Kavanagh seemed best equipped by temperament and background to reject, as he makes clear[178] in 'Spring Day':

Philosophy's graveyard – only dead men analyse   'Spring Day'
The reason for existence. Come all you solemn boys
From out your dictionary world and literary gloom –
Kafka's mad, Picasso's sad in Despair's confining room.

In the opening stanza he also has a dig at Yeats:

Give over T.S. Eliot and also W.B.

It was reported that Kavanagh had said 'Yeats I can do without'. Was this simply Kavanagh's bravado, the iconoclasm of the next generation, a poet trying to make his mark by dismissing an emblematic figure? Or was it more? Was it in fact a facet of Kavanagh as prophet opening up something that goes beyond the confines of the accepted thinking of his times, which Yeats in so many ways represents? It may be a combination of all these things. But I now turn to look at the restrictions of what in Kavanagh's time was thought of as 'modernity'.

Modernity and Polarities
Patrick Kavanagh was born into a rural society which was still largely pre-industrial. It was also a society which was just in the process of passing from an oral to a literate culture. Added to this it had recently

---

[177] op. cit.
[178] p224, Patrick Kavanagh, *The Complete Poems*, The Goldsmith Press, Newbridge, 1992

passed through a dramatic language change from Irish to English. James Kavanagh, Patrick's father, was an Irish speaker but his mother Bridget didn't know Irish. These two major societal shifts must have deeply affected the mindset. The view of what poetry should be must have been coloured by the oral tradition. The Irish language substratum of the adopted English may also have contributed a certain 'hybrid energy'. One way or the other, Kavanagh's upbringing in a lifestyle, which in many aspects was only beginning to emerge from a pre-modern culture to a modern society, may ultimately have helped him to see through and beyond the confines of his times.

When I speak of Modernity, I'm thinking of a particular intellectual view of the world which formed around the Enlightenment in the 17th century and which – in spite of the challenges of Romanticism and Modernism – was dominant until about 1960, when Europe had recovered economically from the Second World War.[179] Again it's debatable where we are from the 1960s on. Some say this is Postmodernism, some say Chastened Modernity and yet others speak of High or Late Modernity. While our present way of thinking casts doubt on any of these overarching or general concepts, in Kavanagh's time, and indeed even still, such broad sweeping and unnuanced divisions have a certain currency. But all that concerns us here is that the poet Kavanagh faced into an era whose general mood was still strongly influenced by the Enlightenment and a belief in rationality, science and endless progress, ultimately in secularism.

One way of viewing Modernity which culminated in the Second World War is to think of it as a society trapped between polarities[180]. Clearly in certain straightforward cases we are faced with opposite polarised choices. If we're suffering, our only choice is to remain in pain or to end the pain. But these kinds of opposites may not be appropriate on other occasions. In richer, more complex cases such polarities go nowhere. For instance: is it nature or nurture? – are we being subjective or objective? – are we free or not free? – does the individual or the community count most? and so on. It seems that we have to mend these false oppositions. How can we look at them with a third eye, somehow discover 'the excluded middle' and repair these damaging divisions,

---

[179] Stephen Toulmin, *Cosmopolis: The Hidden Agenda of Modernity*, The Free Press New York,1990
[180] Peter Ochs, *Another Reformation: Postliberal Christianity and the Jews,* Baker Academic, Grand Rapids, Michigan, 2011

these unwholesome dichotomies. Listen to these prophetic three lines[181] from Kavanagh's 'Canal Bank Walk':

The bright stick trapped, the breeze adding a third
Party to the couple kissing on an old seat,
And a bird gathering materials for the nest for the Word.

'Canal Bank Walk'

I will go on to look more closely at Kavanagh's prophetic role or tease out this extraordinary insight. But by way of contrast, I want now briefly to turn back to Yeats, whom Kavanagh declared he could do without.

Ironically, Yeats was to die the January before the outbreak of the Second World War, which would ultimately undermine the optimistic mindset that believed in rationality and perpetual progress. I say ironically because, in so many ways, this extraordinarily gifted poet exemplified a society which was trapped in its polarities. Yeats famously said 'We make out of the quarrel with others, rhetoric, but of the quarrel with ourselves, poetry.'[182] I suggest that these quarrels sometimes reflect false and, sometimes even insidious opposites.

It could be argued that he was caught in a polarisation between Romanticism and Modernism which is encapsulated in the fascinating 'Sailing to Byzantium'. Certainly, even as a young man in his search for meaning, Yeats chose the strange and often manipulative domain of spiritualism and *séances* rather than any of the world's major religious traditions. In matters of sex, Yeats, who tried an operation which was believed to rejuvenate male sexual potency, implicitly opposed celibacy to full sexual powers, excluding any middle ground. But perhaps the most serious of Yeats's polarities was his flirtation with Fascism. This is the most pernicious polarity of Modernity, the division of the world into 'us' and 'them'.

Philosophers, who see Modernity in terms of polarities, propose a way of escaping these entrapments, or to put it another way, of repairing what went wrong. There are two stages. We need, first, to describe how things are, and then, to find a third way which transcends these dilemmas.

But now I want to ask how does Patrick Kavanagh deal with these polarities which seem to be such a characteristic of his era?

---

[181] p294, Patrick Kavanagh, *The Complete Poems*, Newbridge, The Goldsmith Press, Newbridge, 1992
[182] W.B. Yeats 'Anima Hominis,' *Essays*, Macmillan, London, 1924

Kavanagh Beyond Polarities

Leaving aside for the moment the stance taken in his two longer poems, all kinds of combinations occur in many of his poems which avoid false choices. The Ireland, which Patrick Kavanagh lived in, was a society riddled with oppositions: rational realism or Irish Romanticism, local or universal, rural or urban, clerical or anti-clerical, Catholic or Protestant, sexuality or spirituality, and so on.

After his visit to America and his discovery of the Beats, Kavanagh in his 1958 poem 'To Hell with Commonsense', without any concession to Irish Romanticism, issues his verdict[183] against the controlling rationality of Modernity:

'To Hell with
Commonsense'

More kicks than pence
We get from commonsense
Above its door is writ
All hope abandon. It
Is a bank will refuse a post
Dated cheque of the Holy Ghost.
Therefore I say to hell
With all reasonable
Poems in particular
We want no secular
Wisdom plodded together
By concerned fools. Gather
No moss you rolling stones
Nothing thought out atones
For no flight
In the light.
Let the wear out nerve and bone
Those who would have it that way
But in the end nothing that they
Have achieved will be in the shake up,
In the final Wake Up.

Kavanagh dealt deftly with the false divide between the local and the universal in his celebrated poem[184] 'Epic':

---

[183] p288, Patrick Kavanagh, *The Complete Poems*, The Goldsmith Press, Newbridge, 1992
[184] p238, Patrick Kavanagh, *The Complete Poems*, The Goldsmith Press, Newbridge, 1992

That was the year of the Munich bother. Which
Was more important? I inclined
To lose my faith in Ballyrush and Gortin
Till Homer's ghost came whispering to my mind.
He said: I made the Iliad from such
A local row. Gods make their own importance.

'Epic'

The rural and urban polarity also get short shrift. I always think that
Kavanagh turned the area of Dublin around Pembroke Road and
Raglan Road and Baggot Street, what he liked to refer to as his
Pembrokeshire, into a country village or small town. The Grand Canal
was the river bisecting the town. In 'Canal Bank Walk' we have lines
that, though written about a canal at the heart of a capital city, are as
rural[185] as any of his earlier Monaghan poems:

Leafy-with-love banks and the green waters of the canal
Pouring redemption for me, that I do
The will of God, wallow in the habitual, the banal,
Grow with nature again as before I grew.

'Canal Bank
Walk'

. . . .

O unworn world enrapture me, encapture me in a web
Of fabulous grass and eternal voices by a beech, …

As for the anti-clerical or clerical, Kavanagh, although he had gone
though an anti-clerical phase, in 'Father Mat' or 'Lough Derg' he is
neither the one nor the other. Here's one small example of a sceptical
attitude[186] from 'Lough Derg':

"I renounce the World, the Flesh and the Devil";
Three times they cried out. A country curate
Stared with a curate leer – he was proud.
The booted
Prior passes by ignoring all the crowd.

'Lough Derg'

On the other hand, the ex-monk from Dublin in *Lough Derg* gets

---

[185] p294, Patrick Kavanagh, *The Complete Poems*, The Goldsmith Press, Newbridge, 1992
[186] p107, Patrick Kavanagh, *The Complete Poems*, The Goldsmith Press, Newbridge, 1992

Say but the Word

compassionate treatment and even the prior later cuts a more sympathetic figure accompanying the pilgrims leaving the island[187] in boats:

'Lough Derg'   The Prior went with them – suavely, goodily
Priestly, painfully directing the boats.

As someone who as a teenager 'did Lough Derg' three times, I can well recall ambivalent feelings when we could smell the Prior's fried breakfast wafting across the morning as we fasted on, exhausted after our all-night vigil! However, I'll be returning to the poet's perspective in 'Lough Derg' as a whole shortly, and I turn now to Kavanagh's angle of vision on the world.

Kavanagh's Angle of Vision

What was the poet's viewpoint, his attitude to life and the cosmos? Some don't feel there was any consistent angle of vision.

Among these is his biographer John Nemo,[188] who noted 'Kavanagh's point of view evolved primarily from his response to life, which was emotional rather than intellectual ... In place of the logic that directs the creative vision of poets like T. S. Eliot and W. B. Yeats, Kavanagh's creative faculties rely on inspiration and intuition. Artistically, he reacts rather than acts…'

Another is the poet, novelist and biographer, Anthony Cronin, who knew Kavanagh extremely well and is a perceptive observer. Anthony Cronin wrote in *Heritage Now*[189] 'You can look in vain in his poems for elaborate metaphors, correspondences, symbols and symbolic extensions of meaning ... neither is there in his poems really anything that turns out to be a coherent life-view in the philosophical sense'.

But now I have to come clean. I have been skirting the issue in several of the lines I quoted from his poems. Let me remind you:

'Canal Bank   And a bird gathering materials for the nest for the Word.
Walk'

'To Hell with   It
Commonsense'   Is a bank will refuse a post
Dated cheque of the Holy Ghost.

---

[187] p115, Patrick Kavanagh, *The Complete Poems*, The Goldsmith Press, Newbridge, 1992
[188] John Nemo, *Patrick Kavanagh*, Twayne Publishers, New York, 1979
[189] Anthony Cronin, *Heritage Now: Irish Literature in the English Language*, Brandon, Dingle, 1982

But in the end nothing that they
Have achieved will be in the shake up
In the final Wake Up

Pouring redemption for me, that I do
The will of God ...

Patrick Kavanagh stated in *Self-Portrait*[190] that any poet worth his salt
is a theologian. I find as a reader I have to take him seriously. And I am
not alone in this. There are at least two fine books devoted to viewing
his poetry from a theological perspective: Una Agnew's *The Mystical
Imagination of Patrick Kavanagh: A Buttonhole in Heaven;*[191] and Tom
Stacks' *No Earthly Estate: God and Patrick Kavanagh* in 2002.[192] Two other
theologians David Ford and Daniel Hardy in 1984 had devoted much
of their book *Jubilate*[193] to Kavanagh's poetry. David Ford also discusses
'Lough Derg' in a subsequent article.[194]

I believe that Patrick Kavanagh's theology is not simply a strand in
his work but rather the fundamental attitude which, together with his
difficult and iconoclastic personality, allowed him the prophetic insight
to open up a vision beyond the constricting polarities of his times. This
is true of his work in general but also in particular of his remarkable
longer poems 'The Great Hunger' and 'Lough Derg'.

Kavanagh and Repair

Those who see the failure of Modernity in the light of its false
oppositions see this as being repaired by grace to perceive the
entrapment and then the further gift to go beyond the impasse.

Certainly 'The Great Hunger' perceives the tragedy, the pain and
isolation of lonely bachelor small farmers up and down the country, the
Kavanagh who might[195] have been:

---

[190] op. cit.
[191] Una Agnew, *The Mystical Imagination of Patrick Kavanagh: A Buttonhole in Heaven*, Columba Press, Dublin, 1998
[192] Tom Stack, *No Earthly Estate: God and Patrick Kavanagh*, Columba Press, Dublin, 2002
[193] Daniel W. Hardy and David F. Ford, *Jubilate: Theology in Praise,* Darton, Longman & Todd, London, 1984
[194] David F. Ford, 'Reading texts, seeking wisdom: A Gospel, a system and a poem', *Theology* 114: 173–179, 2011
[195] p91, Patrick Kavanagh, *The Complete Poems*, The Goldsmith Press, Newbridge, 1992

'The Great
Hunger'
Sitting on a wooden gate,
Sitting on a wooden gate,
Sitting on a wooden gate
He rode in day-dream cars.
He locked his body with his knees
When the gate swung too much in the breeze.
But while he caught high ecstasies
Life slipped between the bars.

The poet looks at this world with a third eye, searches for a third way.
Then, in 'Having Confessed' there is the gift to go beyond it:

'Having
Confessed'
                          We must be nothing,
Nothing that God may make us something.
We must not touch the immortal material
We must not daydream tomorrow's judgment –
God must be allowed to surprise us.

As far as Kavanagh's prophetic voice in 'Lough Derg' is concerned let
me quote from David Ford:[196]

The poem sets us in the middle of the pilgrimage, vividly evoking
its atmosphere and rigours, its varied characters, and the
conversations, prayers, personal dramas and transformations that
happen in a short, intense time span. The poet's view of the
pilgrims might be seen as an attempt to see them theologically, as
God sees them. It is a striking, often paradoxical, mixture of realism
and compassion. Again and again the whole group and its
individual members are described in their pettiness, selfishness,
mediocrity and small-mindedness, their vices of envy, jealousy,
greed, smugness, hypocrisy, cold-heartedness and so on, with a
special poet's emphasis on their insensitivity to beauty. Yet again
and again there are also glimpses of grace, transcendence, beauty,
delight, love, generosity, laughter, compassion and wisdom –

'Lough Derg'
A wisdom astonished at every turn
By some angel that writes in the oddest words.

[196] personal communication

Say but the Word

The God's-eye perspective of the poet is above all shot through with mercy and compassion for everyone, however unsympathetic or insignificant, yet without a hint of sentimentality or religious romanticism. It is backed up by an explicit theology of the ultimacy of love – in a vivid vignette bringing the first century into the twentieth, St Paul is identified riding his ass down a Donegal lane, and the gospel is fireside conversation:

Christ was lately dead,   'Lough Derg'
Men were afraid
With a new fear, the fear
Of love. There was a laugh freed
For ever and ever.

This is connected to a sense of providence –

Only God thinks of the dying sparrow   'Lough Derg'
In the middle of a war.

– and of each person as a child of God. This is a God who finds 'a peasant's emotional problem' significant alongside Second World War battles, and writes common people into the unwritten spaces between the lines of major events.

Kavanagh's 'God's-ear' standpoint listening to the prayers of the pilgrims …

In a tour de force of theological poetics he turns the ordinary, mostly self-preoccupied, prayers into a string of beautifully crafted sonnets. Then he sums up the theological wisdom of what he has done:

This was the banal   'Lough Derg'
Beggary that God heard. Was he bored
As men are with the poor? Christ Lord
Hears in the voices of the meanly poor
Homeric utterances, poetry sweeping through.

This is the wisdom he has just performed through sonnets. It simultaneously offers a vision of who God is and radically

challenges the way we see and hear our fellow human beings, but
does so without weighing us down with guilt – rather, we are given
a merciful revelation of who they and we really are in the sight and
hearing of God.'

It seems to me that this description of Ford's catches beautifully the
essence of what is for me Patrick Kavanagh's poetic vision at its most
incarnate, compassionate and prophetic. We are indeed dealing with a
poet whose insight in the light of the past prepares his times to move
on. In a real sense Kavanagh is both poet and prophet.

Conclusion

This is where I should sum up what I've said. But instead I want to read
a poem 'Conversation with Patrick Kavanagh', which echoes and
extends 'Lodestar', a poem I published in a collection call *Globe*.[197]
Appropriately, they[198] are four sonnets, a form so beloved of Kavanagh.
I speak first then Patrick Kavanagh answers. My voice comes again and
Patrick Kavanagh replies:

'Conversation
with Patrick
Kavanagh'

But Kavanagh, anarchic and thin-skinned,
Did you rely on love's own i.o.u.,
A kamikaze trusting in God's wind
To blow each mood and counter-mood in you?
Capricious prophet, your hand-biting gene
Keeps on undoing any debt that binds;
Ezekiel has come from Inniskeen
Demanding God surprise angst-ridden minds.
Such troubled years before the bright stick trapped,
The couple-kissing seat's third party breeze
When you in your new woven world enrapt
Re-trust the bluebell angel glanced through trees.
In hungry times, you pay the prophet's price,
A peeping Tom who lusts for paradise.

It's Kavanagh's comeback now, my friends,
After angst and satire's letting-fly;
My trade I'd learned absorbing all the trends,

---

[197] Micheal O'Siadhail, *Globe,* Bloodaxe Books, Tarset, 2007
[198] p64, *Studies*, volume 102, number 405

Yet had the bluebell angel bid good-bye?
But sit and watch a nesting water hen
And heal here sinless on canal bank seats;
Let Jordan's waters wash your soul again.
Reborn I choose the bebop ease of Beats.
Ambition's bells are always false alarms.
No-caring jag. The jazz of unconcern.
Abandon now all thoughts of poetry biz
And stomp once more in Kitty Stobling's arms;
Like Ibsen's Terje Vigen we return
To praise the way it was, the way it is.

Our green and peasant poet, forlorn Maguire –
So many might-have-beens your spirit fled –
The sour-tongued satirist's unholy fire,
Each sponged up role is first espoused, then shed.
You search like any probing self-taught man
And tunnel every modern mood in turn
To find again the light where you began;
So much unlearned we need once more to learn.
Some kink, a cussedness in you transcends
Each dark impasse, a third eye seeing through
To open up to daylight our dead-ends,
Reshaping older things we thought we knew.
My scathing prophet dares a scapegoat fate;
In wounded light the bluebell angels wait.

So folks, let's leap into the blinding light.
Picasso, Kafka, W.B. et al
Too dour or mad, don't dare the giddy flight
Where angels bless what's ancient and banal.
My theme anonymous Lough Dergs of need,
The girl who's won a lover, girl with none,
Half-saints or souls as black as bluebell seed.
Was justice God until he saw his son?
I'll take this faithful father at his word,
Who means to show me still no matter what,
The fabulous and commonplace unfurled
Into the light of love's audacious plot,
Of death and wake-up to the dancing bird
And laughter loosed across a broken world.

Say but the Word

For any poet in our time Rainer Maria Rilke and William Butler Yeats are two towering figures in early twentieth century poetry. Bringing together in one essay two poets of such eminence and so wide-ranging a body of work, not to mention the criticism and commentary, is an almost impossible task.

A measure of their stature is how the next generation of poets needed to relate to them. Wystan Hugh Auden, another triple name, who was born 27 years after Rilke and 37 after Yeats, revered them and wrote for both what might have been their epitaphs. In 1938, Auden celebrated the hurricane of inspiration which Rilke had experienced during the year 1922 while living in Chateau de Muzot,[199] near Sierre in Switzerland:

'Sonnets from China XIX'

Tonight in China let me think of one

Who for ten years of drought and silence waited,
Until in Muzot all his being spoke,
And everything was given once for all.

Awed grateful, tired, content to die, completed,
He went out in the winter night to stroke
That tower as one pets an animal.

Even better known is Auden's three part[200] 'In Memory of W. B. Yeats':

'In Memory of W. B. Yeats III'

Earth, receive an honoured guest:
William Yeats is laid to rest.
Let the Irish vessel lie
Emptied of its poetry.

In the nightmare of the dark
All the dogs of Europe bark,
And the living nations wait,
Each sequestered in its hate;

[199] p194, W. H. Auden, *Collected Poems*, ed. Edward Mendelson, Faber & Faber, London, 1976
[200] p248, W. H. Auden, *Collected Poems*, ed. Edward Mendelson, Faber & Faber, London, 1976

Intellectual disgrace
Stares from every human face,
And the seas of pity lie
Locked and frozen in each eye.

Perhaps, the first four lines quoted could have been Rilke's epitaph and
the first eight quoted might well have been Yeats's. Auden's unerring
instinct catches the hermit in Rilke. He also proclaims, to use the title of
the second volume of Foster's massive biography, the arch-poet in Yeats.
In fact both Rilke and Yeats chose their own brief epitaphs, something I
will return to later.

There are such strange and fascinating parallels in their poetry and in
their lives, it is at least worth an attempt to look at them together. Both
are absolute formalists and at the same time, particularly in their later
work, both are extremely 'modern' in the way they juxtapose associations,
images and ideas. Indeed both enjoy a friendship with primary exponents
of various oblique approaches: Yeats with the pre-eminent Modernist
Ezra Pound (1885–1972) and Rilke with the Symbolist Paul Valérie
(1871–1945). They both were, at various points in their lives, involved
in theatre. While there are amazing coincidences, there are also the
deepest and most fundamental differences. Before exploring what utterly
distinguishes these two poets from each other, I will try to survey some
of what they have in common, though even the briefest description of
these features will inevitably adumbrate the basic differences between
them. Clearly, common lists of chance similarities are potentially endless.

Both Yeats and Rilke were born in what were provincial cities with
empires: Dublin and Prague; the one into a minority Protestant
community in a largely Catholic country, the other into a German
speaking minority in a Slavic city. Both wrote what is regarded as their
greatest work during the opening decades of the twentieth century. This
was a time when historical events fundamentally changed our cultural
landscape. In 1900, Sigmund Freud's *Traumdeutung* (*The Interpretation of
Dreams*) opened up the vast realms of the subconscious, questioning many
of our take-for-granted assumptions concerning ourselves and our
motives. In 1905 Albert Einstein's Theory of Relativity altered our whole
perception of the relationship between time and space and indeed
causality. The First World War threatened to tear asunder the fabric of
European society. In painting, the first fifteen years of the new century
brought Fauves, Cubist and Expressionists. In 1915 T. S. Eliot published

Say but the Word

'The Love Song of J. Alfred Prufrock' and in 1922 'The Waste Land'. Franz Kafka brought out *Der Prozeß* (The Trial) in 1925 and *Das Schloß* (The Castle) in 1926. James Joyce had begun *Ulysses* in 1914. Clearly, the previously accepted universal axioms and absolutes were shaken and the cultural sphere was in turmoil. It is against this backdrop that both Yeats and Rilke as poets approached the world.

Vocations, Artistic Colonies and Towers

Yeats and Rilke both had an extraordinarily strong sense of their vocation as poets. Both were writing poems during their school years. By age nineteen Yeats, deciding not to follow his father to Trinity College Dublin, was already setting out to be a poet. Rilke, on the other hand, unlike Yeats who had spent three and a half years at the Erasmus Smith High School where he had declined to take examinations, was sent to a military school and at sixteen to attend briefly a business school in Graz. At twenty-one he went to study art history in Munich. From there on he entered into the life of a poet. So seriously did Rilke take his calling that he always referred to his *Auftrag,* which echoes the German phrase *im Auftrag* 'commissioned'. For Rilke the mainspring of his existence was the interplay between ordinary life and turning the daily into poetry.

Another formative experience for both were the times they spent in artistic colonies. Yeats had lived as a boy with his family for a time in the Bedford Park artist colony in England designed by Norman Shaw. Although he had romantic longings for his grandparents' Sligo, it seems to have stamped his imagination. Rilke lived for a time in an artist colony in the village of Worpswede, near Bremen. His inseparable companions here were the painter Paula Becker and the sculptor Clara Westhoff. When Paula suddenly married another painter, almost on the rebound, Rilke married Clara.

In calling these two poets 'towering figures', I am playing on the amusing coincidence that both Yeats and Rilke reached the apogee of their work, while living in towers. For Yeats it was the tower at Ballylee, which provided the title for one of his most powerful collections[201] *The Tower* (1928):

'The Tower' I pace upon the battlements and stare
On the foundations of a house, or where

---

[201] p219, *Collected Poems of W. B. Yeats*, Macmillan, London, 1965

Tree, like a sooty finger, starts from the earth;
And send imagination forth
Under the day's declining beam, and call
Images and memories
From ruin or from ancient trees,
For I would ask a question of them all.

Yeats had purchased this tower and restored it. An American reading tour
had paid for the roof. Already he was writing 'I declare this tower my
symbol' and bringing Joyce, Shelley and Milton to bear as resonances.
'This winding, gyring, spiring treadmill of a stair' would also become
consciously laden with historical symbolism and significance and provide
the title for another weighty collection *The Winding Stair and Other Poems*
(1933).

    In 1922 Rilke was given the castle tower at the Château de Muzot, near
Sierre, in the canton of Valais, Switzerland by a patron Werner Reinhart,
who also provided the money to repair it. Reinhart generously offered it
to him for as long as he wished and Rilke lived out his last four years there.
It was in this tower that he finished the *Duineser Elegien* (The Duino
Elegies) which he had begun in another castle on the cliffs of Duino ten
years earlier. Here also, in an incredible explosion of energy, he wrote his
Sonette an Orpheus (Sonnets to Orpheus) – fifty-five sonnets in memory
of Ouckama Knoop the young dancer, who died of leukaemia aged
nineteen. The two sequences deal with suffering and death, with our
human relationship to the world and the infinite and, maybe above all,
with praise.[202]

Nicht sind die Leiden erkannt,
nicht ist die Liebe gelernt,
und was im Tod uns entfernt,

ist nicht entschleiert
Einzig das Lied überm Land
heiligt und feiert.

'Sonette I xix
SW 743'

---

[202] Rainer Maria Rilke, *Sonnets to Orpheus* with *Letters to a Young Poet,* translated by Stephen Cohn,
Carcanet, Manchester, 2000

Say but the Word

translation by
Stephen Cohn

Love yet remains unlearned;
hardship prevails unseen;
still veiled, still unrevealed

how Death shall take us
Song alone through the land
sanctifies, praises.

The Absent Lover

Here we come to yet another of the strange resemblances between Yeats
and Rilke. They shared a belief in the absent lover, both in theory and
in practice. They also had in common a marvellous gift for keeping
former lovers as friends, confidantes and correspondents.

Yeats had a number of lovers including Olivia Shakespeare and
Florence Farr but the shadow of Maud Gonne came between them.
Even after his marriage to Georgiana Hyde-Lees (with Ezra Pound as
best man) in 1917, when he was fifty-two, that shadow remained in
place.

Yeats had met Maud Gonne in his father's house in London in 1889
and fell irrevocably in love. Despite a half dozen or so proposals over
twenty years, she never yielded to him. He cajoled, mythologized her,
was reproved by her, but she always remained for him Pallas Athene.
His long and complex relationship with Maud Gonne has left many
traces in his work. One of the best known is the stanza that concludes
the second part[203] of *The Tower*:

'The Tower' Does the imagination dwell the most
Upon a woman won or woman lost?
If on the lost, admit you turned aside,
From a great labyrinth out of pride,
Cowardice, some silly over-subtle thought
Or anything called conscience once;
And that if memory recur, the sun's
Under eclipse and the day blotted out.

Rilke found beautiful strong women irresistible, as indeed they seemed
to find him. The most outstanding relationship for him was with Lou

[203] p222, *Collected Poems of W. B. Yeats*, Macmillan, London, 1965

Say but the Word

Andreas-Salomé (1861–1927), a novelist of Russian and Huguenot extraction. She was fourteen years older than Rilke, had been pursued by Nietzsche and had also been a pupil of Freud. She became Rilke's mistress, launched him in Munich society and introduced him to the Russian language and to Russia. When she tired of him, he went back to Worpswede, where he married Clara. They had a daughter, Ruth, and a year later Rilke left. He persuaded Clara that they should live apart. Clara's mother looked after the child. There followed a long line of lovers, among them wealthy patronesses, the wife of his publisher, pianists and a poet. The pattern was always the same; as soon as claims were made on him[204] that threatened his *Auftrag*, he withdrew, though often remaining friends.

Liebende, wäre nicht der andre der
die Sicht verstellt, sind nah daran und staunen ...
Wie aus Versehn ist ihnen aufgetan
hinter dem andern ... Aber über ihn
kommt keiner fort, und wieder wird ihm Welt.

'Die Achte Elegie'

Lovers – were not the others present, always
Blocking the view! – draw near to it and wonder ...
Behind the other, as though through oversight
The thing's revealed ... But no one gets beyond the other
And so the world returns once more.

Fathers and Father Figures

Yeats and Rilke both had fathers whom they deeply respected but took their distance from. Yeats's father, John B. Yeats, the lawyer turned painter, was perpetually improvident, largely unable to complete any work and anxious to ensure that his son did not conform. His mother was a country person, daughter of the well-heeled Sligo merchant family, the Pollexfens and was alien to her husband's urban, artistic and intellectual life.

The father figure for Yeats would be John O'Leary. He had met him with his own father in his late teens at the Contemporary Club, where O'Leary was the leading light. He was a Tipperary man, who, while a law student at Trinity College Dublin, had been part of a plot to rescue

---

[204] p658, *Rainer Maria Rilke Die Gedichte*, Insel Verlag, Frankfurt am Main, 1957, 1986, 1995

leaders of the 1848 rising from Clonmel Jail. After an imprisonment, he studied medicine in Cork before moving to Paris, where he lived with the American painter John MacNeill Whistler. As financial agent for the Irish Republican Brotherhood, O'Leary regularly travelled between London, New York and Dublin. Later he served nine years in an English prison and then returned to Dublin with his wife, the poet Eileen O'Leary.

O'Leary had everything to intrigue the young Yeats. He was Catholic and of native Irish stock. He became for Yeats the symbol of Irish patriotism and much later said of him and the Contemporary Club 'from these debates, from O'Leary's conversation, and from the Irish books he lent or gave me has come all that I set my hand to since'. O'Leary features in the refrain[205] of 'September 1913':

'September 1913' Romantic Ireland's dead and gone,
It's with O'Leary in the grave.

And again in Yeats's final pantheon[206] in 'Beautiful Lofty Things':

'Beautiful Lofty Things' Beautiful lofty things: O'Leary's noble head;

Rilke's father had started out on a military career but due to ill health ended up a disgruntled and disciplinarian railway clerk in the Austro-Hungarian Empire. Like Oscar Wilde, Rilke was initially raised as the girl his mother must have wanted. His parents separated when he was nine, two years before he was sent to military school. The important father figure for Rilke became the sculptor Auguste Rodin (1840–1917).

In 1902, his family in Prague stopped his allowance. Rilke persuaded Clara that they should not live together when they moved to Paris. He was commissioned to write a book on Rodin and she was to study under the master. He spent many hours studying his sculptures and visited Rodin at Meudon. The concept of deep observation, *Schauen* as Rilke called it, grew and grew. He tried in his poetry to achieve the tactile quality, the shape and life of things. Rodin represented the artist *par excellence* and Rilke's own sense of dedication was confirmed by Rodin's 'il faut toujours travailler' (one must always be at work). It was a

[205] p121, *Collected Poems of W. B. Yeats*, Macmillan, London, 1965
[206] p348, *Collected Poems of W. B. Yeats*, Macmillan, London, 1965

Say but the Word

relationship between two men of a different generation and it was not always easy. In 1903, Rilke's book was completed and he acted as a secretary to Rodin until dismissed by him in 1906.

The other figure, though in a much less personal way, was Paul Cézanne (1839–1906). Rilke was overwhelmed by the unsentimental realism of his work, which he first saw at the 1907 *Salon d'Automne*. The extraordinary daily consistent work of Cézanne over the last thirty years of his life appealed to him. Indeed such was Cézanne's dedication that he was unwilling to attend his mother's funeral because he felt compelled to continue work on a painting in which he was absorbed. *La réalisation* ... that which convinces and materialises, the reality that is based on his own experience with his subject and which has been intensified to indestructability, that is what seems to be the goal of his most serious work. That, in so many ways, was a manifesto for the poet's own life's work.

Religion

Both Yeats and Rilke reacted against their respective religious backgrounds. Yeats rejected both the sceptical views of his father, which he had based on his early reading of Charles Darwin and John Mills, and the Protestantism of his mother. The escape route from the choice between the 'grey truth' of his father's scientific rationalism and the Pollexfen low church Protestantism was curious and I cannot help wondering whether it was ultimately a deeply nourishing option. From his first reading of *Esoteric Buddhism* by A. P. Sinnett, through his various stages of Theosophy, Cabbalism and magic, Yeats chose this 'mystical way'. 'I am very religious', he wrote, 'and deprived by Huxley and Tyndall, whom I detested, of the simple-minded religion of my childhood, I had made a new religion, almost an infallible Church of poetic tradition, of a fardel of stories, and of personages, and of emotions, inseparable from their first expression, passed on from generation to generation by poets and painters with some help from philosophers and theologians'. This does indeed sound like a peculiar cocktail.

In London in 1887 he was part of Madam Blavatsky's circle, though seemingly expelled for his emphasis on magic. His biggest influence here was the practicing magician MacGregor Mathers, who had published *The Kabbalah Unveiled* in 1887. In 1890 to 1990, Yeats was involved with The Rosicrucian Society's Order of the Golden Dawn.

This was to influence his poetry and his life for the rest of his days. When he married Georgiana, he was further encouraged in his occultism by her talent for automatic writing. In the eighth part of 'Vacillation', from *The Winding Stair and Other Poems* he gives his last word[207] on his Christian background:

'Vacillation VIII'

Did I become a Christian man and choose for my belief
What seems most welcome in the tomb — play a pre-destined part.
Homer is my example and his unchristened heart.

Rilke, was brought up by his mother as a Catholic. She was apparently very pious and avidly undertook pilgrimages. Rilke put aside all this and renounced Christianity from an early age. However, he had undoubtedly a religious cast of mind and in all of his work there are many different modes in which he names a deity, including the God of the Russian peasants, Buddha, Apollo, The Angels of his Duino Elegies, and, of course, Orpheus. He was not in any way a systematic thinker and had no pretension to be one, though he had written an early essay on Nietzsche and was a close friend of the philosopher Rudolf Kassner (1873–1959). All his life he seems deeply conscious of a yearning for the divine. That longing and sense of a presence is so beautifully caught[208] in 'Liebes Lied' (Love Song) from *Neue Gedichte* (1906):

'Liebes-Lied SW 482 Z.8-13'

Doch alles, was uns anrührt, dich und mich,
nimmt uns zusammen wie ein Bogenstrich,
der aus zwei Saiten *eine* Stimme zieht.
Auf welches Instrument sind wir gespannt?
Und welcher Geiger hat uns in der Hand?
O süßes Lied.

'Love Song'

But everything that touches us you and me
Takes us together like one stroke of the bow
Which draws one voice out of two strings.
On what instrument are we stretched?
And what fiddler has us in his hands?
O sweet melody!

---

[207] p285, *Collected Poems of W. B. Yeats*, Macmillan, London, 1965
[208] p299, *The Penguin Book of German Verse*, introduced and edited by Leonard Forster, Harmondsworth, 1957, 1959.

Say but the Word

Yet for all the similarities, the differences are more profound. Just as any list of likeness could be endless, so too is any list of what distinguishes these two poets. Conscious of the risk of superficiality and of not doing justice to the complexities of their lives, I turn now to some of these differences.

Place and Nowhere

One of the standard ways in which Yeats and Rilke are contrasted is their different locations. The Yeats family, always short of money and perpetually unsettled, moved from place to place. His childhood summers in Sligo allowed him to mythologise that part of Ireland. I suspect that his thematic relation to place is founded in some reaction to the disconcerting effects of the constant upheaval in his childhood. Accompanying a meditation on beauty and Maud Gonne, his wish[209] for his daughter is:

May she become a flourishing hidden tree ...

'A Prayer For My Daughter'

O may she live like some green laurel
Rooted in one dear perpetual place.

Rilke, it is often said, epitomizes the up-rootedness of the modern person. He spoke six languages and quite a lot of his work, including some of his later poetry, was in French. He was at home in German-speaking countries, in Russia, in France and in Scandinavia. While always searching for solitude, he also wandered ceaselessly and travelled almost obsessively, particularly from the age of twenty-eight to thirty-nine (1903–1914). It was only during the last six years of his life that he found peace in the Rhône Valley in Switzerland. Even then, his work was in no real sense concerned with place.

  While this common citing of place is both true and interesting, it is not as basic as other distinctive features.

Difference of Tone

Yeats is the absolute master of the sonorous line that drums into our memory. No poet, in any language that I know, can compare with him for this reverberating tone that he had right from very early on. It's not

---

[209] p213, *Collected Poems of W. B. Yeats*, Macmillan, London, 1965

the playful sparkling memorable Shakespearean phrase but rather self-conscious weighty utterances that echo an inner grandeur. Such is their quality that many are familiar and have a currency as stock quotations:

'The Lake Isle
of Innisfree'

I will arise and go now, and go to Innisfree,
And a small cabin build there, of clay and wattles made:

'He Wishes For
The Clothes
Of Heaven'

I have spread my dreams under your feet;
Tread softly because you tread on my dreams.

'September
1913'

But fumble in a greasy till
And add the halfpence to the pence ...

Romantic Ireland's dead and gone,
It's with O'Leary in the grave.

'Easter 1916'

All changed, changed utterly:
A terrible beauty is born. ...

Too long a sacrifice
Can make a stone of the heart.

'Among School
Children'

O chestnut-tree, great-rooted blossomer,
Are you the leaf, the blossom or the bole?
O body swayed to music, O brightening glance,
How can we know the dancer from the dance?

'The Municipal
Gallery
Revisited'

Think where man's glory most begins and ends,
And say my glory was I had such friends.

'The Man And
The Echo'

I lie awake night after night
And never get the answers right.
Did that play of mine send out
Certain men the English shot?

More and more of these majestic lines loom in the mind. Little wonder a recent study of Yeats's 'technical and aural achievements' by Brian Devine is entitled *Yeats, the Master of Sound.* Tellingly, among his wishes for his daughter is:

Say but the Word

That all her thoughts may like the linnet be,
And have no business but dispensing round
Their magnanimities of sound,

'A Prayer For my Daughter'

Yeats's consummate skill turns what is essentially poetry of argument and rhetoric into these magical lofty and unforgettable lines. It was from the debates in the Contemporary Society came 'all that I have set my mind to since'. He said that out of the struggle with others came rhetoric, out of the struggle with ourselves came poetry. Yeats's grave tone is always that of the grand man pacing the battlements.

Rilke's tone is utterly different. There is a lovely and mysterious timbre I find so hard to word. The poems are for me even more memorable than those of Yeats. The pitch of intensity is achieved not along the battlements of argument but rather by the firm, suggestive yet gentle tone of a friend who insists we never lose sight of ultimate meaning. In 1924, he wrote these lines[210] for his Polish translator Witold Hulewicz:

Glücklich, die wissen, daß hinter allen
Sprachen das Unsägliche steht;

'Fur Witold Hulewicz SW II 259'

Happy those who know that behind all
languages the unsayable stands.

His language has a blend of lightness and seriousness. It is beautiful and intricate. But rather than try to express the inexpressible, just an example first from an early collection[211] *Das Buch der Bilder* (The Book of Images):

Die Blätter fallen, fallen wie von weit,
als welkten in den Himmeln ferne Gärten;
sie fallen mit verneinender Gebärde.

'Herbst SW I 400'

Und in den Nächten fällt die schwere Erde
aus allen Sternen in die Einsamkeit.

Wir alle fallen. Diese Hand da fällt
Und sieh dir andre an: es ist in allen.

[210] p1045, *Rainer Maria Rilke Die Gedichte*, Insel Verlag, Frankfurt am Main, 1986
[211] p346, *Rainer Maria Rilke Die Gedichte*, Insel Verlag, Frankfurt am Main, 1986

Und doch ist Einer, welcher dieses Fallen
unendlich sanft in seinen Händen hält.

'Autumn'
translated by
J. B. Leishman
and Stephen
Spender
The leaves are falling, falling as from far,
as though above were withering farthest gardens;
they fall with a denying attitude.

And night by night down into solitude,
The heavy earth falls far from every star.

We are falling. This hand's falling too –
all have this falling-sickness none withstands.

And yet there's One whose gentle-holding hands
This universal falling can't fall through.

Then, one[212] of the final *Sonnets to Orpheus*.

'Sonnette an
Orpheus
Zwieter Teil
XXV'
Schon, horch, hörst du der ersten Harken
Arbeit; wieder den menschlichen Takt
in der verhaltenen Stille der starken
Vorfrühlingserde. Unabgeschmackt

scheint dir das Kommende. Jenes so oft
dir schon Gekommene scheint dir zu kommen
wieder wie Neues. Immer erhofft,
nahmst du es niemals. Es hat dich genommen.

Selbst die Blätter durchwinterter Eichen
scheinen im Abend ein künftiges Braun.
Manchmal geben sich Lüfte ein Zeichen.

Schwarz sind die Sträucher. Doch Haufen von Dünger
lagern als satteres Schwarz in den Aun.
Jede Stunde, die hingeht, wird jünger.

---

[212] p711, *Rainer Maria Rilke Die Gedichte*, Insel Verlag, Frankfurt am Main, 1986

Say but the Word

Listen: can you hear the first of the harrows
working? Again, men's rhythms are heard
in an Earth still retentive, all silent, whose energies
wait for the spring. Nothing seems tired,

you can sense what is coming: every thing
so often experienced as if now made new.
You could not possess what, in spite of the waiting,
for all your eagerness, now possessed *you*.

Even the leaves of the oaks overwintered
at evening light take tints of the future.
Sometimes one breeze send another sign.

Dark are the hedgerows. Mountains of dung
darker than the darkness brood over the pasture.
Every hour that passes grows ever more young.

'Sonnets to Orpheus Part Two XXV' translated by Stephen Cohn[213]

The delicacies of language and the interweaving of content and form makes Rilke notoriously difficult to translate. Many have translated poems to English over the years, including several poets such as Elizabeth Barrett Browning, Stephen Spender, Randall Jarrell and Robert Bly. Like translations of Dante, broadly they divide into those who attempt to capture content, form and spirit of a poem in translation and those who give precedence to the content and general spirit of the poem at the expense of abandoning the strict formal schemes of his work. The above two poems illustrate both. In 'Autumn', for instance *Gebärde* in the third line of the first stanza is rendered as 'attitude' rather than 'gesture' or 'gesticulation' and gives the rhyme with 'solitude'. By such slight loss of accuracy the magic sense of Rilke's form is echoed. There is no one solution to this crux for translators.

Fantasist and Realist

The most significant distinction between Yeats and Rilke is their approach to the world at large. In so many ways Yeats is not a realist, while it seems to me that Rilke was deeply realistic. Many of the other differences between their work flow from this underlying difference.

[213] p117, *Rainer Maria Rilke: Sonnets to Orpheus* translated by Stephen Cohn, Carcanet, Manchester, 2000

I have already mentioned Yeats's lifelong preoccupation with Maud Gonne, 'the lover lost'. I do not wish to diminish some of his tremendous love poetry but much of it, through all its varied moods, has an unreal air.

The best word I can come up with for a non-realist is a fantasist. For all the outstanding gifts of the great master of sound, he remains at heart an escape artist, a lover of might-have-beens, of imagined grandeurs, of vast theories and myths. It is not hard to understand how Patrick Kavanagh, who came out of the core of rural Ireland and who must have suffered in the shade of the great man, spoke about the 'Celtic Twilight as made up and patented by Yeats and Lady Gregory'.

Some questions must be asked about his stance on rural Ireland. Certainly, his attachment to Sligo as an antidote to his roaming unsettled childhood as the son of a broke portrait painter is understandable. Nevertheless, there is quite a deal of romantic fantasy, particularly in his early work. Even, a fairly early poem[214] such as 'The Fiddler of Dooney' in spite of the lovely quatrain:

'The Fiddler of Dooney'
For the good are always the merry,
Save by an evil chance,
And the merry love the fiddle,
And the merry love to dance:

rather peters out into:

And when the folk there spy me,
They will all come up to me,
With 'Here is the fiddler of Dooney!'
And dance like a wave of the sea.

However, as the common Irish aspired to middleclassery, Yeats was less enamoured of the 'folk'. Always, a shrewd careerist, apart[215] from being accounted

'To Ireland in the Coming Times'
True brother of a company
That sang, to sweeten Ireland's wrong,
Ballad and story, rann and song;

[214] p82, *Collected Poems of W. B. Yeats*, Macmillan, London, 1950
[215] p56, *Collected Poems of W. B. Yeats*, Macmillan, London, 1950

He was also busy from early on in essays and articles appropriating what was known[216] as the Anglo-Irish tradition:

Nor may I less be counted one
With Davis, Mangan, Ferguson,

As time passed he was at pains to mythologise a colonial class of 'old fathers' to which he affected to belong and to move towards his views on eugenics[217] and the indomitable Irishry:

Merchant and scholar who have left me blood
That has not passed through any huckster's loin,
Soldiers that gave, whatever die was cast:
A Butler or an Armstrong that withstood
Beside the brackish waters of the Boyne
James and his Irish when the Dutchman crossed;

'Introductory rhymes', *Responsibilities*

The images of 'Urbino's windy hill' or Byzantium in the poem of that name or in the amazing poem with line after haunting line 'Sailing to Byzantium', are another flight from reality[218] to some idealised perfection:

Nor is there singing school but studying
Monuments of its own magnificence;
And therefore I have sailed the seas and come
To the holy city of Byzantium.

'Sailing to Byzantium'

Yet another facet of Yeats the fantasist is, of course, his fascination with the occult and his sweeping theory of the gyres. The latter, with its escape into the *longue durée*, has the feel of Ferdinand Braudel and the Annalist school. It absolves from the responsibility of action when he paces the battlements as:

Turning and turning in the widening gyre
The falcon cannot hear the falconer;
Things fall apart; the centre cannot hold;
Mere anarchy is loosed upon the world ...

'The Second Coming'

---

[216] p57, *Collected Poems of W. B. Yeats*, Macmillan, London, 1950
[217] p113, *Collected Poems of W. B. Yeats*, Macmillan, London, 1950
[218] p217, *Collected Poems of W. B. Yeats*, Macmillan, London, 1950

Rilke, on the other hand, is a realist. This may at first sound somewhat surprising as he is often thought of as simply ethereal and difficult in comparison with Yeats, who, initially at least, seems more involved and down to earth. Early in his life as a poet, Rilke had a very large readership and gained an almost saintly reputation, despite the unconscionable treatment of his wife and daughter; however, it must be said that though he could not both follow his life's *Auftrag* and live together with them, he remained involved with them all his life.

His perceived disinterest in social matters provoked the opprobrium of Bertolt Brecht (1898–1956) and his circle. It seems that Rilke's executors, censoring some material, promoted an otherworldly image of the poet. With time a more rounded human picture of Rilke emerges, not as the angel-haunted mystic but as a complicated human who during periods of his life was indeed socially concerned.

There is in his work an extraordinary realism. This he learned from the realism of both Rodin and Cézanne and more and more he wanted to achieve *Anschauen*, the ability to really see. Auden caught this side[219] of Rilke:

'New Year's Letter'
And Rilke whom *die Dinge* bless,
The Santa Claus of loneliness.

Auden alludes here to another concept of significance to Rilke *Dinggedichte*. These were poems, which are the result of an intensive observation by the poet of a person or object. The aim was to gain a strong sense[220] of objectivity:

'Der Blinde'
Sieh, er geht und unterbricht die Stadt
die nicht ist auf seiner dunkeln Stelle,
wie ein dunkler Sprung durch eine helle
Tasse geht. Und wie auf einem Blatt

ist auf ihm der Widerschein der Dinge
aufgemalt; er nimmt ihn nicht hinein.
Nur sein Fühlen rührt sich, so als finge
es die Welt in kleinen Wellen ein:

---

[219] p204, *W. H. Auden Collected Poems*, ed. Edward Mendelson, Faber & Faber, London, 1991
[220] p536, *Rainer Maria Rilke Die Gedichte*, Insel, Frankfurt am Main, 1995

Say but the Word

eine Stille, einen Widerstand –,
und dann scheint er wartend wen zu wählen;
hingegeben hebt er seine Hand,
festlich fast, wie um sich zu vermählen.

Watch how he goes, proceeding through the city
(which does not reach his darkness there within),
leaving a dark trace like a crack in porcelain.
Reflected on his surfaces you see

an image of all things, reversed, in negative,
which touches him no deeper than his skin.
And yet sensation stirs in him, as if
the World sent little waves which he takes in:

a stillness, a resistance of some kind.
Whom shall he choose? He pauses to decide
then makes a courtly gesture with his hand –
as one might wave in greeting to his bride.

'The Blind
Man'
translated by
Stephen Cohn

This is realism with all its levels and nuances. However, realism here does not mean just melancholy or a dismal view of things. Realism is a full acceptance of life with all that goes with it, of joy, regret, celebration, grief, delight and death. Rilke took his *Auftrag*, or what I would call his 'ministry of meaning' to heart. This is an invitation to gaze through him at the suspended moment in all its complex glory.

There is here a stern ascetic vision of a man who, gregarious and beholden to patrons, sought out solitude in order to fulfil what he saw as his destiny to find meaning for a world, to be an illuminating go-between. We are invited to share the intimacy[221] of his vision:

Wie er, so
würbest du wohl, nicht minder –, daß, noch unsichtbar,
dich die Freundin erführ, die stille, in der eine Antwort
langsam erwacht und über dem Hören sich anwärmt, –
deinem erkühnten Gefühl die erglühte Gefühlin.

'Die Siebente
Elegie'

---

[221] p653, *Rainer Maria Rilke Die Gedichte*, Insel, Frankfurt am Main, 1995

'The Seventh
Elegy'
translated by
David
Young[222]
Like him you want
         to call forth a still
                  invisible mate
a silent listener
         in whom a reply
                  slowly wakens
warming itself
         by hearing yours
                  to become
your own
         bold feeling's
                  blazing partner.

Between Two Eternities

Though he was seventy-four when he died, Yeats did not grow old with
any real serenity, contentment or wisdom. Like the figure of the black
clad deaconess in Ibsen's *When We Dead Awaken*, Plato's ghost
continued[223] to sing 'What then?':

'What then?'
'The work is done,' grown old he thought,
'According to my boyish plan;
Let the fools rage, I swerved in naught,
Something to perfection brought';
 But louder sang that ghost, 'What then?'

'Are You
Contented?'
Have I, that put it into words,
Spoilt what old loins have sent?
Eyes spiritualised by death can judge,
I cannot, but I am not content.

The obsession with eugenics seems to grow, fuelled by his fantasy of
himself as an Anglo-Irish aristocrat who somehow embodied glories[224]
of ancient Ireland:

'Under Ben
Bulben'
Many times man lives and dies
Between his two eternities,

[222] p123, *Rainer Maria Rilke: Duino Elegies* translated by David Young, W. W. Norton, New York,
       1978, 2006
[223] p347 & p370, *Collected Poems of W. B. Yeats*, Macmillan, London, 1950
[224] p398, *Collected Poems of W. B. Yeats*, Macmillan, London, 1950

That of race and that of soul,
And ancient Ireland knew it all,

He declared that the 'stupider and less healthy' should have their families limited: 'I may be, or it must be, that the best bred from the best shall claim again their ancient omens.' He spoke of the uneducatable masses. And he was flirting with violence:

You that Mitchel's prayer have heard   'Under Ben
'Send war in our time, O Lord!'   Bulben'

Yeats had lost nothing of his sense of superiority. According to Roy Foster's biography, the arch-poet told Dorothy Wellesley that 'a description of my own grave and monument in a remote Irish village ... it will bind my heirs, thank God. I write my poems for the Irish people but I'm damned if I'll have them at my funeral.'

   Rilke died at the age of fifty-one. After a silence of twelve years, at Muzot in 1922 four years before his death, he finished *Duineser Elegien* (*The Duino Elegies*) and the extraordinary *Die Sonette an Orpheus* (*Sonnets to Orpheus*). Though suffering is a pivotal theme, there is nothing lugubrious or morbid. In suffering we discover the wholeness of joy as well as grief. From the famous cry[225] to the angels in the first elegy –

Wer, wenn ich schriee, hörte mich denn aus der Engel   'Die Erste
Ordnungen?   Elegie'

Who, if I cried, would hear me among the angelic   'The First
orders?   Elegy'

– through the following five elegies, in the footsteps of Friedrich Hölderlin (1770–1843) a long established Christian tradition of spiritual apprenticeship progresses from the sense of alienation at the loss of Eden to a knowledge and self-awareness and an acceptance of the interconnectedness of life and death. There is a series of images of puppets, gnats, children, animals, heroes, lovers and poets which suggest the movement towards the angelic consciousness.

[225] p629, *Rainer Maria Rilke Die Gedichte*, Insel, Frankfurt am Main, 1995

The marvellous turning point comes in the seventh elegy. Here Rilke gives up his personal pursuit of angels and transcendence. No cry or any escape from reality will do. He faces the world, the being here, *Hiersein*. His work, his ministry of meaning is to transform[226] the world of men.

'Die Siebente Elegie'

War es nicht Wunder? O staune, Engel, denn *wir* sinds
wir, o du Großer, erzähls, daß wir solches vermochten, mein Atem
reicht für die Rühmung nicht aus.

'The Seventh Elegie' translated by J. B. Leishman

Was it not a miracle? Angel, gaze, for it's we –
O mightiness, tell them that we were capable of it – my breath's
Too short for this celebration.

It is quite astounding to think that Rilke, who wrote those fifty-five Sonnets to Orpheus, in white heat in memory of the young dancer who died from leukaemia, should himself die four years later from a virulent form of the same disease. All his life, he had seen death as one with life and as something that would transform him and spoke of his transmutation being achieved by 'a flame of pure pain'. He died refusing any drugs insisting[227] on being conscious to the end.

'Für Leonie Zacharias; Widmung SW II 249'

O sage, Dichter, was du tust?
                                                    – Ich rühme.
Aber das Tödliche und Ungetüme,
Wie hältst du's aus, wie nimmst du's hin?
                                                    – Ich rühme.

Tell us, poet, what is it you do?
                                                    – I praise.
But the deadly and monstrous things,
how can you bear them, how accept them?
                                                    – I praise.

Two Epigraphs
Both Yeats and Rilke chose their own epitaph.
   The enigmatic three line epitaph which Yeats, in grand style, ordered

---

[226] p656, *Rainer Maria Rilke Die Gedichte*, Insel, Frankfurt am Main, 1995
[227] p1035, *Rainer Maria Rilke Die Gedichte*, Insel, Frankfurt am Main, 1995

in the final lines of the poem 'Under Ben Bulben', which he dated September 1938, four months before his death was:

Cast a cold eye
On life, on death.
Horseman, pass by!

'Under Ben Bulben'

Those final three lines on his gravestone retain inscrutability. Yeats, we know from his biographers, had first written these lines in the margin of a book containing an essay by William Rose on Rilke and Death. Rilke's view of death is in the first two parts of 'Under Ben Bulben', though later it blurs into his eugenic obsessions. The epitaph taken in isolation has a note of almost Stoic indifference. A cold eye! Who is the horseman? It seems, however, to point back to the fourth and fifth line of the poem with 'the indomitable Irishry':

Swear by those horsemen, by those women
Complexion and form prove superhuman,

'Under Ben Bulben'

Rilke's chosen epigraph[228] was the mysterious:

Rose, oh reiner Widerspruch, Lust,
Niemandes Schlaf zu sein unter soviel
Lidern

'Ô Lacrimosa (SW II 185)'

Rose, o sheer contradiction, desire
To be no one's sleep under so many
Lids.

This epitaph too keeps its own secret. The lids in German can only mean eyelids. Some have suggested word play on *Liedern*. However we take it, there is acquiescence at the heart of a rose. The poet is the contradiction of being everybody's heart and nobody's, the realist and seer for all the world's eyes.

---

[228] p971, *Rainer Maria Rilke Die Gedichte*, Insel, Frankfurt am Main, 1995

Say but the Word

It was about 1965 when I first encountered Samuel Beckett. I was in my late teens when I saw a production of *Waiting for Godot* staged by the Dramatic Society of University College Dublin. Oddly, or maybe not so oddly, it's the character of the two tramps Vladimir and Estragon that stuck in my mind, with Beckett's beloved vaudeville turns and the stage as bare as a Yeats Noh play. Somehow, Pozzo and Lucky and the boy made less of an impression. I can still see the lugubrious face of a student known as Spud Murphy, who played one of the tramps.

It is hard to describe how well Beckett's strange sequence of bizarre and ironic comic turns about boots that don't fit, carrots and other trivia, set in – what might be anywhere – drew an audience into a sense of futility, repetitiveness and purposelessness. They wait endlessly for Godot, who we neither encounter, nor are even sure exists. In Godot, there is the very obvious echo of God, who sends the innocent boy as his messenger. Add to this the appearance in both acts of the cruel taskmaster Pozzo and his animal-like Lucky. Pozzo takes pleasure in taunting and bullying Lucky. The master asks his slave to dance and to think in order to entertain the tramps. Here Beckett seems to comment on class exploitation. This potent mixture of tedium and meaninglessness somehow caught the mood of the late fifties and early sixties. It was an eerie thrill, as if we had thrown off all the unnecessary yokes of living. We were like young men driving an open-windowed car at reckless speed, while knowing in the pit of the stomach that it was bound to crash.

The Playwright

John Fletcher in his book *About Beckett* notes, in wonder, that 'unlike most other great playwrights ... Beckett's complete dramatic output can be contained in a single volume ... By the time of his death Beckett had written some three dozen plays, but a high proportion can count only as playlets or what an earlier generation would call "curtain raisers" ...' In fact, there are probably only four full-length plays: *Waiting for Godot*, *Endgame*, *Krapp's Last Tape* and *Happy Days*. Why then does John Fletcher regard Beckett as 'one of the world's foremost practitioners of the art of writing for theatre'? According to Fletcher 'what makes Beckett a great dramatist, not only of the twentieth century but of all time, is not that he presided over the demise of the "well-made" play, but that his contribution is fundamental and original in a way few others have been.' He goes on to compare him to Molière's *The Misanthrope*: 'likewise *Waiting for Godot* has traditional elements (derived from popular forms such as the music hall and the circus), but these are transcended in a play that stands, fifty years after its first production, as the most apt image yet created of our situation in a world without God, deprived of the transcendent confidence that belief in the existence of God confers.'

For me there are a number of questions. Was it the novelty of Beckett's theatricality that, after a deal of bewilderment, hostility and a slow start in January 1953 at the nearly defunct Théâtre de Babylone in Montparnasse made such an impression! Or was it as an image of a post-war world emptied of God? Or the combination of both? It is, of course, endlessly debated whether Beckett wished to propagate a view of the world as empty and meaningless or whether the ambiguities of his ending leaves minimal room for hope. Is his view of life simply a woman squatting over a grave to give birth? Or is 'I must go on' – a kind of bleak stoic persistence?

While Beckett is clearly best known as a playwright, he also published eight novels and four or five novellas and saw himself as a poet as well.

It is interesting to see how Beckett's poetry adumbrates his better known plays and novels. Partly as a practitioner of the art and partly in order to understand the relationship between Beckett and the prevailing intellectual climate, I want to address these questions in the light of his poetry and try to place it in the context of Beckett's life and time.

The Poetry

John Fletcher expressed some amazement at Beckett's relatively small body of work as a dramatist. His reputation as a poet is slighter, so too is the sum of his poetry. His first book *Whoroscope* is a small edition of a 98 line poem published in 1930 by Nancy Cunard's Hours Press. Then came the slim *Echo's Bones and Other Precipitates* (1935). Apart from this there are *Collected Poems in French* (1961), *Collected Poems in English and French* (1977) and *What is the Word* (1989).

Apart from this there is his translation of the substantial *Anthology of Mexican Poems* edited by Octavio Paz (1958). Included in *Collected Poems in English and French* are also a number of translations from Paul Eluard, Arthur Rimbaud, Guillaume Apollinaire together with a number of Sebastien Chamfort's maxims.

I think there are some advantages to looking at the Beckett phenomenon through his poetry. Just as in the theatre, Beckett in his time was perceived and perceived himself as an innovator – certainly as far as the Irish poetic scene was concerned. However, his poetry is so less well known than his plays, or indeed his novels, the same mystique does not surround it.

The Modernist

Anthony Cronin[229] in his biography *Samuel Beckett: The Last Modernist,* quotes an article of Beckett's where discussing the poets Brian Coffey, Thomas MacGreevy and Denis Devlin he praises them for having 'submitted themselves to the influences of ... Corbière, Rimbaud, Laforgue, the *surréalistes* and Mr Eliot, perhaps also to those of Mr Pound, with results that constitute already the nexus of a living poetic in Ireland'. To this day in any discussion of the various schools of modern poetry in Ireland, Beckett gets a mention along with Thomas MacGreevy (1893–1967), Brian Coffey (1905–1995), Padraic Fallon (1905–74) and Denis Devlin (1908–1959), who are felt to be the pioneers of the Modernist movement.

Of course, it's worth stressing that the Modernist movement in Irish poetry was by no means all pervasive. Indeed it simply flowed alongside a more classical mainstream in such figures as Joseph Campbell (1879–1944), Padraic Colum (1881–1970), Austin Clarke (1896–1974), Patrick Kavanagh (1904–1967) and Louis McNeice (1907–1963).

However, one glance at, for example the first half of the poem 'What is the Word' places Beckett squarely[230] in an extremely Modernist mode:

'What is the
Word'

folly –
folly for to –
for to –
what is the word –
folly from this –
all this –
folly from all this –
given –
folly given all this –

---

[229] p112, Anthony Cronin, *Samuel Beckett: The Last Modernist,* Harper Collins, London, 1996
[230] text at http://www.samuel-beckett.net/whatistheword.html with reference from: Grand Street, Vol. 9, No. 2, Winter 1990, pp17–18, N.Y., ISSN 0734-5496

seeing –
folly seeing all this –
this –
what is the word –
this this –
this this here –
all this this here –
folly given all this –
seeing –
folly seeing all this this here –
for to –
what is the word –
see –
glimpse –
seem to glimpse –
need to seem to glimpse –
folly for to need to seem to glimpse –
what –
what is the word –

This repetitive fractured syntax could hardly be more experimental. Though what was once so avant-garde can so easily seem 'old hat' at this distance. But while the broad concept of Modernism may include the experimental, it also has far wider implications.

Modernism and Interiority

The Modernist impulse was a reaction against the Romantic Movement. Yet like the Romantic Movement, it was at odds with the world. It is a protest against a mechanistic, instrumental, view of the world that lacked depth and breath. Charles Taylor in his book *Sources of the Self: The Making of Modern Identity* points out that what they both have in common is their interiority. This means that both the Romantic and the Modernist explore the inner self rather than a community or society. The difference is that Romantics set off the world of nature and human feeling against the debased utilitarian culture and poetry in turn revealed the true spirit of things. The all-pervasive influence of the industrial society, the fact that science now embraced the life sciences and the influence of Schopenhauer's view of nature as an amoral force, all meant that the Romantic vision was rejected as out of date and scorned by the Modernists. Charles Taylor points out how the interiority, the turning inward to the personal psyche of the Modernists, had a double thrust. They both turned inward the self and at the same time were busy fragmenting and decentering what they saw as the controlling rational ego.

The clear danger with this interiority is an opting out of society and a refusal to take any responsibility for shaping a wider meaning. Apart from the risk of solipsism and plain self-indulgence, there is the risk of turning poetry into a kind of private piety, which ends up marginalising poetry or branding it as some kind of academic pursuit not appropriate to the ordinary reader of books.

Anyone familiar with Beckett's plays and novels will know how he plumped for the interiority of Modernism. His poetry prefigures the internal monologues central to his work. The title of his collection *Echo's Bones* tells it own[231] tale. Echo brought down the wrath of Juno and was always allowed the last word but never the first. She was rejected by Narcissus and her bones turned to rocks. The words 'skull', 'head' and 'bone' loom large:

'The Vulture' ... my skull shell of sky and earth

'Euneg I' Above the mansions the algum-trees
the mountains
my skull sullenly
clot of anger
skewered aloft strangled in the cang of the wind
bites like a dog against its chastisement.

. . . . .

in my skull the wind going fetid...

'dread nay' head fast
in out as dead ...

head sphere
ashen smooth ...

[231] p9–33, *Samuel Beckett: Collected Poems in English and French*, John Calder, London, 1977

the highmost
snow white
sheeting all
asylum head

your prayers before the lamps start to sing behind the larches   'Serena II'
here at these knees of stone
then to bye-bye on the bones

the grapples clawing blindly the bed of want   'Cascando'
bringing up the bones ...

This fascination with the head or skull as the centre of all cerebral activity and inner monologue, features throughout all of Beckett's subsequent work. It is as if the Cartesian split between the body and mind, heralded by the famous 'I think, therefore I am', has been taken to almost unimaginable extremes. Likewise, bones as a signal of his fixation with death is a hallmark that those familiar with Beckett's plays and novels will immediately recognise.

Translations of Poetry
As we might expect, given Beckett's fastidious use of language, his translations are crisp, faithful to the spirit of the original, well turned. All the same, there is also a tinge of Beckett's own penchant for rare or older words. Two verses from Rimbaud's famous *Le Bateu Ivre* illustrate[232] his style:

Je sais les cieux crevant en éclairs, et les trombes   'Le Bateau Ivre'
Et les ressacs et les courants; je sais le soir,
L'aube exalté ainsi qu'un peuple de colombes,
Et j'ai vu quelquefois ce que l'homme a cru voir.

J'ai vu le soleil bas taché d'horreurs mystiques
Illuminant de longs figements violets,
Pareils à des acteurs de drames très antiques,
Les flots roulant au loin leur frisson de volets.

[232] p96–97, *Samuel Beckett: Collected Poems in English and French*, John Calder, London, 1977

'Drunken Boat' I know the heavens split with lightnings and the currents
Of the sea and its surgings and its spoutings, I know evening,
And dawn exalted like a cloud of doves.
And my eyes have fixed phantasmagoria.

I have seen, as shed by ancient tragic footlights,
Out from the horror of the low sun's mystic stains,
Long weals of violet creep across the sea
And peals of ague rattle down its slats.

In the first verse, he manages to keep the translation line for line but uses
'phantasmagoria' for the simpler *ce que l'homme a cru voir*. He also chooses
'a cloud of doves' rather that *un peuple de colombes* (a crowd of doves).

In the second verse, he juggles the lines to make it fit. He starts, like
the French, with 'I have seen' but the order is *c, a, b, d*. He introduces
the word 'footlights'. For *figements* (clottings, congealings) he chooses
'weals' and for *les flots* (floods, cascades, etc.) he uses 'peals'. This adds
an internal rhyme. The translation of *frisson* (shiver, quiver etc.) by the
rarer 'ague' (fever, a shivering fit) is very typical of his style.

When Beckett turns to Sébastien Chamfort's sarcastic maxims, he is
caustic and colloquial and in his most bitter[233] vein:

Il vaux mieux être assis que debout,
couché que assis, mort que tout cela.

Better on your arse than on your feet,
Flat on your back than either, dead than the lot.

Il faut vivre au jour le jour, oublier beaucoup,
enfin éponger la vie à mesure qu'elle s'écoule.

Live and clean forget from day to day
Mop life up as fast as it dribbles away.

Beckett's Modernist Models
In his translations Beckett signals very clearly that his models, apart
from the Symbolist Arthur Rimbaud (1854–1891), were Guillaume

---

[233] p126–129, *Samuel Beckett: Collected Poems in English and French*, John Calder, London, 1977

Apollinaire (1880–1918) and Paul Éluard (1885–1952), whose translations he published in 1932. Both of these were founding figures of the Surrealist Movement and indeed Apollinaire is credited with coining the term surrealism. Éluard, like Beckett, would take part in the French resistance during the Second World War. The central tenet of this movement was the sudden juxtaposition, the bizarre *non-sequitur*. This opens up the possibility of what Charles Taylor describes as 'the framed epiphany'. The surprising conjunction, the bringing together of what otherwise would be utterly unconnected jolts us into understanding. This is the modernist epiphany *par excellence* and replaces the Romantic epiphany of nature's spirit. A typical example is the opening line[234] of Éluard's *L'Amoureuse*:

Elle est debout sur mes paupières   'L'Amoureuse'

which Beckett translates as:

She is standing on my lids

Of course, she could not stand on his eyelids and yet we sense the obsession of the poet in this strange and arresting beginning to the poem.

Just as in the example of Beckett already quoted, in *Echo's Bones*, the title poem of Beckett's collection, dated 1935, we see this technique[235] at work:

asylum under my tread all this day   'Echo's Bones'
their muffled revels as the flesh falls
breaking without fear or favour wind
the gantelope of sense and nonsense run
taken by the maggots for what they are

This poem weaves a kind of fantastic chain of associations in the mind and, if I read it correctly, its meaning is fairly clear. To put it crudely and prosaically, the poet, or his persona, is aware that he's walking throughout the day over the now muted lives of the dead as their flesh is disintegrating and rotting flatulently and carelessly. They have run

---

[234] p66–67, *Samuel Beckett: Collected Poems in English and French*, John Calder, London, 1977
[235] p28, *Samuel Beckett: Collected Poems in English and French*, John Calder, London, 1977

the gauntlet of what makes sense and doesn't make sense in life. Since they are no more than flesh, the maggots eat them.

His tight and utterly precise use of language draws the reader into his thought-world. A close reading illustrates so many of the Beckett traits. 'Asylum' is an astonishing word to start with. It has a double sense with resonances of lunatic asylum as well as asylum as a place of safety and refuge (from life?). The rhythm and tone of the first line could be one of the early Dylan Thomas poems from around 1934 like – 'the force that through the green fuse drives the flower'. Beckett too alliterates 'f's in 'flesh fails' and 'fear or favour'. The words 'muffled revels', as though it was a neighbour's party heard through a wall. The use of a quasi-legal phrase 'without fear or favour' along with the equally formal 'breaking wind' is redolent of the way Beckett will use the higher legal, religious or literary registers of language ironically and with black humour in his plays and novels. The noun 'gantelope' for gauntlet fascinates and the final 'taken by the maggots for what they are' with its undertones of vain human pretence is cleverly turned and lures the reader into Beckett's desolate mindscape.

It seems to me in this poem alone, we have the harbinger of the plays and novels that would follow. The obsession with death and the apparent meaninglessness of life are Beckett's hallmark. A glance at some of the themes and motifs of a number of other poems will see how often they announce the concerns of his more widely known works.

Whoroscope

His 98-line poem 'Whoroscope' was written in 1930. As he himself wrote in a letter: 'first half before dinner, had a guzzle of salad at the Cochon de Lait and went back to the École [Normale] and finished it about three in the morning'. Nancy Cunard of Hours Press in Paris advertised a competition for a poem of 100 lines. Thomas MacGreevy tipped off Beckett that same afternoon and suggested that he use the notes, which he had been making from books on René Descartes to compose a poem. According to Anthony Cronin's biography, a large part of the poem is almost straight out of Adrien Baillet's *La Vie de Monsieur Descartes* (Paris 1669). The poem won the prize and was published with notes by Nancy Cunard.

Without the notes, I could not make head or tail of the poem. The title is a play on horoscope, the rest – as emerges from the notes — consists of references to the life and preoccupations of Descartes. T. S.

Eliot had started a vogue for learned notes but James Knowlson, in his biography *Damned to Fame – The Life of Samuel Beckett,* feels that it 'looks as if he saw it not just as an imitation but as a deliberate send up of T. S. Eliot's foot-noting practice in *The Waste Land*'. Whether mimicry or satire, Beckett was 24 years old and showing off his erudition. However, the fragmentary and allusive monologue is not unlike the tone of *Krapp's Last Tape.*

Dominant Themes

The subject of illness and death pervades his poetry. *Enueg* is a twelfth or thirteenth century Provençal troubadour's lament: [236]

Exeo in a spasm   'Enug I'
tired of my darling's red sputum
from the Portobello Private Nursing Home ...

Then follows a natural reaction of anger and resentment at his cousin's fate:

my skull sullenly
clot of anger
skewered aloft strangled in the cang of the wind
bites like a dog against its chastisement.

The body of the poem is a walk up the Grand Canal in Dublin back by the Liffey with mention of barges, Fox and Geese, Chapelizod and hurlers. Although, the air is jaunty, decay dominates the imagery:

... the tattered sky like an ink of pestilence
in my skull the wind going fetid ...

The strange leap of the bleak final lines:

Ah, the banner
the banner of meat bleeding
on the silk of the sea and the arctic flowers
that do not exist.

[236] p10–12, *Samuel Beckett: Collected Poems in English and French*, John Calder, London, 1977

turns out in fact to be a quotation from Rimbaud's 1874 'Poème Barbare' from *Illuminations*:

Le pavillon en viande saignante sur la soie des mers et des fleurs arctiques; (elles n'existent pas.)

This was apparently written after a visit to a beloved cousin who was dying.

'Malacoda' is a poem on the death of his father. Malacoda (Evil-Tail) is the leader of the pack of demons, the Malebranche (Evil-Clawed) whom Dante and his guide Virgil encounter in the eighth circle of the Inferno. Here Malacoda is how Beckett speaks[237] of 'the undertaker's man', an unfortunate figure in modern poetry. (William Carlos Williams had referred to this image in 1917 in 'Tract' as 'the undertaker's understrapper')

'Malacoda'
thrice he came
the undertaker's man
impassible behind his scutal bowler
to measure
is he not paid to measure
this incorruptible in the vestibule
this malebranca knee-deep in the lilies
Malacoda knee-deep in the lilies
Malacoda for all the expert awe
that felts his perineum mutes his signal
sighing up through the heavy air
must it be it must be it must be
find the weeds engage them in the garden
hear she may see she need not

There is a genuine cry of grief for his father: 'must it be it must be it must be' and a wish to shelter his widowed mother. There is an echo of the phrase in Beethoven's last string quartet – *muss es sein?* must it be?

Sex

If Beckett is preoccupied with *thanatos*, with death, there is also *eros*. Anthony Cronin in listing the parallels between the philosopher Arthur

[237] p26, *Samuel Beckett: Collected Poems in English and French*, John Calder, London, 1977

Schopenhauer and Beckett, writes[238] that Schopenhauer

had mixed feelings about his mother but considerable affection for
his father. Probably as a result of his relationship with his mother
he was a considerable misogynist and for his sexual gratification
preferred whores or casual acquaintances with whom he was not
emotionally involved. Whatever he may have felt or been on a
conscious, willed level, Beckett also had strong misogynistic
tendencies; and he too tended to divorce the idea of sexual pleasure
from obligation or emotional commitment.

Little wonder then that such liaisons feature in Beckett's poetry.
    The poem 'Dortmunder', using the name of a German Beer as its
title, is in fact about a visit to a brothel in Kassel with Boss Sinclair, the
father of Peggy, who was his loved one at the time. Like so much of
Beckett's poetry, it is weighted down with allusions to the Old
Testament prophet Habakkuk, who cried out[239] for justice from the
Lord, and to Schopenhauer.

She stands before me in the bright stall   'Dortmunder'
sustaining the jade splinters
the scarred signaculum of purity quiet
the eyes the eyes black till the plagal east
shall resolve the long night phrase.
Then, as a scroll, folded,
and the glory of her dissolution enlarged
in me, Habbakuk, mard of all sinners.
Schopenhauer is dead, the bawd
puts her lute away.

He had in fact since his student days at Trinity College Dublin been a
visitor to brothels such as Becky Cooper's emporium where there was a
picture of Dante meeting Beatrice in the parlour. It seems on one
occasion Beckett was ejected from the establishment for sneering at the
reproduction. This incident comes to the surface in another poem[240]
about brothels *Sanies II*:

---

[238] p123, Anthony Cronin, *Samuel Beckett: The Last Modernist*, HarperCollins, London, 1996
[239] p16, *Samuel Beckett: Collected Poems in English and French*, John Calder, London, 1977
[240] p19, *Samuel Beckett: Collected Poems in English and French*, John Calder, London, 1977

'Sanies II'   the Barfrau makes a big impression with her mighty bottom
                Dante and blissful Beatrice are there
                prior to Vita Nuova ...

                ... a bitter moon fessade la mode
                oh Becky spare me I have done thee no wrong spare me damn thee

                spare me good Becky
                call off thine adders Becky I will compensate thee in full
                Lord have mercy upon
                Christ have mercy upon us

                Lord have mercy on us

Religion

Beckett's religious background looms large right from the beginning with what the footnotes to 'Whoroscope' describe as 'His Eucharistic sophistry, in reply to the Jansenist Antoine Arnauld, who challenged him[241] to reconcile his doctrine of matter with the doctrine of transubstantiation.'

'Whoroscope'   So we drink Him and eat Him
                and the watery Beaune and the stale cubes of Hovis
                because He can jig
                as near or as far from His Jigging Self
                and as sad or lively as the chalice or the tray asks.
                How's that, Antonio?

The mocking tone of his references indicates not only how profoundly his upbringing was ingrained but also how, at the deepest level, he is unable to leave it behind. There is a sense in which he uses allusions to shock or cause a sudden disjunction. In his third *Serena* (a Provençal evening song) which seems to involve a walk[242] over Dublin's Butt Bridge, along by Misery Hill and the Gasometer out by Ringsend, Irishtown, Sandymount, Merrion and on to Booterstown and Blackrock:

---

[241] p3, *Samuel Beckett: Collected Poems in English and French*, John Calder, London, 1977
[242] p25, *Samuel Beckett: Collected Poems in English and French*, John Calder, London, 1977

the Merrion Flats scored with a thrillion sigmas   'Serena III'
Jesus Christ Son of God Saviour His Finger
girls taken strippin that's the idea

Clearly the juxtaposition of Christ's finger (inscribing the sand on the
Merrion Flats with a t(h)rillion ripples?) and girls caught while
stripping cause a frisson in Beckett's subconscious, which he wants to
pass on to his reader. Often this fixation expresses itself in gallows-
humour. 'Habbakuk, mard of all sinners', the Biblical prophet in a
Kassel brothel or in the second part of his lament for his cousin dying[243]
in the Portobello Nursing Home:

world world world world   'Enueg II'
and the face grave
cloud against the evening

de morituris nihil nisi

and the face crumbling shyly
too late to darken the sky
blushing away into the evening
shuddering away like a gaffe

veronica mundi
veronica munda
give us a wipe for the love of Jesus

Erudition

Yet another tension in Beckett's psyche is the sense that he cannot quite
leave academia behind. There may be a touch of guilt at the undoubted
disappointment of his parents when, after an unhappy period, he
abandoned his post as lecturer in Trinity College. It may also just be the
natural tendency of a learned young man to want to exhibit the breadth
of his knowledge. Anthony Cronin commenting on 'Whoroscope',
notes that despite Lawrence Harvey, a scholar of Beckett's poetry,
devoting sixty-six pages to a three-page poem, 'a contemporary reader
is more likely to be struck by how ably Beckett has, in Vivian Mercier's

---

[243] p13, *Samuel Beckett: Collected Poems in English and French*, John Calder, London, 1977

words, "caught up with the international avant garde on his first flight"; and to agree with Mercier that it is "No wonder he had a great deal to unlearn later'". Cronin refers to 'Dortmunder' as 'a learned affair'. The quotation above from *Enueg II* is Beckett at his cleverest and punning in Latin. He is echoing the Latin tag *de mortuis nil nisi bonum*: 'say nothing but good of the dead'. Whatever about a readership being familiar with the original, to substitute a future participle in *de morituris* 'of those who will die' is certainly a display of erudition. Yet even that pales beside his play on *veronica mundi* 'Veronica of the world' beside *veronica munda* 'clean Veronica'. This is worthy of *Finnegan's Wake* and indeed may be the hand of James Joyce laid too heavily on Beckett. In a one verse poem he faces this side of himself in the poem[244] dated 1934:

'Gnome'   Spend the years of learning squandering
           Courage for the years of wandering
           Through a world politely turning
           From the loutishness of learning.

Wide-ranging allusion can lend depth and texture to a poem, but Beckett is almost too anxious to impress. Even the titles of his poems seem to flaunt scholarship: the Provençal songs 'Enueg', 'Alba' and 'Serena' alongside 'Sanies' (thin discharges from wounds or sores), 'Malacoda', 'Da Tagte Es' (an echo of a German poem by Walther von der Vogelweide), 'Cascando' (decreasing in volume and tempo and later the title of a radio play in 1961), 'Ooftish' (*oof tisch* 'on table', according to a note a Yiddish expression for 'put your money down on the table').

Poems in French
It is significant that the poems he wrote in French are somewhat less loaded down by references. They are clearly very much in the Modernist mode and bear the stamp of his modes. Some[245] he translated himself:

'1. Poemes   elles viennent
1937–1939'   autres et pareilles
              avec chacune c'est autre et c'est pareil
              avec chacune l'absence d'amour est autre
              avec chacune l'absence d'amour est pareille

[244] p7, *Samuel Beckett: Collected Poems in English and French*, John Calder, London, 1977
[245] p38–39, *Samuel Beckett: Collected Poems in English and French*, John Calder, London, 1977

they come
different and the same
with each it is different and the same
with each the absence of love is different
with each the absence of love is the same

In this we encounter an expression of an extraordinary absence at the
heart of Beckett. There is almost a sense that he achieves this directness
through writing in French. Take this poem[246] which is not translated
by Beckett:

à travers la mince cloison   'Ascension'
ce jour où un enfant
prodigue à sa façon
rentra dans sa famille
j'entends la voix
elle est émue elle commente
la coupe du monde de football

toujours trop jeune

en même temps par la fenêtre ouverte
par les airs tout court
sourdement
la houle des fidèles

son sang gicla avec abondance
sur les draps sur les pois de senteur sur son mec
de ses doigts dégoûtants il ferma les paupières
sur les grands yeux verts étonnés

elle rode légère
sur ma tombe d'air

which seems to translate as:

through the thin partition   'Ascension'

---

[246] p42, *Samuel Beckett: Collected Poems in English and French*, John Calder, London, 1977

this day where a child
prodigal in his own way
returns to his family
I hear the voice
it is emotional it commentates
the soccer world cup

always too young

in the same time through the open window
through the very brief airs
dully
the swell of the faithful

her blood spurts with abundance
on the sheets on the sweet pea on her fellow
with his fingers he shuts her eyelids
on the big green surprised eyes

she runs in lightly
on my tomb of air

While this poem is full of Modernist disjunctions, there is an unmistakable air of hurt and sadness. Has the fact that Beckett has written it originally in French given him the distance to face some childhood memory that is ineffably painful? It is as if in all of Beckett's work there is a process of distancing himself from his own feelings. He makes every effort to both observe meticulously and at the same time to keep all at arm's length. Every device, intellectualism, erudition and maybe even writing an acquired language distances Beckett from any emotional contact. In his social life he also distanced himself to the point of preferring casual relationships or prostitutes for sexual gratification to any committed intimacy. There is a sense in which Beckett is a chilly observer in a mind that eschews the warmth of embodiment and life.

Schopenhauer
The preoccupation with death, sex, religion, erudition and black humour all anticipate the themes of his later plays and novels. There is to a certain extent an intellectual hinterland to the overwhelming role

which suffering plays in all of Beckett's work. Both Anthony Cronin and James Knowlson highlight his interest in Arthur Schopenhauer. In a letter to Thomas MacGreevy in September 1937 he wrote of Schopenhauer: 'I always knew he was one of the ones that mattered most to me'. The consequences of Schopenhauer's philosophy of the Will, which make suffering the human norm and regard any fleeting happiness as mere relief, underpin much of Beckett's oeuvre. However, I think that Cronin is right when he suggests that, more than any conviction about the actual philosophy, Beckett found much of his own personality coincided with that of Schopenhauer. Apart from their shared disinterest in politics and public affairs, their misogynist tendencies and dislike of sexual commitment, they both had great affection for their fathers and a deal of ambiguity concerning their mothers.

Beckett's obsession with human suffering and decay is, as in the case of most artists, the confluence of a personal background and the intellectual climate that shaped him. There was a lack of real warmth in his restrained and unengaged bourgeois upbringing, which predisposed him to disengagement and distance and the *Zeitgeist* encouraged a hard-bitten distrust.

Upbringing

There is a general view abroad that Beckett grew up in a happy and sheltered home in the wealthy South Dublin suburb of Foxrock where he lacked for nothing. Lawrence Harvey, the greatest authority on Beckett's poetry, in his chapter 'A Poet's Initiation' (in a book of critical essays *Samuel Beckett Now*, Chicago 1970), says 'this happy and propitious climate extended beyond hearth and home, for Sam followed his older brother Frank to the best private schools ...' He quotes Beckett as saying 'You might say I had a happy childhood ... although I never had much talent for happiness. My parents did everything possible to make a child happy but often I felt very much alone'.

Knowlson acknowledges 'the inhibitions and prohibitions' of a Protestant professional class home where his mother May 'attempted to live up to the standards of the big house in which she had been brought up'. He concludes that 'Beckett's childhood was mainly a happy one.' He does advert to his mother's aim 'to mould her children to her own design' and to 'the stormy conflicts which would blow up between them'. In his view, what Beckett himself referred to as her 'savage loving' resulted in his feeling 'the weight of her moral condemnation and disappointment'. They hardly ever saw eye to eye on anything concerning himself.

On the other hand, Cronin is more penetrating. He quotes the writer Mary Manning, a neighbour whose mother and May were close, 'There wasn't much loving going on in the Beckett household'. Mary Manning also described the young Beckett as 'under-nourished ... he suffered from emotional malnutrition'. She remembered May Beckett as 'a very moody person', as 'very deeply Protestant' and as 'virginal, a nun, a manly nun'. Cronin suggests that 'she suffered from mood-swings, periods of often acute depression, balanced by occasional and less obviously noticeable elated states'. While there is no doubt about May Beckett's love for her son, it seems to me that Anthony Cronin's insight rings true when he assumes that 'much of Sam's later anxiety about his mother and his desire to please her were probably fostered in childhood by these alternations of personality, the apparent warmth and approachability of one phase being horribly followed by silence and seeming hostility'. Cronin may also be accurate in his opinion that 'the length and frequency of her unapproachable periods also created a need for mother substitutes, which had an influence on his later sexual development'.

Given his mother's temperamental behaviour and his parents' deteriorating marriage, we begin to understand why Beckett 'never had much talent for happiness'. His father avoided his home and began to brood more on the Catholic woman he had been prevented from marrying. At the same time, his mother was openly sarcastic and hostile to her husband in the presence of others. Inside the privileged suburban Foxrock house there must have been a lot of silent desperation. Little wonder then that Beckett 'often felt very much alone'.

If we add the 'distancing', which was part of the comfortable middle class Protestant life of the time, we can see how Beckett was conditioned from childhood to opt for cool superior, observation and withdrawal. For the most part, again to cite Cronin, 'like the aristocracy, the Protestant business communities of the towns and cities looked down on Catholics as, in general, rather feckless, lazy and dishonest ... it was a boast among the denizens of Foxrock ... that one could pass one's day without speaking to any Catholic other than the railway company's employees'. Cronin goes on to cite[247] Vivian Mercier:

---

[247] p9, Anthony Cronin, *Samuel Beckett: The Last Modernist*, HarperCollins, London, 1996

The males and some of the females of the typical Protestant family took the train every weekday to office, school or university in Dublin. In all these places they were likely to be associating almost exclusively with fellow Protestants. The females who stayed at home spent their leisure time with other Protestant ladies, though their maids and gardeners were usually Catholic. If one preferred to think of oneself as English there was really no reason not to.

There was nothing in Beckett's schooling from the kindergarten of the disciplinarian Elsner sisters through Alfred le Peton's Earlsfort House School or Portora College that would have compensated for a want of emotional warmth at home.

Beckett arrived as a callow youth at Trinity College Dublin in October 1923. After a long period of adjustment, he encountered the spirit of the times in the form of R. B. Rudmose-Brown, who ahead of his time took an interest in contemporary French poetry and introduced his students to Verlaine, Larbaud, Fargue, Jammes and he had doctoral students exploring the like of Valérya and Péguy. Rudmose-Brown claimed in an unpublished biography to be against any ideology of any hue, opposed patriotism or nationalism and any organised religion. He and his wife Furry held weekend parties for students at their home in Malahide, where they encouraged their students 'to pair off'. They themselves bickered constantly and each had affairs. Ultimately a love of whiskey got the better of them both and they had to be dried out. Furry put an end to her life with an overdose. Rudmose-Brown, as Anthony Cronin put it 'made an intellectual out of a cricket-loving schoolboy'. Yet as teacher and patron his effect on a highly impressionable and unsure young man was hardly entirely wholesome. Intellectual prowess is one thing, emotional growth is quite another.

Zeitgeist

However it was in intellectual circles in Paris of the 1920s, he came in contact with the nihilism, despair and suicide that came in the wake of the Dadaists. Their reaction to the barbarity of a world war was to try to destroy out of disgust what they saw as the bourgeois artistic values. Following their rejection of society and ultimately of writing, many of them debated whether it was worth going on living. Apart from a number of flamboyant suicides, the consensus was, as Marcel Arland wrote 'the limit of daring is not destruction, but abstention; a violence greater than saying No is to be found in silence … so the real despair lies in acceptance rather than in suicide'. Anthony Cronin rightly points out that here is the 'fore-echo of the preoccupations that would one day be central to Beckett's work'. Clearly his consuming fascination with James Joyce (1882–1941) also left indelible marks on his character.

And all the more so, with the humanist loss of nerve following another World War with all the unspeakable savagery of the Holocaust. Beckett's temperament and upbringing coincided with the *Zeitgeist.* He read the novel *La Nausée* by Jean-Paul Sartre (1905–1980) with approval. However, while Sarte and Albert Camus (1913–1960) were making waves as existentialists Beckett was still unknown. Nowhere is that echo so clear than in the closing lines[248] of *The Unnamable:*

'The
Unnamable'

It will be I, it will be the silence, where I am,
I don't know, I'll never know,
in the silence you don't know,
You must go on, I can't go on, I'll go on.

The argument goes on as to whether Beckett simply wishes to draw us into his own baleful vision of the human condition or whether he allows for hope. Some argue that much of Beckett is wonderful black comedy. Others, like Charles Taylor, suggest that the 'negation borders on something else again, a purpose beyond stoic lucidity of vision. As with the *via negativa* in theology, the counter-epiphanic can be embraced not in order to deny epiphany altogether, not just to find a place for the human spirit to stand before the most complete emptiness, but rather to force us to the verge of epiphany. This is one way of reading the work of Samuel Beckett, perhaps also a way of understanding some of the work of Paul Celan'. In our consumer society where even the questions tend to be lost, it must be said that Beckett was, at the very least, concerned with ultimate meaning.

Stature as a Poet
How are we to think of Beckett as a poet? In some ways the small amount of poetry he published will mean that his name as a poet will always be mentioned as a sort of footnote to the early Irish Modernists:

[248] http://en.wikiquote.org/wiki/Samuel_Beckett#The_Unnamable_.281954.29 accessed 17th September 2014

Brian Coffey, Thomas MacGreevy, Denis Devlin or Padraic Fallon. On the other hand, for aficionados of his plays or novels or indeed for his biographers, the poems illustrate the themes and preoccupations of his later works.

I remember how my own professor at Trinity College, David Greene, while sighing that poetry was something that he always associated with his youth, pointed out how many writers of prose had begun as poets. So perhaps Beckett joins the long list of writers whose apprenticeship with words was served in poetry and who apart from an occasional poem, make their way in prose. On the other hand, Beckett did a considerable amount of translation including the anthology of Octavio Paz, which was only published in 1958.

What is it that pushes a would-be younger poet in the direction of fiction and drama? I am sure that it has often been economic pressure. But in some cases, it must be that the inner drive, the urge to write poetry disappears. Beckett omitted several previously published poems from *Echo's Bones and Other Precipitates.* Knowlson tells us that he wrote to Thomas MacGreevy:

Genuinely my impression was that it was of little worth because it did not represent a necessity. I mean that in some way it was 'Facultatif' [optional] and that I would have been no worse off for not having written it. Is that a very painless way of thinking of poetry? Quoi qu'il soit [Whatever it may be] I find it impossible to abandon that view of the matter. Genuinely again my feeling is, more and more, that the greater part of my poetry, though it may be reasonably felicitous in its choice of terms, fails precisely because it is facultative whereas the 3 or 4 I like, and seem to have been drawn down against the really dirty weather of one of those fine days into the burrow of the 'private life '...

He goes on to mention 'Alba' and the long 'Enueg' and 'Dortmunder' among those that 'do not and never gave me the impression of being constuit.' Whatever about the sentiments of 'Dortmunder', there is a passion in his grief over his cousin's impending death in 'Enueg'. I do also sense in 'Alba', that there was passion about his loss[249] of Ethna McCarthy, for whom 'Alba' was written:

[249] p15, *Samuel Beckett: Collected Poems in English and French*, John Calder, London, 1977

'Alba'   grave suave singing silk
         stoop to the black firmament of areca
         rain on the bamboos flower of smoke alley of willows

Conclusion

But I return to Vladimir and Estragon over forty years after I was first
thrilled and drawn into their repetitive world of meaninglessness. This
time it is another Murphy, the actor Johnny Murphy as Estragon. I
suppose I owe these tramps a certain debt of gratitude. They forced me
as a young man to look down into the dark pit of their obsession and to
come to understand the slow paralysis of despondency, the torpor of
despair. When, for lack of a rope they don't hang themselves, I wonder
if the audience, laughing nervously at this gallows humour, have ever
gazed into the abyss of despair. But now I'm neither shocked nor
startled. I feel a great sadness. I think of a sensitive eager young boy
rescuing an endangered hedgehog. And then I hear the adult Beckett
speaking of his 'existence by proxy', a sense of 'being absent', 'an
unconquerable intuition' of 'a presence, embryonic, underdeveloped,
of a self that might have been but never got born, an *être manqué*'.

Beckett's translations of Octavio Paz's Mexican poetry had been a
journeyman's job arranged through a friend for UNESCO when money
was short. The unilingual volume took eight years to appear. 'That
lousy Mexican Anthology was undertaken to take the chill off the pot
in the lean winter of 1949–50', Beckett grumbled, 'nine years later … it
comes rattling its doggerel at me'. Apparently it galled him that anyone
should think he, rather than Paz, had chosen the poems. I cannot help
wondering if he saw the irony in the final lines of a poem by that
extraordinary Mexican poet Juana de Asbaje (1651–1695) which he also
translated:

'Describes   Beguiled perhaps by grief
Rationally the   I presume without reason
Irrational   no fulfilment can ever
Effects of Love'   my passion assuage.

                And though nigh disabused,
                still the same grief assails me,
                that I suffer so sore
                for so little a cause.

Say but the Word

Perhaps the wounded soul sweeping
to take its revenge
repents it and wreaks
other vengeance on me.

In my blindness and folly
I, gladly deceived,
beseech disenchantment
and desire it not.

If I had to choose a favourite period in the history of poetry in English, I would plump for the Elizabethan and Jacobean poets. Of course such general labelling of eras is too sweeping and all boundaries blur. But there is a quality to these years, which seems so contemporary. I think it is because we, like them, are living through great changes. Just as they knew the thrill of a world opening up – *Both th'old discoveries, and the new-found seas* – we are in the middle of a technological revolution and a globalisation which may have hardly yet begun.

All the poets within a given time differ in their gifts, their thought and craft, and will appeal to our changing moods and needs at various stages of our life. But if I absolutely had to choose one poet from this tradition, in the way we name someone our best friend ... ? At this point in my life, provided I was allowed share his company with other good friends, I would choose George Herbert (1593–1633). No poet that I know of can combine such depth and richness of thought with such dazzling subtlety of language, expression and structure. His work is a consummate example of the Greek ideal of art where content and form are seamlessly one.

I am not a George Herbert scholar but I simply want to delight a little in my friend.

Reception

Ironically, the quality which is Herbert's outstanding gift is also why his genius has frequently been ignored or unacknowledged. His great poetic work *The Temple* contains almost all his poems in English. In *The Temple* profound theological thinking is combined with daring imagination and form by one of the greatest lyric poets ever. In a superb study called *George Herbert: His Religion and Art,* Joseph H. Summers gives a masterly account of the reception of Herbert's work. He points out that 'with some notable exceptions, those who have admired the poems in the immediate as well as in the distant past can be roughly divided into two groups; the religious readers who bowed to Herbert's piety and the literary men who praised the "wit and ingenuity" or perhaps the form and language. Each group often had strong reservations: the *dévot* could sometimes ignore the wit for the sake of the piety; and the *litterateur* might be able, reluctantly, to do the reverse. In either process both the poetry and religion suffered, for they are intimately and inextricably interrelated in *The Temple*'.

Summers shows that past images of Herbert's poetry 'are formed by Laudians, Puritans neo-Classicists, Evangelicals, Romantics, Transcendentalists, Anglo-Catholics and modern apostles of Donne', who 'bring partial if valuable illumination'. Herbert seems to have constantly run up against the literary *Zeitgeist*. His use of the conceit was soon taboo to the Augustan poet John Dryden and the flatter 'age of reason' style with its heroic couplet. Addison roundly condemned the pattern poems of Herbert as 'an aberration' and looked for 'congruity of ideas'. No new edition of *The Temple* appeared for ninety years between 1709 and 1799.

Then Samuel Taylor Coleridge was to rediscover George Herbert, much in the way somewhat later Felix Mendelssohn would rediscover Johann Sebastian Bach. Coleridge in his later years, combining his literary with his religious understanding, managed somewhat to restore Herbert's literary credibility. However, he felt that to appreciate Herbert 'even poetic sensibility' was not enough, 'unless he be a *Christian* ... for religion is the element in which he lives and the region in which he moves'. And Coleridge went further in thinking you had to be a certain kind of Christian, which I read as: you had to belong to the Anglican tradition. This is not so. Later Christina Rossetti and Gerard Manley Hopkins were admirers of both Herbert's content and form.

Ultimately it was the renewal of interest in the poetry of John Donne that directed attention to Herbert, though as an interesting but lesser contemporary. Nevertheless once more Herbert ran foul of the *Zeitgeist*. Donne was a more tortured soul and, in accordance with the taste of the time, was therefore seen as less limited and much more sophisticated, complex and inclusive. The *Zeitgeist* also demanded that the poet be seen as personal and authentic. What T. S. Eliot, another admirer of Herbert, called 'a unified sensibility', was not the thing.

However, all this still forces us to ask two questions. Firstly, is it possible to appreciate Herbert's rich thought and not be a Christian? And secondly, are the times now ripe for a more general appreciation of Herbert's poetry?

It is very difficult to answer the first question. Clearly, to understand and be deeply moved by the content, a Christian belief and background might be seen as a prerequisite. In the case of a non-Christian, it would undoubtedly demand a generous act of empathy and a hospitable imagination. But it must surely be possible for a genuine poetic sensibility to be moved by such exquisite poetry.

It is difficult to be certain but I do sense that the mood of our times is shifting. Certainly Summers, when he published his book on George Herbert in 1954, was confident that 'during the past twenty years … an atmosphere is forming more congenial to the appreciation of Herbert as well as Milton'. Such moods shift slowly and yet in the 21st century there may be a new seriousness about religion, partly due to its emergence both for good and for bad, as a major global dynamic. It may be that more poetry lovers will be able to relish the inextricable mix of theological thought and beautiful form.

Didactic
Apart from matters of content and form, particularly when separated, standing in the way of a real acknowledgement of Herbert's poetry, there is the question of Herbert's openly didactic purpose. 'The Church-porch', the seventy-seven stanza poem[250] which forms the first part of *The Temple* begins:

'Perirrhanterium'   Thou, whose sweet youth and early hopes inhance
Thy rate and price, and mark thee for a treasure;
Harken unto a Verser, who may chance
Ryme thee to good, and make a bait of pleasure.
 A verse may finde him, who a sermon flies,
 And turn delight into a sacrifice.

This is an unambiguous declaration of intent. Of course, this may be anathema to a certain widespread belief that the most a poem should dare is to allow images to faintly suggest something. But this certainly was not the Elizabethan or Jacobean view. Many of Shakespeare's best sonnets end with a couplet summing up his message. Take his Sonnet XCIV, which I read as a meditation on power

For sweetest things turn sourest by their deeds;
Lilies that fester, smell far worse than weeds.

It is still very much part of the poetic tradition. Robert Frost, probably the most popular of all modern American poets, famously remarked

---

[250] p33 *The English Poems of George Herbert*, ed. C. A. Patrides, J. M. Dent, London, 1974

Say but the Word

that a poem 'begins in delight and ends in wisdom.'

Even so, it is well worth posing the question how poetry, which is so palpably didactic and unashamedly Christian, does not end up being simply tedious moralism. What makes the difference is the mastery of craft and language, the architectonics of his book and the layered intensity of thought which invites us into a world of meaning. It is not a command; it is a voice beckoning us into the temple. The excitement of language which Herbert offers is already apparent in that line:

Ryme thee to good, and make a bait of pleasure.

Many of the other seventy-six stanzas of *The Church Porch* have lines, which start with an imperative. It is the imperative of the Proverbs so beloved of Herbert, whose own collection of proverbs was first published in 1640 seven years after his death. There is a gnomic tone that reminds me of 'Hávamál' in the Edda poems or indeed, of the Biblical proverbs, which recommends[251] the best ways to live wisely:

Drink not the third glasse, which thou canst not tame,   'Perirrhanterium'
When once it is within thee; but before
Mayst rule it, as thou list; and poure the shame,
Which it would pour on thee, upon the floore.
   It is most just to throw that on the ground,
    Which would throw me there, if I keep the round.

Or two stanzas later and still on the same theme, the final couplet is in the imperative mood of wisdom:

Shall I, to please anothers wine-sprung minde,
Lose all mine own? God hath giv'n me a measure
Short of his canne, and bodie; must I finde
A pain in that, wherein he findes a pleasure?
   Stay at the third glasse: if thou lose thy hold,
    Then thou art modest, and the wine grows bold.

Mention of the Biblical proverbs and their influence brings us to the unique degree of intertextuality in Herbert's work.

[251] p34, *The English Poems of George Herbert*, ed. C. A. Patrides, J. M. Dent, London, 1974

Say but the Word

Intertextuality

Herbert was steeped in the scriptures and *The Temple* is highly intextextual. Poem after poem resonates with Biblical texts. His favourites are the Psalms and the Wisdom tradition. Herbert praises, implores and importunes God as the author(s) of the Psalms had done. Anyone who has read Herbert will have recognised echoes of the Bible. The conclusion[252] of the sonnet 'The Sinner' illustrates this beautifully.

'The Sinner'   And though my hard heart scarce to thee can grone,
Remember that thou once did write in stone.

This fine couplet is clearly addressed to God. On the surface this is simply a well-crafted couplet. In fact Herbert is summoning up all kinds of resonances for those who, like many of his readers, are immersed in the Biblical tradition. Such as Ezekiel 36: 26

 A new heart also will I give you, and a new spirit will I put within you: and I will take away the stony heart out of your flesh, and I will give you an heart of flesh.

or Jeremiah 24:7

And I will give them an heart to know me, that I am the LORD: and they shall be my people, and I will be their God: for they shall return unto me with their whole heart.

as well as Exodus 31:18

And he gave unto Moses, when he had made an end of communing with him upon mount Sinai, two tables of testimony, tables of stone, written with the finger of God.

St Paul in 2 Corinthians 3:3 echoes both Ezekiel and Jeremiah:

Forasmuch as ye are manifestly declared to be the epistle of Christ ministered by us, written not with ink, but with the Spirit of the living God; not in tablets of stone, but in fleshy tables of the heart.

[252] p59, *The English Poems of George Herbert*, ed. C. A. Patrides, J. M. Dent, London, 1974

Another example of intertextuality is found[253] in the poem 'The Bunch of Grapes':

I did towards Canaan draw; but now I am
Brought back to the Red sea, the sea of shame.

.   .   .   .   .

But can he want the grape, who hath the wine?
   I have their fruit and more.
Blessed be God, who prosper'd *Noahs* vine,
    And made it bring forth grapes good store.
    But much more him I must adore,
Who of the Laws sowre juice sweet wine did make,
Ev'n God himself being pressed for my sake.

'The Bunch of Grapes'

Look at the density of the last verse about Christ and how the allusion to the Eucharist is made.

In 'The Holy Scriptures II' Herbert refers[254] to the intertextuality within the Bible:

Oh that I knew how all thy lights combine,
    And the configurations of their glorie!
    Seeing not onely how each verse doth shine,
But all the constellations of the storie.

'The Holy Scriptures II'

This verse marks that, and both do make a motion
    Unto a third, that ten leaves off doth lie:
    Then as dispersed herbs do watch a potion,
These three make up some Christians destinie:

Such are thy secrets, which my life makes good,
    And comments on thee: for in ev'ry thing
    Thy words do finde me out, & parallels bring,
And in another make me understood.

    Starres are poore books, & oftentimes do misse:
    This book of starres lights to eternall blisse.

---

[253] p139, *The English Poems of George Herbert*, ed. C. A. Patrides, J. M. Dent, London, 1974
[254] p77, *The English Poems of George Herbert*, ed. C. A. Patrides, J. M. Dent, London, 1974

A single verse does not shine alone but all the constellations of the story shine and the verse marks another verse which in turn points to yet a third verse ten pages away. There is, of course, another dimension to all of this: Herbert is also telling us how to read his own poems and to look out for secrets. Indeed, the intertextuality of any poet is well worth exploring. In the case of Herbert this leads naturally to questioning Herbert's own theological understanding.

Herbert's Theology
While he was certainly an Anglican, Herbert's theological perspective was no easy formulaic Anglicanism. He crafted meaning out of his contemporary circumstance. Since the Reformation, his England had oscillated between extremes. Elizabeth I declared, however, that she had 'no desire to make windows into men's souls'. Herbert was persuaded by a middle course between the pre-Reformation Catholic tradition and the Reformists.

This *via media* is there at all sorts of levels. As a Reformist he would not approve of what Charles Taylor in *A Secular Age* refers to as Christianity 'at several speeds' with a complementary relationship 'between the laity, the clergy and other religious "virtuosi" like monks or hermits or wandering saints'. Yet the pre-Reformation monastic order and rule were important for Herbert. There is a circular time inherent in the feasts of the church in such poems as: 'Good Friday', 'Easter I', 'Easter II', 'Whitsunday', 'Trinity Sunday'.

Herbert reflects the Reformation emphasis on the *Word* as celebrated[255] in 'The Holy Scriptures I' (below) and 'The Holy Scriptures II' (quoted above):

'The Holy Scriptures I'

Oh Book! infinite sweetnesse! let my heart
Suck ev'ry letter, and a hony gain,
Precious for any grief in any part;
To cleare the breast, to mollifie all pain.

However, he does not neglect the sacramental. For Herbert, in keeping with the Protestant tradition, there are only two sacraments. The first[256] is Baptism:

---

[255] p76, *The English Poems of George Herbert*, ed. C. A. Patrides, J. M. Dent, London, 1974
[256] p64, *The English Poems of George Herbert*, ed. C. A. Patrides, J. M. Dent, London, 1974

on my infancie
Thou didst lay hold, and antedate
   My faith in me.

        O let me still
Write thee great God, and me a childe.

'H. Baptisme (II)'

The second is the Eucharist. This is, of course, in his time a fraught theme and he delicately seeks to find some vague and underdetermined middle ground between Catholic transubstantiation and a Puritan focus on the symbolic. Not only does Herbert here show extraordinary subtlety of mind, but he produces a really fine poem, 'The Agonie', with its wonderful[257] final six-line stanza:

Who knows not Love, let him assay,
And taste that juice, which on the cross a pike
Did set again abroach; then let him say
   If ever he did taste the like.
Love is that liquour sweet and most divine,
Which my God feels as bloude; but I, as wine.

'The Agonie'

What was a theological bone of contention is for Herbert less a puzzle or a church-dividing issue than a mystery, which leads to God.

Again, while he is in the *sola gratia* 'grace alone' Reformation tradition, Herbert wants both doctrine and life to 'combine and mingle', as he tells us in a fascinating extended image[258] in 'The Windows':

LORD, how can man preach thy eternall word?
   He is a brittle crazie glasse:
Yet in thy temple thou dost him afford
   This glorious and transcendent place,
   To be a window, through thy grace.

'The Windows'

But when thou dost anneal in glasse thy storie,
   Making thy life to shine within
The holy Preachers; then the light and glorie

---

[257] p58, *The English Poems of George Herbert*, ed. C. A. Patrides, J. M. Dent, London, 1974
[258] p84, *The English Poems of George Herbert*, ed. C. A. Patrides, J. M. Dent, London, 1974

Say but the Word

More rev'rend grows, and more doth win;
    Which else shows watrish, bleak, and thin.

Doctrine and life, colours and light, in one
    When they combine and mingle, bring
A strong regard and aw: but speech alone
    Doth vanish like a flaring thing,
    And in the eare, not conscience ring.

Herbert also deals brilliantly with this theme of grace, showing a more introspective, intimate side of Christianity. He knows that the more he trusts God to provide, the more liberated he feels himself in the world; the more he depends on grace, the more freedom he has. This he expresses, with the complex back and forth play[259] he is capable of, in 'Clasping of Hands':

'Clasping of Hands'

Lord, thou art mine, and I am thine,
If mine I am; and thine much more,
Then I or ought, or can be mine.
Yet to be thine, doth me restore;
So that again I now am mine,
And with advantage mine the more.
Since this being mine, brings with it thine,
And thou with me dost thee restore.
    If I without thee would be mine,
    I neither should be mine nor thine.

So opulent is Herbert's thought that a theologian would find endless further aspects to explore. I cannot do justice to this trove. I will just glance at one other facet; his angle on sin. Fundamentally he sees sin, along with the many earlier thinkers, as an absence of good. Here again is a middle way. While the Creator is all powerful, as humans we have responsibility for what we do. He makes this clear[259.1] in the opening two stanzas of his thirty-eight stanza 'Providence':

'Providence'

O Sacred Providence, who from end to end
Strongly and sweetly movest! shall I write,

[259]   p164, *The English Poems of George Herbert*, ed. C. A. Patrides, J. M. Dent, London, 1974
[259.1]   p129, *The English Poems of George Herbert*, ed. C. A. Patrides, J. M. Dent, London, 1974

And not of thee, through whom my fingers bend
To hold my quill? shall they not do thee right?

Of all the creatures both in sea and land
Onely to Man thou hast made known thy wayes,
And put the penne alone into his hand,
And made him Secretarie of thy praise.

There is nothing holier-than-thou about George Herbert. This can be seen in a poem like 'Sinnes Round' where the form too goes round, opening and closing[260] with the echoing 'Sorrie I am, my God, sorrie I am':

Sorrie I am, my God, sorrie I am,   'Sinnes Round'
That my offences course it in a ring.
My thoughts are working like a busie flame,
Untill their cockatrice they hatch and bring:
And when they once have perfected their draughts,
My words take fire from my inflamed thoughts.

My words take fire from my inflamed thoughts,
Which spit it forth like the Sicilian hill.
They vent the wares, and passe them with their faults,
And by their breathing ventilate the ill.
But words suffice not, where are lewd intentions:
My hands do join to finish the inventions.

My hands do join to finish the inventions:
And so my sinnes ascend three stories high,
As Babel grew, before there were dissentions.
Let ill deeds loyter not: for they supplie
New thoughts of sinning: wherefore, to my shame,
Sorrie I am, my God, sorrie I am.

This brings me to a side of Herbert's outlook, which like most of his work, could be viewed theologically, but which I see also as a side, which speaks especially to us today. I am thinking of how he copes with the

---

[260] p134, *The English Poems of George Herbert*, ed. C. A. Patrides, J. M. Dent, London, 1974

temptation to despair and with the overwhelming world of knowledge, prestige and power.

George Herbert Today

Herbert's poems understand where I am and where I have been. All of us, who grew up in an era where despondency was almost a *sine qua non* of literature, had to struggle with despair. If we listen carefully, there is in Herbert, what the scholar C. A. Patrides famously called, a 'controlled turbulence'. Yet without losing his ultimate anchoring in his belief, like the author of Psalm 80, Herbert faces the utter mystery of affliction[261] in 'Confession':

'Confession'
O What a cunning guest
Is this same grief! within my heart I made
   Closets; and in them many a chest;
   And, like a master in my trade,
In those chests, boxes; in each box, a till:
Yet grief knows all, and enters when he will.

No scrue, no piercer can
Into a piece of timber work and winde,
   As Gods afflictions into man,
   When he a torture hath design'd.
They are too subtill for the subt'llest hearts;
And fall, like rheumes, upon the tendrest parts.

We are the earth; and they,
Like moles within us, heave, and cast about:
   And till they foot and clutch their prey,
   They never cool, much lesse give out.
No smith can make such locks, but they have keyes:
Closets are halls to them; and hearts, high-wayes.

It is almost as though, in being securely anchored, Herbert can describe affliction in a deeper and more vivid way than a Kafka or a Beckett.

We do not know why Herbert, the highflying worldly wise former Public Orator and Member of Parliament, decided that earthly and

---

[261] p137, *The English Poems of George Herbert*, ed. C. A. Patrides, J. M. Dent, London, 1974

heavenly ambition were incompatible and why he spent the last three years of his life working hard as a parson in Bemerton, near Salisbury. His belief in peace, the loss of patrons and the turning tide of politics played a part. His desire from boyhood had been a life 'based on divinity'. Between 1626 and 1629 he seemed to suffer from ill health and there was no prospect of gainful employment. Listen to the anguish in the two final stanzas[262] from 'The Employment II':

Oh that I were an Orenge-tree
   That busie plant!
Then should I ever laden be,
   And never want
Some fruit for him that dressed me.

But we are still too young or old;
   The man is gone,
Before we do our wares unfold:
   So we freeze on,
Untill the grave increase our cold.

'The Employment II'

Herbert's world, like ours, is in flux. There are all the power games, the prestige and pleasures of academic or court life, which Herbert had known from his background as well as in his career. He knew them, but ultimately chose another love. Could 'The Pearl' yet be an anthem[263] for our 21st century?

I know the wayes of learning; both the head
And pipes that feed the presse, and make it runne;
What reason hath from nature borrowed,
Or of it self, a good huswife, spunne
In laws and policie; what the starres conspire,
What willing nature speaks, what forc'd by fire;
Both th' old discoveries, and the new-found seas,
The stock and surplus, cause and historie:
All these stand open, or I have the keyes:
   Yet I love thee.

'The Pearl'

---

[262] p95, *The English Poems of George Herbert*, ed. C. A. Patrides, J. M. Dent, London, 1974
[263] p103, *The English Poems of George Herbert*, ed. C. A. Patrides, J. M. Dent, London, 1974

I know the wayes of honour, what maintains
The quick returns of courtesie and wit:
In vies of favours whether partie gains,
When glorie swells the heart, and moldeth it
To all expressions both of hand and eye,
Which on the world a true-love-knot may tie,
And bear the bundle, wheresoe're it goes:
How many drammes of spirit there must be
To sell my life unto my friends or foes:
    Yet I love thee.

I know the wayes of Pleasure, the sweet strains,
The lullings and the relishes of it;
The propositions of hot bloud and brains;
What mirth and musick mean; what love and wit
Have done these twentie hundred yeares, and more:
I know the projects of unbridled store:
My stuffe is flesh, not brasse; my senses live,
And grumble oft, that they have more in me
Then he that curbs them being but one to five:
    Yet I love thee.

I know all these, and have them in my hand:
Therefore not sealed, but with open eyes
I flie to thee, and fully understand
Both the main sale, and the commodities;
And at what rate and price I have thy love;
With all the circumstances that may move:
Yet through these labyrinths, not my groveling wit,
But thy silk twist let down from heav'n to me,
Did both conduct and teach me, how by it
    To climbe to thee.

I can revel in the richness of the imagery of wine making 'both the head
and pipes that feed the presse and make it runne', the imagery of the
commercial world – 'the stock and surplus'; 'both the main sale, and
the commodities' – 'And at what rate and price I have thy love' or the
musical metaphors – 'the sweet strains, the lullings and the relishes of
it'. As has often been pointed out, strains and relishes were precise

musical terms. This brings me to Herbert's use of language and imagery.

Language and Imagery

Herbert, who was a master of the Classics, employed the fertile mix of Anglo-Saxon and Latinate vocabulary in the same way as Shakespeare. Yet in spite of his vast learning and of the carefully worked allusions to the classical myths in his early Latin poetry he chose to avoid such references altogether in *The Temple.* For all its Latinate usage, this poetry is down to earth in the sense that, apart from the constant resonance with scriptures, it employs ordinary imagery of law or commerce or music and so forth. What is so remarkable is not the every day domain where he sought his imagery but the panache with which he extends his metaphors. Here is just one stanza from 'Easter' with the daring musical image of Christ's body as the strings[264] stretched on a wooden instrument:

Awake, my lute, and struggle for thy part   'Easter'
   With all thy art.
The crosse taught all wood to resound his name,
   Who bore the same.
His streched sinews taught all strings, what key
Is best to celebrate this most high day.

I always feel that when Herbert gives us an extended image and the complex logic of a conceit, it does not have either the hectic or indeed sometimes showy quality we find in John Donne. Herbert has a precise wildness, what in patristic times was called 'sober intoxication'. The conceit holds its aim and is subordinated to his purpose. Everything remains substantive and grounded in his relation to God.

   I know of no poet who can astound me over and over again with such infectious imagery. Look how the initial two stanzas[265] of 'The Discharge' take off:

Busie enquiring heart, what wouldst thou know?   'The
   Why dost thou prie,   Discharge'
And turn, and leer, and with a licorous eye
   Look high and low;
And in thy lookings stretch and grow?

[264] p61, *The English Poems of George Herbert*, ed. C. A. Patrides, J. M. Dent, London, 1974
[265] p153, *The English Poems of George Herbert*, ed. C. A. Patrides, J. M. Dent, London, 1974

Hast thou not made thy counts, and summ'd up all?
   Did not thy heart
Give up the whole, and with the whole depart?
   Let what will fall:
     That which is past who can recall?

Yet, renowned as Herbert's conceits are, he can also surprise us with a fanfare of images. The well-known sonnet 'Prayer I' is a dazzling example where image leaps to image[266] without so much as a main verb throughout:

'Prayer I' Prayer the Churches banquet, Angels age,
     Gods breath in man returning to his birth,
     The soul in paraphrase, heart in pilgrimage,
The Christian plummet sounding heav'n and earth;

Engine against th' Almightie, sinners towre,
     Reversed thunder, Christ-side-piercing spear,
     The six-daies world-transposing in an houre,
A kinde of tune, which all things heare and fear;

Softnesse, and peace, and joy, and love, and blisse,
     Exalted Manna, gladnesse of the best,
     Heaven in ordinarie, man well drest,
The milkie way, the bird of Paradise,

     Church-bels beyond the starres heard, the souls bloud,
     The land of spices; something understood.

This sonnet alone is testimony to Herbert's astonishing vaults of imagination. There are so many striking and memorable combinations of words that several have provided titles for books and programmes. Apart from the second line of the couplet which supplied the title of Kate O'Brien's novel *The Land of Spices* and Mark Tully's long running BBC radio programme 'Something Understood', 'The Soul in Paraphrase', 'Reversed Thunder' and 'Heaven in Ordinary' have all been used as titles of books on religious topics. Clearly, both the

---

[266] p70, *The English Poems of George Herbert*, ed. C. A. Patrides, J. M. Dent, London, 1974

religious implication and the imaginative impact endure.

There is, of course, more than the imagery involved: there is also the mastery of form, to which I now want to turn.

Mastery of Form

Herbert is one of the greatest masters of form in the whole of the English language poetic tradition. He is such a virtuoso that it is difficult to know where to begin to describe his extraordinary gift.

In the first place, there is the architectonics of *The Temple*. And architectonics is the appropriate term, as *The Temple* is an intricate structure with all the tiers of Biblical and other allusions and resonances we expect from Herbert. As C. A. Patrides has pointed out, the three parts of *The Temple*: 'The Church-porch', 'The Church' and 'The Church Militant' represent the progress of the human soul but also refract the Hebraic temple in the porch, the holy place and the Holy of Holies. Then again it can be thought of as the invitation, an ordering of Christian life and the workings of God. There are further echoes of the temple not only as a place, but in the idea of the human body as a temple of the Holy Ghost. And we must not forget that underpinning all this is the plain and simple architecture of the church as a building.

At the level of the single poem Herbert's two 'pattern' or 'shaped' poems, 'The Altar' and 'Angels Wings', are widely known. Although disdained by the Augustans, this type of 'exhibition' poem continues to have an appeal and is used by such poets as Bertolt Brecht, Dylan Thomas, e. e. cummings and Denise Levertov.

Another pyrotechnical device is the acrostic. The letters from the column to the extreme left in 'Prayer I' quoted above, if read vertically from top to bottom, give PTEAST. This was a standard abbreviation for 'point east'. It is the imperative that is, if you like, the missing main verb in the poem. Herbert is pointing east to the land of spices.

One further 'exhibition' form is the 'paring' device, which we see in *Paradise* and for all its exotic quality[267] fits the theme:

I Bless thee, Lord, because I G R O W   'Paradise'
Among thy trees, which in a   R O W
To thee both fruit and order   O W.

---

[267] p143, *The English Poems of George Herbert*, ed. C. A. Patrides, J. M. Dent, London, 1974

Say but the Word

What open force, or hidden C H A R M
Can blast my fruit, or bring me H A R M,
While the inclosure is thine   A R M?

Inclose me still for fear I   S T A R T.
Be to me rather sharp and   T A R T,
Then let me want thy hand & A R T.

When thou dost greater judgements S P A R E,
And with thy knife but prune and P A R E,
Ev'n fruitfull trees more fruitfull   A R E.

Such sharpnes shows the sweetest F R E N D:
Such cuttings rather heal than   R E N D:
And such beginnings touch their E N D.

Apart from the firework displays of skill, Herbert uses traditional forms such as the sonnet, but is also constantly inventing form and rhyme schemes appropriate to his subject matter. Each poem seems new and different.

For all the array of rhyme schemes in Herbert's poems, perhaps the most exciting feature of his form is his metrics, especially his use of what Joseph H. Summers labels counterpoint. About half of the poems in *The Temple* use a conventional rhyme scheme. The others do not and a quarter of the poems have counterpoint with patterns where no lines of the same length rhyme, or where in an elaborate rhyme scheme only one pair of the same length rhyme. This is an approach he noticed in Sir Philip Sidney's translations of the Psalms, which he greatly admired. These were begun by Sidney and completed by his sister, Countess of Pembroke, Mary Herbert. Take for instance[268] Psalm XX:

'Psalm XX'   Let God the Lord heare thee,
Ev'n in the day when most thy troubles be;
      Let name of Jacob's God,
       When thou on it dost cry,
Defend thee still from all thy foes abroad.

---

[268] http://www.luminarium.org/renascence-editions/sidpsalms.html#psalmes accessed
        16 September 2014

Or Psalm XXXVIII:

Lord, while that Thy wrath doth bide,   'Psalm
   Do not chide,   XXXVIII'
Nor in anger chastise me
For Thy shafts haue pierc't me sore,
   And yet more
Still Thy hands vpon me be.

In many ways this is Herbert's formal trademark. It gives freshness to poem after poem as in the wonderful rhythms[269] of 'Complaining':

Do not beguile my heart,   'Complaining'
   Because thou art
My power and wisdome. Put me not to shame,
   Because I am
  Thy clay that weeps, thy dust that calls.

  Thou art the Lord of glorie;
   The deed and storie
Are both thy due: but I a silly flie,
   That live or die
  According as the weather falls.

  Art thou all justice, Lord?
   Shows not thy word
More attributes? Am I all throat or eye,
   To weep or crie?
  Have I no parts but those of grief?

  Let not thy wrathfull power
   Afflict my houre,
My inch of life: or let thy gracious power
   Contract my houre,
  That I may climbe and finde relief.

There is such beautiful sway to his poem 'Longing'. Here are just the first two[270] stanzas:

[269] p153, *The English Poems of George Herbert*, ed. C. A. Patrides, J. M. Dent, London, 1974

Say but the Word

'Longing'   With sick and famisht eyes,
With doubling knees and weary bones,
        To thee my cries,
        To thee my grones,
To thee my sighs, my tears ascend:
            No end?

    My throat, my soul is hoarse;
My heart is wither'd like a ground
        Which thou dost curse.
        My thoughts turn round,
And make me giddie; Lord, I fall,
            Yet call.

This constant variation in the metrics seems to suit Herbert's thought and temperament so well.

Conclusion

All I can hope to succeed in doing is to share my love of this marvellous work and to convey, at least to some degree, why he appeals so strongly to me. I am sympathetic to his themes and thought and at the same time I am attracted by this consummate skill. His ability to combine content and form is unique. He does this with an intensity and flair that never loses its focus or swaggers self-indulgently. I love the way he wrestles with ideas of his own time, and am utterly intrigued that a man who died at forty achieved all he did. As the years pass I find myself drawn again and again to his work. The more I read him the more I find in him and the more he sustains me. There is always a freshness to his poems, which is astounding and he remains rooted[271] in what is greater than himself:

'Love II'   Immortal Heat, O let thy greater flame
        Attract the lesser to it: let those fires,
        Which shall consume the world, first make it tame;
And kindle in our hearts such true desires,

---

[270] p157, *The English Poems of George Herbert*, ed. C. A. Patrides, J. M. Dent, London, 1974
[271] p73, *The English Poems of George Herbert*, ed. C. A. Patrides, J. M. Dent, London, 1974

As may consume our lusts, and make thee way.
 Then shall our hearts pant thee; then shall our brain
 All her invention on thine Altar lay,
And there in hymnes send back thy fire again:

Our eies shall see thee, which before saw dust;
 Dust blown by wit, till that they both were blinde:
 Thou shalt recover all thy goods in kinde,
Who wert disseized by usurping lust:

 All knees shall bow to thee; all wits shall rise,
 And praise him who did make and mend our eies.

For those who do not share his faith or cannot make the required hospitable leap of imagination, he will remain a counter-cultural poet. For the mindset of modernity, his quiet confidence that 'All knees shall bow to thee' is scandalous and offends the secular self-sufficiency that cannot conceive what it cannot see. Our autonomy is impugned by the recognition of something beyond ourselves. Our eyes do not need mending; they see all there is to see. For my own part, as I go daily to my table, I hear Herbert's magnificent poem 'The Flower' reverberate[272] in me:

And now in age I bud again,   'The Flower'
After so many deaths I live and write;
 I once more smell the dew and rain,
And relish versing: O my onely light,
  It cannot be
  That I am he
 On whom thy tempests fell all night.

 These are thy wonders, Lord of love,
To make us see we are but flowers that glide:
 Which when we once can finde and prove,
Thou hast a garden for us, where to bide.
  Who would be more
  Swelling through store,
 Forfeit their Paradise by their pride.

[272] p172, *The English Poems of George Herbert*, ed. C. A. Patrides, J. M. Dent, London, 1974

'You can only take my word for it':
Denise Levertov's Poetic Witness

The poet Robert Creeley in an introduction to Denise Levertov's *New Selected Poems* said 'poets are a company and poetry must finally be a tribal art despite the fierceness of contest, which sometimes preoccupies its persons'. Too often however, probably due to Ezra Pound's dictum 'make it new', we tend to concentrate on current modes or contemporary cabals and lose sight of the longer tradition. I have got to say that I am much more interested in the fellowship of poets across generations, in a community of relationships over time. I find myself less concerned with the constant search for novelty than with reshaping and renewal.

A summons passes along an unpredictable and regenerative grapevine. All our antennae are up to catch the signal. I want to be part of some long rumour of wisdom.

Our second 'Thirty Years War', culminating in the Holocaust, unleashed a crisis in humanism which had been brewing in intellectual European circles, particularly throughout the second half of the previous century. Poetry is always of its time, our words are waves sent from our time and place. They may bounce off some universal Heaviside layer above us and be picked up far away, resonating with the reality of another time and place. When I take this broad perspective I'm bound to think through how the poets, whose company I keep or avoid, relate to this crisis, this temptation to despair, which so often threatens to blot out the light, to silence a long rumour of wisdom.

Brief Biography

I want to look briefly at the life of Denise Levertov whose work throughout the second half of the twentieth century has kept the long rumour of wisdom alive. She is part of a company of poets where I would like to belong, a community I want to be woven into. Hers is a vision and a voice which attracts me. I feel sure that she would understand my desire. She has pointed towards that fellowship and baton-passing and the wonder[273] of an inherited language in her poem 'September 1961':

---

[273] p186, *The Collected Poems of Denise Levertov,* eds. Paul A. Lacey & Anne Dewey, New Directions, New York, 2013

This is the year the old ones,
the old great ones
leave us alone on the road.

'September
1961'

.   .   .   .   .

They have told us
the road leads to the sea,
and given

the language into our hands.
We hear
our footsteps each time a truck

has dazzled past us and gone
leaving us new silence.

Born in Ilford in Essex, a London suburb, in 1923, her mother was reared in a mining village in North Wales and her father was a Russian immigrant Hasidic Jew, who had taught at the University of Leipzig. Held under arrest during World War I, her father subsequently emigrated to Britain where he became an Anglican priest. She was educated at home and from an early age was taken by ballet, writing and the piano. In her short essay 'What We Remember' she described some of the cultural figures that touched her childhood: her parents having tea with Paul Robeson, the American bass-baritone known for his radical outlook; her father translating Franz Werfel, the expressionist German language playwright and contemporary of Franz Kafka in Prague, whose wife had once been Gustav Mahler's wife; her early exchange of a letter with T. S. Eliot. In another short piece 'An Encounter – and a Re-Encounter' she describes, at twelve alongside her elder sister Olga who was twenty-one, asking to join the Communist Party. Too young, she was refused membership but was allowed sell copies of the *Daily Worker* on Saturdays. Denise Levertov's teenage years were spent in wartime London and she worked as a civilian nurse during the blitz. Two years after the war ended she met the American writer Mitchell Goodman in a youth hostel in Switzerland. She married him and moved to the United States of America. She worked at various universities including Tufts, Brandeis and Stanford. She spent her final years in Seattle where she moved in 1989.

Say but the Word

Themes

One biographical paragraph opens onto the major themes of Denise Levertov's work. It's of course impossible to compress a life's work which was so long and rich into an easy scheme and yet it seems to me that the three major themes of her work are love, justice in society and the doubts and struggles concerning life's meaning. Let me look at each of these in turn.

Love

Her love poems are so beautiful in their quiet intensity and sensuality. Take her two companion poems[274] 'The Marriage':

'The Marriage'

You have my
attention: which is
a tenderness, beyond
what I may say. And I have
your constancy to
    something beyond myself.
The force
of your commitment charges us – we live
in the sweep of it, taking courage
one from the other.

and 'The Marriage (II)':

'The Marriage (II)'

I want to speak to you.
To whom else should I speak?
It is you who make
a world to speak of.
In your warmth the
fruit ripen – all the
apples and pears that grow
on the south wall of my
head. If you listen
it rains for them, then
they drink. If you
speak in response

[274] p58, *The Collected Poems of Denise Levertov,* eds. Paul A. Lacey & Anne Dewey, New Directions, New York, 2013

the seeds
jump into the ground.
Speak or be silent: your silence
will speak to me.

What a lovely evocation of the ease of a marriage! And there is the
trademark extended image in the ripening fruit. Here is another fluid
image in 'Losing Track' which touches both the depths and ebbings of
sensuous togetherness[275] from her sixth collection *The Jacob's Ladder*
published in 1961:

Long after you have swung back   'Losing Track'
away from me
I think you are still with me:

you come in close to the shore
on the tide
and nudge me awake the way

a boat adrift nudges the pier:
am I a pier
half-in half-out of the water?

and in the pleasure of that communion
I lose track,
the moon I watch goes down, the

tide swings you away before
I know I'm
alone again long since,

mud sucking at gray and black
timbers of me,
a light growth of green dreams drying.

What is astonishing is that though her marriage to Mitch Goodman
ended in divorce in 1974, twenty-seven years after they had first met,

[275] p226, *ibid.*

she could write such a poised and movingly generous poem as
'Divorcing' which appeared[276] in her collection *The Freeing of the Dust*
which appeared in 1975:

'Divorcing'   One garland
of flowers, leaves, thorns,
was twined round our two necks.
Drawn tight, it could choke us,
yet we loved its scratchy grace,
our fragrant yoke.

We were Siamese twins.
Our blood's not sure
if it can circulate,
now we are cut apart.
Something in each of us is waiting
to see if we can survive,
severed.

The magnanimity of this love by extension leads us naturally to her
engagement with justice in society and her refusal to accept an unfair
world which is the second significant theme in Denise Levertov's work.
The girl of twelve seeking to join the Communist Party becomes the
mature woman crying out against all the cruelties of war, hunger and
the destruction of life and of the human habitat. You can hear her
dismay[277] at injustice and poverty as the inverse of a dream for the world
'3 a.m., September 1, 1969':

'3 a.m.,   Warm wind, the leaves
September 1,   rustling without dryness,
1969'   hills dissolved into silver.

It could be any age,
four hundred years ago or a time
of post-revolutionary peace,
the rivers clean again, birth rate and crops
somehow in balance…

[276] p481, *ibid.*
[277] p412, *ibid.*

In heavy dew
under the moon the blond grasses
lean in swathes on the field slope. Fervently
the crickets practice their religion of ecstasy.

Yet she could be more strident in her righteous impatience at the
barbarities of our world and given her time, the Vietnamese War
loomed large. Here are the opening lines[278] of 'Advent 1966':

Because in Vietnam the vision of a Burning Babe   'Advent 1966'
is multiplied, multiplied,
                    the flesh on fire
not Christ's, as Southwell saw it, prefiguring
the Passion upon the Eve of Christmas,

but wholly human and repeated, repeated,
infant after infant, their names forgotten,
their sex unknown in the ashes,

set alight, flaming but not vanishing,
not vanishing as his vision but lingering,

cinders upon the earth or living on
moaning and stinking in hospitals three abed; ...

This insistent sympathy with the suffering will persist right through
her work and even in her final volume *The Great Unknowing: Last poems*
published posthumously where she achieves such a beautiful serenity,
a poem[279] such as 'Fugitives' still occurs:

The Red Cross vans, laden with tanks of   'Fugitives'
drinking water, can go no further:
the road has become a river.
The dry, dusty, potholed road
that was waiting the rainy season
is flowing with men and women
(especially women) and children.

[278] p342, *ibid.*
[279] p995, *ibid.*

What is notable here is that in spite of her obvious shock and disgust at the inequity and the unnecessary misery in our world, her sense of balance as a poet always keeps her on the right side of the fine line between poetry and an angry harangue. There is little doubt her own quest for a purpose in life, with the inherent misgivings and qualms, helped her to avoid any temptation to allow any poem turn into a tirade. This brings us to the third strand in Denise Levertov's work which deals with questions of doubt and meaning.

After her conversion to Christianity in 1984, faith becomes the dominant theme of her later work. Questions of meaning were woven through her poetry from the start. Phrases such as 'in the pleasure of that communion' or 'the crickets practice their religion of ecstasy' or the reference to Southwell in 'Advent 1966' illustrate this. The consistency of this aspect throughout her life and spiritual journey is highlighted in *The Stream & the Sapphire: Selected Poems on Religious Themes* (1997).

I hear her youthful agnostic questioning in the second[280] of 'Three Meditations' from *The Jacob's Ladder* published in 1961:

'Three
Meditations ii'

Who was it yelled, cracking
the glass of delight?
Who sent the child
sobbing to bed, and woke it
later to comfort it?
I, I, I, I.
I multitude, I tyrant,
I angel, I you, you
world, battlefield, stirring
with unheard litanies, sounds of piercing
green half-smothered by
strewn bones.

Many doubts and struggles with meaning occupy her thought and poems. After her move to Seattle in 1989, she became a Catholic. As we will see when looking at her vision, it is in *A Door in the Hive* (1993), *Evening Train* (1993), *Sands of the Well* (1996) as well as in the marvellous posthumous *This Great Unknowing* (1999) that she reaches an

[280] p153, *ibid.*

extraordinary peace and acceptance as her own life and probably the most turbulent century of all time were both coming to a close. Yet even in this last phase a little of the questioning struggle still echoes. A mountain sometimes visible, sometimes not, becomes a constant motif and emblem of the great unknowable. There are reverberations of old questionings[281] in 'Mirage':

Ethereal mountain   'Mirage'
snowwhite foam hovering
far above blue, cloudy ridges –
can one believe you are not a mirage?

In 'The Blind Man's House at the Edge of the Cliff' there is also another motif which suggests daring to live[282] on the edge 'not from ignorance, not from despair' but:

He knows that if he could see   'The Blind
he would be no wiser,   Man's House at
High on the windy cliff he breathes   the Edge of the
face to face with desire.   Cliff'

I will return later to this deep-seated need for meaning and will look at how it blossoms into a more confident vision but now I want to comment briefly on her approach to writing.

Shift from Formal to Open Verse
The poetry in Denise Levertov's first two books has a more classical formal style[283] as we see in 'Listening to Distant Guns':

The roses tremble; oh, the sunflower's eye   'Listening to
Is opened wide in sad expectancy.   Distant Guns'
Westward and back the circling swallows fly,
The rooks' battalions dwindle near the hill.

However after she settled in America she became for the rest of her life an American poet – moving in the opposite direction to Anne

---

[281] p896, *ibid.*
[282] p788, *ibid.*
[283] p3, *ibid.*

Stevenson, an American who became a British poet.

But in terms of style, what kind of an American poet? I once saw in a book a drawing, I think by Richard Wilbur – whose work I love – where there were three signposts. One signpost had 'Black Mountain' on it, another had 'Beats' and a third had 'Parnassus'. I reckon 'Parnassus' stood for a certain classic formality which, following the Greeks, saw art in the creative tension between content and form. This is what in 1986 Ronald Baughman's *A Field Guide to Recent Schools of American Poetry* described rather unfortunately as 'Academic'. But Denise Levertov was prior to the Beatnik poets who came to prominence in the 1960s. This meant her choice was between the more classical approach with which she started out and the Black Mountain approach named after a group of poets who studied at Black Mountain College with Charles Olsen in the 1950s, who wanted 'projective verse' and had theories about 'open form' and composition by 'fields'. Olsen's theory stemmed from Ezra Pound and William Carlos Williams. He felt that rhyme and metre were largely the result of print and wanted to compose in an 'open field' with no form to guide the work. It should be guided by breathing and syllables juxtaposed with one perception immediately and directly leading to a further perception. The form should only be an extension of content. Though Denise Levertov never claimed membership of the Black Mountain School, as an admirer of William Carlos Williams she certainly came under its influence.

Robert Creeley in his introduction to her *New Selected Poems* writes movingly of how during a year when they were neighbours in the south of France they had 'talked as only the young can – of our master Williams' line, of how to locate stress, how to *measure*, to keep the physical fact of sound and rhythm explicit'. It must have seemed attractively progressive, even revolutionary, in its time. During her life many different schools would come and go – Baughman describes another five: the Concretists, the Confessionalists, the Deep Imagists, the New York School, the New Black Aesthetic. While all of these leave a trace in subsequent generations, the choice which faced Denise Levertov is basically the same today: either formal or open form. The only difference is that the so-called Neo-Formalist School may now be as countercultural as the Black Mountain School seemed then. Modes of form – syllabic, metrical or open – will wax and wane or simply be chosen by a poet's time and temperament, but what matters in the end is a poet's voice and vision.

Say but the Word

Voice

A voice is a tone, a pitch that speaks the truth. There is an amazing autobiography of Jacques Lusseyran, a blind member of the French Resistance under the Nazi occupation called *Et la lumière fut* (translated as *And there was light*). Blinded in childhood, he, as he described it 'could read voices like a book'. When interviewing prospective underground recruits he could immediately detect any falseness in a voice, any trace of weakness or treachery. The one time he went against his instinct, his group was betrayed, arrested and sent to Buchenwald. Such is the importance of a voice ringing true. There is no defining it and yet we recognise it when we hear it.

In a memorable essay called 'Voice' in her book *Tessarae*, Denise Levertov tells how as a young woman hitch-hiking in France she'd strayed into a church in Montélimar. There behind a grille a hidden choir of nuns from an enclosed order were singing *a capella*, 'but one voice began to mount like a skylark and detach itself from the rest, from the mingled voices which together sounded well, but from whose conjunction this single one soared in an intensity of beauty – a voice so clear and just, yet vibrant with such sweetness, I have remembered it always. Or have remembered at least what words and images might have described it: the pure, silvery cold quality of a coloratura conjoined with something dark, honeyed, sensuous, such as one expects to find only in mezzo-sopranos and contraltos ... the fact that this great, this glorious and rare voice was singing behind bars, that the face and identity of the singer would be forever unknown to us and the world, shadowed the music ... We did not consider "the greater glory of God," or the fact that the nun may have been perfectly content in her chosen cloister.'

And that 'voice' is, through its Latin origin in *vox*, a cognate of the second element in Calliope, 'beautiful voice' and daughter of Zeus and Mnemosyne, who was Homer's muse. Denise Levertov did not write an epic in the classical sense of one extended narrative poem and yet you get a feeling that poem after poem over a lifetime added up to a personal epic which spanned the second half of the twentieth century. She kept that beautiful voice singing.

The word 'epic' itself is also ultimately related to *vox,* to voice. The Greek word *epos* meant word or song. Indeed 'voice', again through *vox* is a cognate of the Irish word *focal* meaning word. One of Denise Levertov's most beautiful poems[284] is called 'Credo' from her 'Mass for the Day of St Thomas Didymus', which begins:

---

[284] p674, *ibid.*

'Credo'   I believe the earth
          exists, and
          in each minim mote
          of its dust the holy
          glow of thy candle.
          Thou
          unknown I know,
          thou spirit,
          giver,
          lover of making, of the
          wrought letter,
          wrought flower,
          iron, deed, dream.

Or there are those often quoted three lines[285] from 'The Unknown':

'The   The awakening is
Unknown'   to transformation,
           word after word.

The word can also reverberate with the full scope[286] of the opening of
John's Gospel as in 'On the Mystery of the Incarnation':

'On the   It's when we face for a moment
Mystery of the   the worst our kind can do, and shudder to know
Incarnation'   the taint in our own selves, that awe
                 cracks the mind's shell and enters the heart:
                 not to a flower, not to a dolphin,
                 to no innocent form
                 but to this creature vainly sure
                 it and no other is God-like, God
                 (out of compassion for our ugly
                 failure to evolve) entrusts,
                 as guest, as brother,
                 the Word.

Then again 'voice' comes from the Latin word *vox* from which vocation

[285] p244, *ibid.*
[286] p818, *ibid.*

Say but the Word

is also derived. Here is a reflection on that call[287] again in 'For Those Whom the Gods Love Less' from the last original collection published while she lived:

When you discover
your new work travels the ground you had traversed
decades ago, you wonder, panicked,
'Have I outlived my vocation? Said already
all that was mine to say?'

    .   .   .   .   .   .

it's the way
radiant epiphanies recur, recur,
consuming, pristine, unrecognized —
until remembrance dismays you. And then, look,
some inflection of light, some wing of shadow
is other, unvoiced. You can, you must
proceed.

'For Those Whom the Gods Love Less'

Now a final, and maybe the crucial *midrash* on 'voice'! Once more[288], through *vox*, 'voice' is cognate with the Icelandic word *vottur* which means witness:

a trace, of certainty, promise
broader than slender
tapir's disappearing
sturdy back, the
you can only
take my
word for it, a life,
a phase
beyond the
known geography, beyond familiar

'Visitation. Overflow.'

Those lines are from 'Visitation. Overflow.', and are the words of a witness. *You can only take my word for it.* Indeed there is a poem[289] called 'Witness' in *The Almost Island*: where her mountain motif again features

[287] p956, *ibid.*
[288] p1000, *ibid.*
[289] p897, *ibid.*

Say but the Word

as she bears witness to a witnessing presence:

'Witness' Sometimes the mountain
is hidden from me in veils
of cloud, sometimes
I am hidden from the mountain
in veils of inattention, apathy, fatigue,
when I forget or refuse to go
down to the shore or a few yards
up the road, on a clear day,
to reconfirm
that witnessing presence.

For a poet the true voice follows a love of language word after word – no matter whether in fixed syllabic counts, rhyme and metre or juxtaposition – the epic of a lifetime's vocation, even, if need be, to become a soaring witness behind a grille of anonymity.

Vision and Culminating Concerns
Vision is the main driver of a poet. How does the poet desire the world to be? What is the poems' horizon? Of course it can simply be the sudden mood of inspiration or what was called in Irish *tinfeadh*, the breath blow in, or the blitz of insight, the spark and gleam of understanding that the Japanese call *hirameki.* But I mean here something broader and bigger, an attitude, a point of view that becomes the primus motor of life devoted to writing poetry.

I think we can think of the vision towards which Denise Levertov grew and which and in the end fulfilled her as having three major aspects which are culminations of the major themes we have already discussed. Firstly there is serenity and a faith which evolves from the doubts and struggles for meaning. Secondly, there is a calmer sense of an individuality and society mediated by her Christian viewpoint to which she came gradually from her political activism. Thirdly, there is an earned wisdom of self-surrender which seems to flow naturally from the poise and generosity so apparent in her earlier love poems.

In an era of workshops and a rather naïve trust in technique, we're often given to understand that, shown the right bag of tricks, everyone will write great poetry. I believe that there is an intangible quality to a work which is driven by an inner need for the artist to make some sense of things, to achieve a certain peace. Often it's a sense of wonder and awe, a feeling of deep involvement in the world and beyond the world. There is no doubt that this urge is there in the poetry of Denise Levertov from the very start. An early and previously uncollected poem[290] which is included in her *New Selected Poems* called 'Childhood's End' begins:

The world alive with love, where leaves tremble,
systole and diastole marking miraculous hours,
is burning round the children where they lie
deep in caressing grasses all the day,
and feverish words of once upon a time
assail their hearts with languor and with swans.

'Childhood's End'

Immediately you know that elusive mark of awe and layered insight is present. I'm not thinking here only of the explicated faith which runs through her work right from the amazing *The Jacob's Ladder* and is a particular characteristic of her later work. There is too a profound element of mystery which pervades her earlier poetry. Think, for instance, of these lines[291] from 'The Secret' in her collection *O Taste and See* published in 1964:

Two girls discover
the secret of life
in a sudden line of
poetry.

'The Secret'

I who don't know the
secret wrote
the line.

   . . . . .

a thousand times, till death
finds them, they may
discover it again, in other
lines

in other
happenings. And for
wanting to know it,
for

[290] p19, *ibid.*
[291] p193, *ibid.*

Say but the Word

assuming there is
such a secret, yes,
for that
most of all.

But in her final years this feeling for the mystery of life ripens into the serenity[292] of a 'From Below' in *The Great Unknowable*:

'From Below' I move among the ankles
of forest Elders, tread
their moist rugs of moss,
duff of their soft brown carpets.
Far above, their arms are held
open wide to each other, or waving –

what they know, what
perplexities and wisdoms they exchange,
unknown to me as were the thoughts
of grownups when in infancy I wandered
into a roofed clearing amidst
human feet and legs and the massive
carved legs of the table,

the minds of people, the minds of trees
equally remote, my attention then
filled with sensations, my attention now
caught by leaf and bark at eye level
and by thoughts of my own, but sometimes
drawn to upgazing – up and up: to wonder
about what rises
so far above me into the light.

There are also superb longer mediations on openly religious themes 'El Salvador: Requiem and Invocation', 'A Calvary Path', 'What the Figtree Said', 'Ascension' which always are lit by Levertov's own angle of vision and yet grounded in lived human life.

The belonging to society, the sense of responsibility towards

[292] p979, *ibid.*

humanity is well known from her poems which oppose oppression, cruelty and war. But after her discovery of Christianity a new dimension to this feeling of answerability emerges. In one of her most explicit expressions of this she, like George Eliot in *Middlemarch*, turns to the web as a metaphor. Here[293] is 'Web' from *A Door in the Hive* published in 1989:

Intricate and untraceable   'Web'
weaving and interweaving,
dark strand with light:

designed, beyond
all spiderly contrivance,
to link, not to entrap:

elation, grief, joy, contrition, entwined;
shaking, changing,
                forever
                        forming,
                                transforming:

all praise,
        all praise to the
                great web.

Anne Dewey in her *The Art of the Octopus: The Maturation of Denise Levertov's Political Vision* has pointed out how Levertov comes to see Christianity as a bridge between individuals and society, and is preoccupied by how society can be transformed by its values.

Finally there is what I see as her yielding to the wisdom of letting go. Robert Creeley has astutely written: 'In the very last years of her life she became a Catholic, and I wondered about that for my own reasons, curious that she should, as a woman, accept the situation of that belief. Very probably I missed the point entirely – and assumed that her choice was among possibilities, whereas I now see it was to come into a company, a gathering of all, a determined yielding of such distinction

[293] p829, *ibid.*

Say but the Word

and isolating privilege, which may well have persuaded her'. Yet like much of her later humility, trust and wisdom, the seeds were there right from the outset. We see this in the final lines[294] of her poem 'Action' published in *Overland to the Islands* in 1958:

'Action'   Deep water.
Little by little one comes to know
The limits and depths of power.

But this deepens into the modesty of the unseen nun singing *a capella* in a cloister in Montélimar. It's a similar self-knowledge burnished by another thirty-four years and finds expression[295] in the lovely 'Whisper' from her late collection *Evening Train*:

'Whisper'   Today the white mist that is weather
is mixed with the sallow tint
of the mist that is smog.
And from it, through it, breathes
a vast whisper:
the mountain.

This poise and humility which is present in her love poetry now re-emerges[296] in, for instance, the magnificent poem 'Suspended', the final one in *Evening Train*:

'Suspended'   I had grasped God's garment in the void
but my hand slipped
on the rich silk of it.
The 'everlasting arms' my sister loved to remember
must have upheld my leaden weight
from falling, even so,
for though I claw at empty air and feel
nothing, no embrace,
I have not plummeted.

This for me expresses the ultimate yielding of the self, the final letting-

[294] p81, *ibid.*
[295] p897, *ibid.*
[296] p911, *ibid.*

Say but the Word

go where there is no attempt to grasp or control. Denise Levertov no longer needs to try to achieve anything. She simply basks in a calm certitude that no matter what, she is sustained.

Introduction

The poet Mary O'Donnell in her wide intellectual range and international perspective has panache and a startling confidence. She combines this with an honesty and a daring vulnerability that refuses to hide behind verbal dexterity or clever irony. This is what makes her work so moving a testimony to her generation. While her novels and short stories in many ways reflect her poetic themes, and though a study of how they are interwoven would indeed be fascinating, I am confining myself almost exclusively to her poetry. I want here to explore how her poetry to date describes the arc of a life lived with intensity and rich engagement.

Perhaps the best point of departure is Mary O'Donnell's own tentative definition of what a poem might be. She has described a good poem 'as having a lot to do with anxiety'. A poet has 'a central anxiety, something which agitates and preoccupies him, which will not let him go until he has addressed it and faced it down'. She goes on to say 'if the anxiety is the trigger-mechanism which creates the poems, we could perhaps speculate that a poem is a kind of resolution, a very open-ended one'.

This contrasts somewhat with Robert Frost's classic statement that 'a poem begins in delight and ends in wisdom'. Both attempts to define a poem are valid for different poets and even for the same poets at various points of their lives. But it seems to me that Mary O'Donnell's particular take, her trajectory from anxiety to open-ended resolution, might be a fascinating way of seeing her whole poetic journey to date and to understanding the extraordinary energy which her poems exude. Some of what might be called anxieties are a series of tensions, of deep pushes and pulls which the poet experiences in her own life and in society and which she needs to try over and over again to resolve. If we stand back and take an overall view of her work, it may reveal the same pattern of tension and open-ended resolution. Let us now probe some of those tensions which in different forms express a conflict between restraint and spontaneity.

Tensions

Societal Constraints and Full Womanhood
There is a tension between domestic constraints and a full sensuous
flourishing of womanhood.

   From the earliest work this concern exercises the poet and provokes
poems. Sometimes it finds expression in genuine fellow feeling with
women curbed by society, as in 'Excision' which twice[297] speaks of:

Razor in Sudan,   'Excision'
yashmak in Tehran,
purdah in India,
two tongues for Japan.

But beside this worldwide solidarity with subdued women, there is the
threat of an excision much nearer home than the Sudan:

Here, veiled tranquillity, the   'Excision'
splice and fever of diet and clean
hair, fragrance, spruce linen;
children, gleaming, scrubbed clones,

excised like her, the genie in
little heads mopped of mystery
till they too live a crisp anxiety.
Neither goddess nor woman inhabit

this temple for which earth is carved,
but diamond fortitude, covert moments
trickling to crow's feet, gimlet eyes
which mirror sparkling smiles. It rots

the brightest soul until she
is too cuntless to dare, too numb
to snare the trancing of
voluptuous years that bled her

---

[297] pp16–17, Mary O'Donnell, *Reading the Sunflowers in September*, Salmon, Galway, 1990

white and loathe to fight.
Her torpor fractures the wall.
fissures creep, the sun-tide
rises even as she sleeps.

This is a strong statement and clearly driven by a deep-seated dread of being sucked into deadening patterns under societal pressure. Yet this stops short of the type of 'protest-verse' which Mary O'Donnell rejects. Right from her first book, *Reading the Sunflowers in September*, any crying out against the world's cruelties is offset by a wonderful enhancing sensuousness which celebrates what she mourns the lack of in 'Excision'. I still remember how struck I was when I first read her love poem 'Cycling with Martin'. In it she and her husband Martin 'whirr across terrain once dreamt of, cautious immigrants in the land of forgotten love.' There[298] are 'tumbling thickets' and 'blackberries' and so:

'Cycling with Martin'

I sample your body on such trips,
draw urgent images from leaves,

long, pushing mushrooms, flaming rosehip,
idle on the hours we've spent,
the heat of your buttocks

as you break within me.

And then the poem concludes with:

This bawdy autumn, I quicken,
feel vintage warmth in the sun,
unsprung from myself as the year drowses.

Hungry for peaches and plums,
flesh lustily cloven,
I repeat my cyclist's mantra,

Brute labials like *love, my love…*

---

[298] p113, Mary O'Donnell, *Reading the Sunflowers in September*, Salmon, Galway, 1990

Say but the Word

Here is another tender love poem in the voice of Eve, one of a beautiful mini-series of poems[299] featuring Eve. It is called 'Eve, Discovering Frost':

I had slept in this place,
having heard the voice of a man,
lay openly, pondered a song
that kept galaxies glinting
from chill carousels.
Feeling safe, I rested.

At dawn his touch had plaited
my hair, my shoulders bore
skins of filigree.
All around, the tamarind, the carambola,
in bright sheaths, their fruits
crystalled in the sun.

Mists rose from the garden,
a silver orb split to halves of light.
My dreams having spun the world
to flosses, I cried out,
then uttered one quiet word:
Beloved.

Of course these tensions, which I'm tracing in Mary O'Donnell's work, intersect and overlap, as one would expect. Sometimes, as in the 'Spiderwoman's Third Avenue Rhapsody', the title poem of her second collection, the celebration of female sexuality is in a frenzied urban setting – 'O wild Manhattan'. More often, as in 'Cycling with Martin' or 'Eve, Discovering Frost', there is an association of the lushness of nature with carnal delight. This leads me to another unease which energises poems: an opposition between the stability of institution and an anarchical life-force.

Institutions and Life-Force
Mary O'Donnell attended university at Maynooth, which has its origins

---

[299] p25, Mary O'Donnell, *Spiderwoman's Third Avenue Rhapsody*, Salmon, Swords, 1993

in St. Patrick's College which was a major seminary for Catholic priests. Maynooth features in a number of poems and the institution has a certain fascination which both appeals and repulses. It is 'a cloistered place' and there are[300] 'new clerics, peach-fuzz on chin like sleep in the eyes of children fervently soutaned':

'Maynooth College, August'

I love and loathe such places:

echoes of purple twilights
on crumbled tennis-court,
the occult haunt of bats and owls.
A hard game, watched, applauded
           by tubercular boys
           from a silent century,
their graves and little crosses
the resting place of swallows.

The 'trigger-mechanism' is in the loving and loathing. She is drawn towards the cloistered peace, the 'doves, pampas grass' and 'a sundial' and at the same time she is repelled by the tamed enclosure. In her fear of the moribund side of institutions she turns to the wildness of nature[301] in 'The Crows Rewrite the Gospels in Maynooth':

'The Crows Rewrite the Gospels in Maynooth'

By late October, crows write poems
in the clouds, unadulterated texts
for anyone who dares to look

     . . . . . .

each wingbeat exhorts, contradicts
in soaring eternity –
I am not the Messiah! The End is not nigh!
Do not repent –
the lines are scattered,
freeform subversions lost to the eye.

The same ambivalent view of institutions recurs in a much later poem in her collection *The Place of Miracles* called 'Over Clongowes Castle'.

---

[300] p60, Mary O'Donnell, *Spiderwoman's Third Avenue Rhapsody*, Salmon, Swords, 1993
[301] p48, Mary O'Donnell, *Spiderwoman's Third Avenue Rhapsody*, Salmon, Swords, 1993

Clongowes is the Jesuit-founded boarding school where her husband[302]
taught for thirty-eight years:

October crows in uproar,
six o'clock evening armies lay siege
to one another above slate and battlements

   .   .   .   .   .   .

Dead leaves swirl and rattle towards gutters.
A door scrapes shut. Inside the castle, all is quiet,
boys, unknowing, at study for principles
of things to come: leadership, the cult
of uniform and strategy for men in black
or grey. The old priests settle

in a breathing space between hours
– at desks, on chairs – lamps aglow,
the scent of decades on their prayer-books.

No uproar, yet still in siege,
the world gone eerily still,
beyond their hearing.

'Over Clongowes Castle'

But I want now to turn to yet another aspect of the opposition between
restraint and spontaneity which finds expression in the tension between
the local and the wider world.

Home Contrasted with Abroad

This conflict appears first in Mary O'Donnell's earliest work. In a poem
entitled 'Histories' Europe is set off against Ireland. Certainly, Europe
scores over Ireland in having[303] 'stuccoed ceilings, frescoed façades' and
a 'casual abundance of cornices, architraves, rose-windows' and:

you read a story in stone, feel the breath
of incubi from 14th-century gargoyles
that dance in a sunlit cupola, perch
on symmetries of a Gothic arch.

'Histories'

302 p185, Mary O'Donnell, *The Place of Miracles: new and selected poems*, New Island, Dublin, 2005
303 p12, Mary O'Donnell, *The Place of Miracles: new and selected poems*, New Island, Dublin, 2005

On the other hand, home is by comparison cramped and disappointing:

Coming home to Ireland is to feel deprived
in the pretty reds of a Georgian square,
the tamed aesthetic of wrought-iron balconies,
to sense this place an afterthought
of recent history, straggled haphazardly
across the ramparts of a few square miles.

It is to drive through a country village
know every house was once a servant's hovel,
to let your anger leak on sodden thatches,
on scutched acres at the edge of a bog –
written about, loved like a mistress,
but – for all the cant – triflingly.

Ireland reads no glorious hieroglyph beyond
a code of cashels and scarred fields,

In 'Savignyplatz, Enniskillen', the poem which follows this, once again Ireland's Enniskillen and Berlin are contrasted. In a poem from her fifth collection *The Place of Miracles* called 'New York Days', which is a companion piece to her earlier 'Spiderwoman's Third Avenue Rhapsody', the theme[304] recurs:

'New York
Days'
Freed again from the predictable, this time it's
antennae all the way, no mad spiderish
scramble to understand it all. On Times Square
I stand like any mesmerised country-woman,
then comes the old familiar rising of the self

from all that keeps me in my place,
against all that instructs on how to live
at fifty, as if the past half-century
were infancy.

Another later poem 'Country Neighbours' from the same collection

---

[304] p182, Mary O'Donnell, *The Place of Miracles: new and selected poems*, New Island, Dublin, 2005

catches in a calm but sad tone the semi-isolation of the Irish countryside. This contrasts with the previously described excitement of New York and echoes Robert Frost's use of the proverb[305] 'good fences make good neighbours':

High walls and hedges   'Country
make friends of them.   Neighbours'
Heavy snow means parties,
shared candles in blackouts,
milk and bread broken
in the silence of
a winter evening.

Smooth roads and sunlight
make strangers. Two cars
mean independence. Sometimes,
we meet out walking,
but there is little to say.

So far I have been looking at what Mary O'Donnell might speak of as 'a central anxiety', where restraints and spontaneity create an internal dissonance. I want to turn now to where I sense a resolution, not just in individual poems but in the progression of her work as a whole.

Embracing the Ordinary
It seems to me that in the course of Mary O'Donnell's superb second and third collections, in *Spiderwoman's Third Avenue Rhapsody* and *Unlegendary Heroes* something amazing happens. Although there are hints of earlier anxieties in the second collection, in a poem like 'Kildare' or '53.23° North' the poet views the foreign and adventurous from her roots in the ordinary. There is a remarkable tenderness and acceptance in the final section of *Spiderwoman's Third Avenue Rhapsody* and in the first section of *Unlegendary Heroes*. A fresh espousal of the ordinary and a delight in the unspectacular is perhaps not so surprising. It has been there from the epigraph dedication to Martin in *Reading the Sunflowers in September* and in subsequent love-poems.

---

[305] p177, Mary O'Donnell, *The Place of Miracles: new and selected poems*, New Island, Dublin, 2005

Arrival of Her Daughter Anna

The advent of the poet's daughter Anna heralds a phase which combines a fresh realism with extreme gentleness. There is a beautiful and subtle sequence of poems entitled *The Journey* which describe the conception, the pregnancy, the preparation of house, the pre-birth and birth, the arrival, the suckling, the pram-walking.

What I love about these poems is how they combine a contemporary awareness with genuine depth of feeling. Conception[306] is in 'The Moment':

'The Journey: I
The Moment'
It is not like the old masters.
No wavering halo,

like jellyfish
in a sea of grace;

no wingbeat brushing close,
or tremor of lilies

from some heart-lurching emissary.

Instead 'the May sun shoots bronze rivets at buttercups' and 'she hears a distant circus cross the fields from the east with drums and trumpets'. And we sense the circus might be a riotous sperm-troupe:

as they break the young corn
in a noisy caravan,

the riot and ring-dance
of naked acrobats

cartwheeling close
to her indolent flesh.

Each phase of pregnancy is caught so magnificently. The first[307] in 'The History of Seasons':

---

[306] p77, Mary O'Donnell, *Spiderwoman's Third Avenue Rhapsody*, Salmon, Swords, 1993
[307] p79, Mary O'Donnell, *Spiderwoman's Third Avenue Rhapsody*, Salmon, Swords, 1993

Say but the Word

Even if I forget,
already the child is remembering.
Its head inverts thought,
absorbs memories from bones,
sockets, the softening ligaments.

'The History of
Seasons'

Her need for affirmation is so delicately expressed[308] in 'Third Trimester
Interlude':

I linger more than usual over the
planes of your back and thighs,
want to be petted, stroked, held,
kissed, licked, sucked and juiced,
till I am shining silver.

'Third
Trimester
Interlude'

And then the move to new awareness[309] in 'The Shadow World':

I admit the world has changed

.   .   .   .   .   .

At least dreams are lush
with everything I miss

.   .   .   .   .   .

Did I really live there?
Did I eat that tack?

When can I go back?

'The Shadow
World'

This is followed by her juxtaposing the preparation of their home for
their child with a television programme about the last great herd of
elephants. In 'The Liberty of Elephants' she nimbly questions the
relationship between freedom and responsibility[310] (a theme which
pervades her novel *The Virgin and the Boy*):

and how, in coming years,
amidst chinoiserie and cowslip prints,
we will convey

'The Liberty of
Elephants'

[308] p80, Mary O'Donnell, *Spiderwoman's Third Avenue Rhapsody*, Salmon, Swords, 1993
[309] p81, Mary O'Donnell, *Spiderwoman's Third Avenue Rhapsody*, Salmon, Swords, 1993
[310] p82, Mary O'Donnell, *Spiderwoman's Third Avenue Rhapsody*, Salmon, Swords, 1993

Say but the Word

the liberty of elephants,
the true stampede for freedom
on the mind's savannah

In 'Pre-Birth Flirtation with Self and Others', she is 'flailed into battle'
and is fighting[311] for existence:

'Pre-Birth
Flirtation with
Self and
Others'

I pushed
to the edge of oblivion,
pushed to the edge of my life,
pushed for her,
only for her.

The poem 'Daughter' is so lovely[312] and so moving:

'Daughter'

For years I have called
across great distances,
feeling her hover

   . . . . . .

Now she sets out
from some wild galaxy:
as I sleep, she nears,
testing glints of starlight,
nights of hollow soul.
I have called her to be human.

Now she comes.

The poems describing suckling, 'Survival Tactics', ends with the
accepting line 'And so are mothers'. Yet the serene final lines of
'Cinnabar Candles and Cinnamon Trees', which portray pram-driving
and conclude both the sequence and the book, embrace in the ordinary
the paradoxical freedom[313] of responsibility:

'Cinnabar
Candles and
Cinnamon
Trees'

Do not question the driver's motives,
do not ask if she is free,

[311] p83, Mary O'Donnell, *Spiderwoman's Third Avenue Rhapsody*, Salmon, Swords, 1993
[312] p85, Mary O'Donnell, *Spiderwoman's Third Avenue Rhapsody*, Salmon, Swords, 1993
[313] p90, Mary O'Donnell, *Spiderwoman's Third Avenue Rhapsody*, Salmon, Swords, 1993

Say but the Word

if this she has chosen.
She has crossed rivers and mountains,
travelling songlines and desert
in search of herself.

Listen.
Ask nothing.
Judge nothing.
Only then will she stop.

I have dwelt on this sequence as it seems to me that this event is pivotal in the poet's life and in her artistic endeavour. This sequence is etched against the vivid 'Antarctica', the third poem in her first collection and the one she chose to open her selected poems. The title, which echoes the title of a well-known poem by Derek Mahon (in fact, her first collection was to have been called 'Antarctica' until she became aware that Mahon's book was about to be published), is a startling image for the position of a childless woman. Childlessness is also a major theme in her novel *The Light-Makers.* Her concern with the notion of freedom and what it means is already present[314] in 'Antarctica':

"But you are free," they cry,   'Antarctica'
"You have no child" – bitterness
from women grafted like young willows,
forced before time, In Antarctica,
who will share this freedom?

The calmer note of assent which characterises the conclusion of *Spiderwoman's Third Avenue Rhapsody* spills naturally over into *Unlegendary Heroes,* which is in many ways a celebration of the day-to-dayness of our humanity.

Unlegendary Heroes
As the title suggests, the unlegendary heroes are the people who lived out their lives without fanfare. Not unlike her fellow Monaghan-born poet Patrick Kavanagh in his great poem 'Lough Derg', she enlists the lives of ordinary souls from a 1938 folklore survey to record the local

[314] p3, Mary O'Donnell, *The Place of Miracles: new and selected poems*, New Island, Dublin, 2005

Say but the Word

people who occupied the South Ulster parish[315] landscape.

'Unlegendary
Heroes' Kathleen McKenna, Annagola,
who was able to wash a week's sheets, shirts
and swaddling, bake bread and clean the house
all of a Monday.

There is only one man mentioned among these heroes. Her motherhood opens up a particular sympathy for her parents, her grandmother, children playing, her own home, her own growing-up and her Monaghan background. It seems that many of the anxieties surrounding the ties of society and full womanhood have been partly assuaged. But this is no bland or sentimental assuagement. In a fine poem named 'Materfamilias' which deals with her grandmother, she is still conscious[316] of the tension:

'Materfamilias' My grandmother had thirteen pregnancies,
Nine full-term. She, who came orphaned
At nineteen from Clogher to Monaghan,
Fell to undreamt streams of constant parenting:
Keeper of children's needs, keeper of spouse,
Two uncles, a doting, whispering grandmother.

In a tall-storied town house 'she learned to rule an embattled roost'. Later 'when grandchildren came along, and she grew mild', and two of her sons were dead, she had her own slant on things:

Would she do all again,
My mother once asked. No chance, she said,
Womanhood, the struggle between self and others,
Was costly; to deal once with the rise and fall

Of life, of death, enough.

By the same token, there is perhaps a new and gentler perspective, a slackening of tension between institution and the need for spontaneity. In 'Latin, 1963', she recalls[317] schools days and learning Latin:

[315] p22, Mary O'Donnell, *Unlegendary Heroes*, Salmon, Cliffs of Moher, 1998
[316] p32, Mary O'Donnell, *Unlegendary Heroes*, Salmon, Cliffs of Moher, 1998
[317] p30, Mary O'Donnell, *Unlegendary Heroes*, Salmon, Cliffs of Moher, 1998

The pattern of school days –
terraces of future marvels,
hints of bedazzlement in the glint
of a *gloria*, a blatant *adoremus*.

Mass was learned in third class
piled like enchanted gold
in the mind's bunker,
a section for every week until
we could respond to entire runs
of wide-vowelled spells.

Some habits take root through the tongue;
translation becomes automatic.
Something else too:
a gift to augment the spoken word,
to enter an hour, a life,
rigs and rushes of pleasure,
childhood's dilating toils,
the senses open to
adoremus, adoremus…

The unease about the home tracts seeming insipid besides the outside world or as a source of restraint has also diminished. In fact it is turned upside down by titling a poem about her home place with the German *Heimat*. Here[318] she makes of townlands her own in a way reminiscent of Patrick Kavanagh:

Kilnadreen was our patch,   'Heimat'
south of Griggy, Drumgarn or Tirnaneill,
north of Coolshannagh, Tullyhirm, Kilnacloy.
Our hill, our fields, our stream.
The avenue buckled towards the outside world,
flinging dogwood and nettles,
docken leaves to cure a sting,
foxgloves, peonies, a neglected lily.
Summer after summer, *Philadelphus*

[318] p20, Mary O'Donnell, *Unlegendary Heroes*, Salmon, Cliffs of Moher, 1998

Say but the Word

perfumed my white days.
In Kilnadreen I learnt about peace,
how it thrived where soil was settled.
Kilnadreen was older that me.

Throughout this whole first section there is indeed a well-earned peace, a settlement. But as in Mary O'Donnell's attempt to define a poem, the resolution is very definitely open-ended.

In the second section of *Unlegendary Heroes*, there are many voices and masks: a woman who it appears is travelling from Ireland for an abortion, a supermodel, Rodin's Crouching Model, Camille Claudel (who was a sculptor apprenticed to Rodin), Jean Ingres's *La Grande Odalisque*, Sylvia Plath, Saint Colman, Emilia Mary (who was daughter of the Duke and Duchess of Richmond) and the Bog-Witch's daughter. The questioning, the examination of a woman's role is still crucial, though now from what is a more settled, though certainly not sedate viewpoint.

In Compassion's Light

Summer Elegies
In both *September Elegies* and *The Place of Miracles*, her fourth and fifth collections, the sense of resolution in the two previous books broadens into a mood of deep compassion and wisdom. Early in the first of these two books an elegiac note is struck. Here are the closing stanzas of the opening poem which is an elegy[319] for the poet Eithne Strong:

'Goodbye' But love rides on the brink of nothing.
Hope, when none of it will matter – that glance,
that afternoon by a lake of humming dragonflies –

is a route to the best peace of all,
the undressed, the fleshless, the unplagued,
beyond what we imagine is immeasurable –

solitude   silence

Early in this collection 'Triathlon, Cooley Peninsula' sets off a triathlon

[319] p99, Mary O'Donnell, *The Place of Miracles: new and selected poems*, New Island, Dublin, 2005

Say but the Word

against the background of the Irish epic Táin Bó Cuailgne (Cattle Raid of Cooley) and her ageing parents and concludes with the fundamental[320] questions:

Inexplicable that they
once lived so. The story of their lives,
that second, invisible skin, reads like
the myth of Maeve before the facts of history
chased it to the edge – the matter of who owned what,
and who was strongest, such trifling with the spirit,
diversions from what they needed to know:
how to live, and why.

'Triathlon,
Cooley
Peninsula'

There are some more marvellous love-poems for her husband Martin, 'Homes', 'Solstice' and 'Summerhouse Dream', scattered through the book which you feel earth her for the other elegiac poems. At the heart of *September Elegies* is a profoundly moving series of poems about her father's death: 'Dawn Rain', 'Doctors, Daughters', 'The Haircut', 'Holy' and 'Pietà'. The poem[321] 'Holy' is quite extraordinary:

Every venerable ancient seeks out his body,
every ancestor who once struggled
and, themselves inhabited, dwells there.
He almost weeps each time we leave,
then laughs through fear of this encounter
that nothing, no-one, can lift.

'Holy'

His frailty, a habitation for the wise and good,
is suffered in by a suffering god
who waited for a time, a moment,
patient while this son lived in the vastness
of life's green garment, exploring its folds.
Now he draws it down, tightly, closer,
so that the spirit, that vast, tumbling
greenness, the momentous motion of every cell
of his eighty years, are no longer divided,
but live intimately and as one.

[320] p103, Mary O'Donnell, *The Place of Miracles: new and selected poems*, New Island, Dublin, 2005
[321] p107, Mary O'Donnell, *The Place of Miracles: new and selected poems*, New Island, Dublin, 2005

Each of these poems is exquisite and has a fine mixture of clinical realism and fellow feeling, culminating[322] in 'Pietà':

'Pietà'   Later everything slows. This day,
           he will be born to death. His work
           finished, each cell leaf-light. Only the shape
           of his skull gives itself still to our hands
           as we lean down, down to touch,
           to kiss.

           This, Pietà, the death-slumped head
           falling to a slant of shoulders, nest
           of breastbone. 'He's gone,' someone says,
           and we look around, bewildered.

The Place of Miracles
The expansive and generous tone continues in *The Place of Miracles* which is the overall title of her new and selected poems and of the collection of new poems. Once again there is a really fine love-poem, 'The Derries, 1976', which I will take up again later, and another delightful poem for her daughter, 'Your Heart'. Her daughter, Anna, also features – as a teenager now – in 'Meditation' and in 'The Swimming Pool', which explores their relationship. This mother-daughter poem is in sharp contrast to the very early 'Women's Rites' where her relationship with her own mother was extremely edgy. Here there is another poem about her mother, 'Speed', which is gentle and solicitous. Another feature of this collection is the inclusion of two prose poems, one of which deals with lupus, an illness which the poet contracted.

The collection begins with a powerful poem of about 190 lines which opens with a grandfather's death and then goes on to tell about her relationship to an adopted sister. The conclusion of the poem in addressing her adopted sister gives explicit expression[323] to what I earlier called settlement:

'The Place of   Up there, Ulster-bound, down here Leinster-wise,
Miracles'   we hold fast and live. Steady. Steadfast.
                 Making daily poems of the ordinary.

[322] p109, Mary O'Donnell, *The Place of Miracles: new and selected poems*, New Island, Dublin, 2005
[323] p134, Mary O'Donnell, *The Place of Miracles: new and selected poems*, New Island, Dublin, 2005

This acceptance of the ordinary allows for poems[324] such as 'Ritual of the Blackberry':

In the end, what matters
is the harvesting, the savouring....

'Ritual of the Blackberry'

or such as[325] 'Birches in October':

Leaves faithful
to the cooling sky, drop invisibly
during the night, nudging out
to the curling, noiseless tips. Fallen.
Another season driven out to sea,
leaving land, making room.
Time folding over.

'Birches in October'

This does not mean that there is any lack of sensuousness, of delight in the carnal, as we're reminded[326] in 'The Bare Branch' or in 'Tattoo':

Sometimes I'm a girl in boots
With blue tattoos on her thighs,
Crossing the city,
Finding him in the long red car
Where I murmur quietly …

'Tattoo'

In another longer poem in six parts, 'New York Days', which I quoted from previously, she takes a cooler, more meditative look at New York than in 'Spiderwoman's Third Avenue Rhapsody', and comes to this[327] conclusion:

I'm holding, holding, unable to let flow,
open my mouth so that you know, you,
dear friend who needs to hear my words. But I'll come
home. A half-century of living's not for dumbing-
down. I'll cross the ocean one more time, considering

'New York Days'

[324] p139, Mary O'Donnell, *The Place of Miracles: new and selected poems*, New Island, Dublin, 2005
[325] p146, Mary O'Donnell, *The Place of Miracles: new and selected poems*, New Island, Dublin, 2005
[326] p137, p136, Mary O'Donnell, *The Place of Miracles: new and selected poems*, New Island, Dublin, 2005
[327] p184, Mary O'Donnell, *The Place of Miracles: new and selected poems*, New Island, Dublin, 2005

the climate that I leave, the one that lies ahead,
where, for now, I must face down the congenital
root, land, suburb, parish, home. I've done my thinking,
mental gymnastics that cure nothing. If I were male

.   .   .   .

But women just come home
and now like some choleric Kathleen I'll cross the foam
and do the best I can with the compartments
of my life, what I'd gladly trade for tenements
if feeling – like chemistry – ran the route it should
and the pulse of love beat true, eternal and good.

The Ireland which she has been briefly away from has changed
fundamentally over the previous decade. The immigrant population is
seen in the light of compassion and their variety, including an eastern
girl, a Lithuanian, a Russian, a Yugoslavian and a Polish evening, is
celebrated and included in a short series of poems called *Exiles.* Her
compassion extends historically to include a two-angled approach to
Jewish history in 'The Confession of Agimet of Geneva, Châtel,
October 20th, 1348, recounted by a Witness' and in 'The Cremation of
Strasbourg Jewry, St Valentine's Day 1349'. It seems to me that this
concern about the history of European Jews shows her deep awareness
of the pivotal significance of the Holocaust and its long-term cultural
and moral impact on our humanity.

The Ark Builders
Mary O'Donnell's latest book *The Ark Builders* is divided into four
sections Among other themes, the first section deals largely with
women resisting age and change. An example of its theme[328] is
'Following Frida':

'Following   *Old, old!* we shout the words he hates,
Frida'   *Loose and old, not tight and old!*
Senses, raging, in need of colour
as we behold ourselves, mirror-wise,
the woman we always were,
just older, looser, still there.

[328] p14, Mary O'Donnell, *The Ark Builders*, Arc, Todmorden, 2009

Say but the Word

The poem[329] 'Ageing Girls' is another example:

They parade the avenues,   'Ageing Girls'
stroll below storks
in high trees,
enjoying quiet nights,
nets of stars.
Prolapses repaired,
faces tightly injected,
they dress to kill
so they can live.
When they strip
 by the shore,
nobody cares,
nor if they spend, gamble,
drop twenty years …

The second section is largely still in a public and somewhat satiric vein
and looks[330] askance at Celtic Tiger Ireland. In 'Les Français sont arrivés,
Die Deutschen auch':

Fish-loving français gobble   'Les Français
all the salmon, the Germans   sont arrivés,
cannot walk enough beneath   Die Deutschen
cloud-sailed skies, where limestone   auch'
ribs encase the Burren,
and we in our tented streets
of emerald cabbages, fearing stone walls
might fall and fill again
the fields despised by Cromwell.

So, hairy sweaters all the way,
fiddle-me-flagrant on the flagstones,
jig-em-to-hell at dolmens, cliff paths,
wherever life-smudged innocents
are drawn to beauty or
a long note, cast out as if to say
whatever you sing, sing nothing.

[329] p15, Mary O'Donnell, *The Ark Builders*, Arc, Todmorden, 2009
[330] p28, Mary O'Donnell, *The Ark Builders*, Arc, Todmorden, 2009

Forget the lament in the shape of a road,
how fairies cursed one house
but danced at another, Don't reveal
the changeling self as the knit-wit island
laughs all the way to Dun an Airgid,
just thank the times,
forget the memory of mists and mires,
cloaked crones and weed-winkled
cross-roads, …

The same lack of memory is targeted[331] in 'An Amnesiac in Dublin':

'An Amnesiac
in Dublin'
After-hours faces in trams are work-dazed;
taxis dodge O'Connell Street,
        the Battle of the Burger,
            Little Africa
                and *Bejing Nua*.
        Amnesiac to the present,
we avert our faces, try to recall older struggles:
Lockout, Rising, the death of Collins;

The third section strikes a calmer note. There is a splendid love poem 'Taking the Measure' dedicated to her husband in which she flashes back to their handholding courtship and then returns[332] partly to the present:

'Taking the
Measure'
Last night on our country road you
took my hand beneath a golden moon
that bowled across the threshed fields.
We walked. We talked. Household politics.
Gardening dilemmas. A midterm trip
to Kerry. As before, you increased your grip,
as if afraid that I would slip. But
you got the girl. You got her
when we joined evening queues
for communal hand-to-hand-secrets,

---

[331] p34, Mary O'Donnell, *The Ark Builders*, Arc, Todmorden, 2009
[332] p65, Mary O'Donnell, *The Ark Builders*, Arc, Todmorden, 2009

intent on warmth, lightness,
the end of the treasure hunt.

Once again peace is found in the glories of sensual routine[333] in 'The Bread-Maker Speaks':

My fingers glide
Beneath your thinly floured
Mound, I learn again how days

And dreams fatten in warmth,
Wetness, barely dusted by
What contains them:

Routine acts, healing
In work, pleasure
In slit and cut.

'The Bread-Maker Speaks'

There is more probing of questions of meaning and negotiation with her Catholic upbringing in 'Santiago de Compostela' where on arrival at the cathedral the group scatters 'some for confession, others seek James and prayer is public.' The pilgrims 'are not shy to cross themselves and kneel'. Then:[334]

Some rod in your soul runs resistant,
though there are instances you could unravel
for a priest, testing the deep ear,
adding to his store of secrets.
Instead, you wander between pillars during Mass,
draw down ropes of miraculous legend.

'Santiago de Compostela'

A similar motif occurs in 'Random Questions' where a dead person is being quizzed about the other[335] side:

Now that I'm fifty, should I go to Confession
about the one sin I want rid of? Is there a time

'Random Questions'

---

[333] p73, Mary O'Donnell, *The Ark Builders*, Arc, Todmorden, 2009
[334] p51, Mary O'Donnell, *The Ark Builders*, Arc, Todmorden, 2009
[335] p70, Mary O'Donnell, *The Ark Builders*, Arc, Todmorden, 2009

to officially say 'sorry', or is that superstition
of the most primitive kind?

There are two excellent poems dealing with clothes belonging to the
dead. Her father's clothes are simply left until 'even the human odour
of clothes fade'. There's 'no mystery to this', it's simply 'time does its
work'. On the other hand, some clothes[336] are passed on:

'Dead People's Clothes'

Carrying it along
with every step; father's silk socks;
mother-in-law's scarf, those old,
dead people's clothes.
The smell of inheritance
lingers in our nostrils.

The final brief section contains three poems. It opens with 'Pentacle', a
personal elegy for the poet and writer John O'Donohue. The second
longer five-part poem 'The Beekeeper's Son' is a meditation which
opens with the burial of John O'Donohue in Ballyvaughan and which
plays on the original un-anglicised name *Baile Uí Bheacháin* which may
contain the element *beach* 'bee'. This poem also takes up again the image
of an ark, which was used earlier in the title poem 'The Ark Builders'.
The book closes with the stunning 'Lines to an Ancestor before An
Operation' where[337] she says:

'Lines to an Ancestor before An Operation'

Watch as I sleep, stay the surgeon's hands
as he raises this quiet part of me

like a new-slung ceiling
in the sagging rafters of my pelvis.
No more nor less than the rest of me,
let me inhabit womb, kidney,

jolting heart, restless brain, small nose,
bright eyes, long fingers, worn,
curling toes, the blunts of my teeth
within whitened crowns, all of me,

---

[336] p69, Mary O'Donnell, *The Ark Builders*, Arc, Todmorden, 2009
[337] p89, Mary O'Donnell, *The Ark Builders*, Arc, Todmorden, 2009

what's left for living in without
the burden of reflection.
Stay close now. Bind an adventurous spirit
to a home that sweetens with every month.

The Shape of Poems

I have concentrated so far on the content of the poems. But what about
the form? Even a cursory reading of Mary O'Donnell's poems and you
know that they are carefully crafted. It is not quite as easy to see in what
way they hang together. So I'd just like to make some general
comments.

Firstly, for the most part, she eschews what we might call classical
forms. Yet, like an abstract painter who just occasionally shows that they
can actually draw, she can use rhyme at will. Just look at how she slips
in and the out of rhyme *à la* T. S. Eliot in part six[338] of 'New York Days':

It dawns on me this morning as I groan awake
to blades severing chinks in hotel curtains,
that Hamlet-like, I have thought, thought
but never done the one thing that I ought.
Outside, the city rises, yeasty dough
in a September fug. I do not want to go,
yet know I must, a day early, that I perceive
things to be held together as I pick my way
through what's to come, play for time
to gather all my small change, shift that sublime
hair's breadth forward, forward. All around,
conversational couples make warning sounds,
not unkind, not in judgement. The habit of holding
deep ingrained, all together, together as one,
yet pained. It will not do, of course, and I
am bereft. Brief consolation in a diner,
I gulp some coffee, then pick my way
through eggs and bacon, make small talk with the
waitress at her station, watch families and weekend
un-*chic* gals join together in this warmth.

'New York
Days'

She employs all kinds of devices to keep the poetic tension and does not

[338] p183, Mary O'Donnell, *The Place of Miracles: new and selected poems*, New Island, Dublin, 2005

allow the non-rhyming lines descend into mushy verse. The reader also knows instinctively that this is not just 'chopped-up prose'. In the first place, the iambic rhythm carries us forward along with the jaunty conversational tone of the language. The word 'sounds' is the last (broken) rhyme. In the next line 'not' is repeated and there 'habit' and 'hold' alliterate. In the next line 'together' is repeated. Then 'bereft' and 'brief' give us an internal broken rhyme. After that there is whole series of 'w's: 'way', 'with', 'waitress', 'watch', 'weekend', 'warmth'. Furthermore 'bacon' and 'station' is a broken rhyme between two lines. One other feature which is so typical of her style is the enjambments she chooses. Look, for instance, at the very deliberate breaking up of 'I' and 'am' or of 'with' and 'the' between two lines.

Very occasionally, she chooses a classical form. For example, 'The Derries, 1976' is a sonnet with the pattern AABB CCDD EEFF GG. This is quite a strict form. There is one broken rhyme between F and F ('haunt / jaunts') and there is a startling enjambment to allow G rhyme with G ('wine / line'). I quote those final lines at the end of this essay.

She also uses the *haiku*. This is a syllabic form $(5 - 7 - 5$ with the last line containing something connected with nature) which was originally a classic Japanese form but which has now become part of the western repertoire. There are *10 Haikus on Love and Death* in *Unlegendary Heroes* and *Seven Monaco Haiku* in *The Ark Builders*. Many of these are very beautiful. Here are two[339] from the later series:

'Seven Monaco Haiku'

Though my basket fills,
I empty to less and less,
light as a petal.

The high labyrinth,
your shutters hung with bright flowers,
graceful pollen-fall.

But apart from the instinctive/deliberate use of alliteration, internal rhyme, rhythm or enjambment which I described above, Mary O'Donnell is formal in the sense that she often tends to employ stanzas of similar lengths throughout the poem. Those stanza lengths may vary from a couple to much longer stanzas.

[339] p62, Mary O'Donnell, *The Ark Builders*, Arc, Todmorden, 2009

Say but the Word

Conclusion: A Refusal to Toe the Line

Mary O'Donnell has a wide-ranging restless intelligence and an extraordinary poetic gift. She is both local and global, realistic and imaginative, probing and rooted, learned and passionate. By the same token, it is impossible to pigeonhole her. She eludes all the easy critical categories. She will disappoint feminists in that she is post-feminist and writes beautiful poems for her husband as well as for her daughter. She will fail any simplistic post-colonial analysis in that she sees the insecurities and the amnesia and yet succeeds in accepting and rejoicing in the present without overcompensation. She won't fit nicely as a post-modernist either as, although she can be biting, satiric, as well as being extremely playful, she refuses to hide behind a screen of irony. She is vulnerable and engages life with all her being.

This poet is of her time – as we all are – and she struggles creatively with the strands of anxiety which I outlined at the opening of this piece. As well as offering a general glance at her poetry I have attempted to sketch a growth throughout her work towards an accommodation with a series of tensions which she expressed so often and so well. There is a trajectory from unease to a certain settlement, even though those underlying tensions never entirely disappear. Any resolution is indeed open-ended. Even given her own definition of poetry as being driven by a central anxiety, the arc of her life brings her poetry somewhat nearer Robert Frost's dictum 'a poem begins in delight and ends in wisdom'.

Scattered in her collections, the love-poems for her husband Martin Nugent run like a red thread. I suspect that this love for him, and for her daughter have been a vital part in that movement across the arc of Mary O'Donnell's life. In one of these poems, 'The Derries, 1976', from *The Places of Miracles,* she describes haymaking on Martin's father's land. In spite of nervousness in the home place, there were sexual high jinks. The final line of this sonnet gives us a clue[340] to this writer's life:

---

[340] p149, Mary O'Donnell, *The Place of Miracles: new and selected poems*, New Island, Dublin, 2005

Even rapture deceives, never
as imagined, the world still spinning; I see you lover, as ever
worrying about being caught in thick clouds of hay, our haunt,
I, laughing my head off at the notion, foreseeing the jaunts

I'd lead you on, the naked swims, unchoreographed, wine-
drenched dances, my best, my precious gift, a refusal to toe the line.

Her precious poetic gift makes her the outstanding poet of her
generation.

19   Conclusion

Let me, crudely and with far too broad strokes, sum up what I've tried previously to say at length in other essays. Rainer Maria Rilke, who like W. B. Yeats would die in the lull between world wars, with some extraordinary searching and compassionate gift seemed in his own time to illuminate a greater perspective: 'und ich kreise jahrtausendelang' 'I orbit for thousands of years' or 'und welcher Geiger hat uns in der Hand? O süßes Lied' 'and which fiddler has us in his hand? O sweet song!' Yeats, on the other hand, would yield to the fascistic attitudes of the period, although he predicted that 'things fall apart, the centre cannot hold; Mere anarchy is loosed upon the world'. But, with his repetitive and predictable gyres, Yeats did not have the creativity and surprise which Rilke's melody implies. Essentially his view was tragic: 'We that look on but laugh in tragic joy'.

Patrick Kavanagh and Samuel Beckett, born within two years of each other just as the twentieth century began, would both in very different ways come to prominence after the Second World War. Kavanagh had the grounded humour and panache of his almost pre-industrial rural upbringing that would transcend the pervasive post-war mood of intellectual despondency. He could demand that all 'solemn boys' come out 'from your dictionary world and literary gloom – Kafka's mad, Picasso's sad in Despair's confining room'. Instead he would choose 'overflowing speech':

For this soul needs to be honoured with a new dress woven   'Canal Bank
From green and blue things and arguments that cannot be proven.   Walk'

Beckett, who had taken part in the French Resistance, would become a major symbol and purveyor of the sense of absurdity and meaningless which dominated the western world during the second half of what was probably the bloodiest century in the history of humankind.

Denise Levertov's journey is different. She didn't have the gift which Rilke seemed to have to soar over and beyond the twentieth century or the *élan*, humour and extraordinary and determined ebullience of Kavanagh's pre-industrial upbringing. On the other hand, she had a vision which transcended the trends and moods of her time in a way that neither Yeats nor Beckett did. What seems to me to be unique about her is that she neither escaped nor yielded to her times; she lived through and beyond them. And it somehow seems appropriate that a poet who carried a long rumour of wisdom to the edge of a new century should be the daughter of a Russian Hassidic Jew turned Anglican and a Welsh mother with a Congregational upbringing and had Russian, Hebrew, German, Welsh and English hovering in the background. She told of how in London she was Welsh while in Wales she was English, how in America she was English and then in England American. She travelled through agnosticism, anti-war protests and the environmental movement. This was the twelve-year-old who applied to join the Communist Party in London and who would live her last years as a Catholic in Seattle.

And it also seems particularly fitting that this beacon carrier should be a woman. For all the savagery of the twentieth century it will be remembered for liberating, at least in Europe and North America, a panoply of women into the main stream cultural life and giving us, to name just a few as favourites, Anna Akmatova, Elizabeth Jennings, Adrienne Rich, Karin Böye, Maya Angelou, Hilda Domin, Vassar Miller, Halldis Moren Vesaas, Anne Stevenson, Mary O'Donnell and Tess Gallagher.

From the window of my attic study where I'm writing this I can see Three Rock Mountain. There are masts there that receive and beam radio signals. I stare at the mountain and I'm glad a long rumour of wisdom has been transmitted from Seattle and that I have picked it up. For all the distortions and the garbling as the message was passed across a century with its stumbling doubts and despondencies, I catch[341] the vast whisper of 'Primary Wonder':

---

[341] p976, *The Collected Poems of Denise Levertov*, eds. Paul A. Lacey & Anne Dewey, New Directions, New York, 2013

Say but the Word

Days pass when I forget the mystery.   'Primary
Problems insoluble and problems offering   Wonder'
their own ignored solutions
jostle for my attention, they crowd its antechamber
along with a host of diversions, my courtiers, wearing
their colored clothes; cap and bells.
                              And then
once more the quiet mystery
is present to me, the throng's clamor
recedes: the mystery
that there is anything, anything at all,
let alone cosmos, joy, memory, everything,
rather than void: and that, O Lord,
Creator, Hallowed One, You still,
hour by hour sustain it.

Say but the Word

Index